THE SOCIAL WORLD OF BIBLICAL ANTIQUITY SERIES

General Editor
James W. Flanagan

THE
EMERGENCE
OF
EARLY ISRAEL
IN HISTORICAL PERSPECTIVE

ROBERT B. COOTE
&
KEITH W. WHITELAM

The Almond Press · 1987

Copyright © 1987 Sheffield Academic Press

Published by Almond Press
Almond Press is an imprint of
Sheffield Academic Press Ltd
The University of Sheffield
343 Fulwood Road
Sheffield S10 3BP
England

Typeset by Sheffield Academic Press
and
printed in Great Britain
by Dotesios (Printers) Ltd
Bradford-on-Avon, Wiltshire

British Library Cataloguing in Publication Data

Coote, Robert B.
    The emergence of early Israel in historical
    perspective.—(The Social world of
    biblical antiquity, ISSN 0265-1408; 5).
    1. Jews—History—To 586 B.C.   2. Jews—
    History—Babylonian captivity, 598-515 B.C.
    3. Israel—History
    I. Title   II. Whitelam, Keith W.
    III. Series
    933   DS121

    ISBN 1-85075-073-4
    ISBN 1-85075-072-6 Pbk

CONTENTS

ACKNOWLEDGMENTS

Our thanks are due to the following for permission to use published material: Almond Press for the use of Map 2, Hopkins (1985:326); the *Bulletin of the American Schools of Oriental Research* for the use of Figures 1 and 2, Gonen (1984:67); the Fränkische Geographische Gesellschaft for the use of Map 1, Hütteroth and Abdulfattah (1977:57); the Society of Biblical Literature and Scholars Press for the use of significant portions of Coote and Whitelam (1986) in Chapters 1, 4, and 5 of the present work. Our thanks are also due to J. Mabry for discussing with us and allowing us to refer to results of work still in progress (1984).

PREFACE

In this book we suggest that attempts to understand the origin of Israel have been unduly influenced by categories of analysis which are more or less extraneous to the history of Palestine.[1] The same could be said of ideas that have loomed large in the minds and desires of rulers. In the end we fear that we may not have been sufficiently critical of our own susceptibility in this regard. As our work has progressed we have become less sure of general assumptions about the unity of early Israel. The tendency has been to assume that the single name Israel referred to a single entity even in origin. There is little in our own investigation that would justify this assumption, and it goes far beyond what is known. It is our view that further work will have to take more seriously than hitherto the posssibility that the unity of Israel implied by the name is a notion applicable to little more than the reign of David, if that. We have become more sceptical despite the various solutions to this problem familiar to biblical historians.

Since much of the material included in this study might be unfamiliar to many readers and stand well outside the normal confines of biblical studies, a short explanation and justification of the organization and progression of the argument is in order. We have deliberately tried to extend the scope of the discussion beyond the more normal and acceptable boundaries of biblical studies in order to provide a different perspective and so raise fresh questions about the nature of early Israel and its development. The present study attempts to move from a broad treatment of the issues of historiography and Palestinian history to a more focussed discussion of the emergence and transformation of early Israel.

Chapter 1 provides an important methodological foundation for the subsequent discussion. It deals with the nature of history writing in general and particular assumptions that have shaped previous research into the history of Israel. In particular, the direction of much research has been dictated by the interpretation of biblical texts. This has imposed strict limits on the discussion thereby prejudicing the ways in which the emergence and development of Israel have been understood. We suggest an alternative approach, advocated by a growing number of scholars, which assigns priority to interpreting archaeological data within a broad interdisciplinary framework. For these reasons, Chapters 2 and 3 address aspects of Palestinian history in the very broadest terms.

The concerns of these chapters may be unfamiliar to many and distracting to others, yet they form an essential part of the argument as a whole. A major assumption, following the work of the French historian F. Braudel, is that complex problems such as those involved in the emergence and transformation of Israel can take centuries to work out. Therefore, in Chapter 2 we have attempted to provide a broad overview of settlement patterns and social relations throughout Palestinian history from the middle of the third millennium BCE to the present in order to illustrate how the emergence of Israel in the early Iron Age fits into the march of time. In trying to synthesize the vast archaeological literature on these periods we have had to make conscious and perhaps controversial decisions in presenting some of the evidence and arguments. Nevertheless, the difficulties we have encountered are more than justified in our opinion since it seems to us that unless this material is reviewed it is impossible to fully understand the nature of the settlement changes that took place in the early Iron Age. Chapter 3 offers a similar broad perspective on the nature of social and geographical relations in Palestine. Here the attempt is made to show how interregional trade affects local political and economic relations. We pay particular attention to the bedouin element in Palestinian history, because of its political significance along settlement margins, and because of the recent propensity to disregard this element in biblical studies. Chapters 2 and 3 paint a broad and schematic picture of significant patterns in Palestinian history, the possibilities and limitations of the past, which have shaped the history of the region and which are essential in trying to understand the fragmentary and ambiguous evidence for the emergence and development of early Israel.

The focus of the work is sharpened in Chapters 4 and 5 by a discussion of the specific problem of the emergence of Israel in Palestine during the early Iron Age[2] and its transformation to a centralized state in a relatively short space of time. In particular, the appearance of dispersed settlements in the highlands and steppes of Palestine at the beginning of the early Iron Age and the ensuing rapid centralization of this area, i.e. the emergence of Israel and the rise of the state, are to be set firmly in the context of the recurrent patterns of Palestinian history as described in Chapters 2 and 3. The growing body of archaeological data, of which much still remains to be published, offers, when interpreted in comparative perspective, a different picture of early Israel from that found in standard textbooks which proceed from the interpretation of the biblical texts. The fourth Chapter deals with the probable circumstances attending and influencing the spread of village culture in the highlands and dryland margins of Palestine in the twelfth and eleventh centuries BCE, the first two centuries of the early Iron Age. The fifth Chapter discusses the formation of the state over the peoples of highland villages during this period and into the tenth century. These two Chapters are meant to represent a continuum of historical change rather than a sharp demarcation between first a supposed 'emergence of early Israel' and only later a supposed 'formation of the Israelite state'. Instead, these two events are understood to be inextricably linked to each other.[3]

In the sixth Chapter, we return to some of the hermeneutical concerns raised at the opening of the book and ask how the historiographical categories that until recently dominated the discussion of early Israel developed over the whole period from the emergence of the first 'Israel' until now. We consider this issue from the projection of the self-understanding of the Davidic state to the nationalist historiography of the nineteenth and twentieth centuries.

We have placed great confidence in a panoramic view of history to inform and support our interpretation of the emergence of Israel and the rise of the state. Here we have tried to follow, however inadequately, the bold enterprise advocated by F. Braudel and his followers, like I. Wallerstein, in trying to chart the flow of world history before returning to the medium- and short-term fluctuations of specific periods or locations. Some may view this as overly ambitious or merely naive, and we recognize that it leaves us open to criticism from specialists in many areas. Nonetheless, it appears to us to be an important direction of research for the study of Palestinian history. Despite the inadequacies of our own presentation or understanding of so vast a subject, we offer this programmatic essay in the hope that it might stimulate others to consider the methodological issues and to revise or correct our interpretation of the emergence of Israel from the wider perspective of the ebb and flow of Palestinian history.

This work has changed considerably in scope and nature since our initial collaboration. Perhaps the most noteworthy deviation from our original plans has been the abandonment of our hope to discuss the religious culture of early Israel. This omission has been brought about by our increasing doubts about the unity of early Israel. Many will view this as a serious omission. However, our interpretation of the emergence of early Israel has led us to believe that more work will have to be done on the folk religious cultures of Palestine from a comparative perspective down to the 1920s, when good evidence was last available, if such a treatment is to be possible.

The work has always been exciting and challenging, particularly because of the considerable geographical distance at which the authors have been forced to operate. Our collaboration could not have been brought to fruition without the help and encouragement of many individuals and institutions. Our research has been generously supported by our home institutions of San Francisco Theological Seminary and the University of Stirling. Both of us are grateful for the assistance of the staff of Glasgow University Divinity Faculty, particularly Professor Robert Davidson, Robert Carroll and Alastair Hunter. Their generosity and hospitality were instrumental in making it possible for us to begin this joint work during the sabbatical leave of Robert Coote as Research Fellow at the University. The Sociology of the Monarchy Seminar sponsored jointly by SBL and ASOR has proved especially stimulating for our work. We are indebted to our colleagues in that group and especially its co-chairpersons Jim Flanagan and Frank Frick. The British Academy has been generous in the support of Keith Whitelam's participation in the SBL/ASOR seminar. David Clines, Philip Davies and David Gunn have offered valuable support and encouragement for which we are most grateful. Helen Steven and Mary McCormick Maaga have read various drafts of the manuscript and made valuable suggestions for improvement. A special debt is owed to Norman Gottwald and Marvin Chaney for their support, critical comments and generous sharing of ideas.

Chapter 1

REWRITING THE HISTORY OF EARLY ISRAEL

The Debate

The emergence of Israel in Palestine has been described by the great French biblical historian R. de Vaux (1978:475) as 'the most difficult problem in the whole history of Israel'. The past quarter of a century has witnessed an intense dialogue and polemic as three major reconstructions have vied for centre stage. The nomadic infiltration model of A. Alt (1966b), M. Noth (1960), and M. Weippert (1971) characterized early Israel as land-hungry nomads or semi-nomads in the process of gradual and mostly peaceful settlement in the sparsely populated hill country of Palestine. Central to this argument was the need to resolve the problem of the nature of the biblical narratives, especially the discrepancy between what appeared to be a pan-Israelite blitzkrieg conducted by Joshua and described in Joshua 1–12 and a more complex and gradual process of settlement described in Judges 1 and elsewhere in Joshua. This produced a heated response from across the Atlantic, where W.F. Albright (1935; 1939), G.E. Wright (1962) and J. Bright (1956; 1981) argued that archaeology had demonstrated the essential historicity of the biblical narratives. These American scholars posited a large-scale external invasion by Israelites who destroyed numerous Canaanite urban centres, very much as described in Joshua. Albright appealed to the destruction of the cities, the emergence of poorer settlements in the hill country and at some of the destroyed urban sites, and the appearance of a seemingly new pottery type, the collared-rim ware, as evidence for such an invasion.

These two reconstructions, quite at variance with each other, have informed the understanding of the origin of Israel of an entire generation of students of the Bible, through the now standard histories of Noth (1960) and Bright (1981). The underlying assumption of both models is that the emergence of Israel in Palestine, identified in the main with the emergence of settlements in the central hill country at the beginning of the Iron Age, is to be explained by a major external nomadic invasion or infiltration. The point at issue between the proponents of these two views is how to read the biblical narratives, particularly in the light of archaeological evidence for the period of the transition between the Late Bronze Age and the early Iron Age.

Fresh stimulus was eventually given to the debate with the appearance of G.E. Mendenhall's seminal essay 'The Hebrew Conquest of Palestine', published in 1962 but not much noticed for nearly a decade thereafter. Mendenhall rejected the notion of a major nomadic invasion of Palestine or the radical replacement of the indigenous population. His controversial view was that the origin of Israel lay in an internal peasants' withdrawal from or revolt against the Canaanite cities. The catalyst for this movement, Mendenhall believed, was a numerically small group carrying ideologically potent traditions of escape from slavery in Egypt. This 'exodus group' played a crucial role in Mendenhall's reconstruction. The peasant population of Palestine could easily identify with such traditions following their own subjugation and exploitation by the urban elite who held nominal control of Canaan for Egypt. Israel was a community based upon religious ethic owing voluntary allegiance to the one true overlord Yahweh, while rejecting the social and religious system of Late Bronze urban Canaan, which Mendenhall characterized as paganism, or the worship of power. Mendenhall has repeated his views with slight modification in subsequent publications (1973; 1983), during which time his reconstruction has gained growing support, particularly in the USA.

Mendenhall's arguments were considerably revised and extended by N.K. Gottwald in his *Tribes of Yahweh* (1979). Gottwald diverged significantly from Mendenhall's portrayal of Israel as an 'apolitical theocracy' bound in covenant relationship with Yahweh. Like Mendenhall, however, he rejected what he labelled the 'domain assumption' of Israel's supposed nomadic origins. Indeed, his decisive arguments against the nomadic factor have been widely received as one of the most convincing aspects of his treatise. Employing recent anthropological literature, he demonstrated that nomadism, or more particularly pastoral nomadism, was not the evolutionary forerunner of agriculture but rather a specialized offshoot of agriculture undertaken to reduce risk in the event of crop shortage or failure—common to the arid Middle East—as well as to avoid taxation and conscription by the state. Along with his predecessors, Gottwald identified the emergence of Israel with the rapid settlement of the hill country at the end of the Late Bronze Age. Against Mendenhall, he stressed the relations of power, the demands and struggles of the peasantry in their fight to throw off the yoke of their Canaanite oppressors.

It has become clear in recent years that there are now major theoretical differences between Mendenhall and others such as Gottwald who support the revolt hypothesis (see Mendenhall, 1983). Most recently, M. Chaney (1983) reviewed these three models in a thorough and judicious manner as the basis for favouring the cogency of the peasant revolt model over the other two. Chaney, however, developed the category of the frontier society introduced into the discussion by G. Lenski (1981) in a review of Gottwald's major work, and analyzed the *apiru* mentioned in texts from Late Bronze Age Canaan in terms of Hobsbawm's work on social banditry (1972).[1]

Despite the deep disagreements among the protagonists of these models, it is possible to identify an important underlying assumption shared by all in the debate. The problem of the origin of Israel as it has previously been formulated has been heavily influenced by the issue of literary interpretation. The beginning and end have been the biblical text. The chief question has been, how are the biblical texts pertaining to the origin of Israel to be understood? How are they to be illuminated by the archaeological evidence, as well as sociological and anthropological studies? This has played such an influential role in the historiography of early Israel that it merits considerable attention.

The Bible has been the most influential source of the prevailing ideas about the nature of Israel from its inception to the present. Yet the Bible itself is largely a product of such ideas (and their historical basis) in effect during the lengthy period of composition, formation, and selection of the biblical documents, and among the limited socio-political groupings primarily responsible for its development. This observation applies with equal force to all periods of the Bible's formation and of its ostensible referents. Hence we assume as a starting point that the critique of biblical history should be a function of a critique of Palestinian history rather than the other way around, as is so often the case. Any discussion about the nature of Israel has been determined by the fact that for the past two thousand years the Bible has been interpreted primarily within the context of and in the service of two interpretative communities broadly defined, the Jewish and Christian, or more correctly, by the intellectual elites of those communities.

The traditions of the Hebrew Bible, with their theological stances and complex and largely hidden history of development, transmission, adaptation and reformulation spanning a millennium or more, provide an immense obstacle for the historian. As often pointed out, the Hebrew Bible was not written to record the type of social scientific or historical data historians might wish to have. It cannot be stressed too strongly that what we are dealing with in the Bible are the religious traditions of early Israel. It is ultimately a document of faith that preserves the life, shape and identity of many communities of faith. By the same token, the traditions have developed along with the communities and been shaped accordingly. Kierkegaard's dictum has been aptly applied to these traditions: 'It is no use remembering a past that cannot become a present' (Blenkinsopp, 1977:152).

The significance of this observation for historical reconstruction can be illustrated from the long narrative complex that begins the Hebrew Bible (Gen—2 Kgs). The final shape of the canon as it addresses the identity and problems of the communities that preserved Israelite traditions in the sixth century BCE has become the subject of intense study in recent years through the work of J.A. Sanders, B. Childs, J. Blenkinsopp, R.P. Carroll, and many others. The narrative about the nomad ancestors in Genesis 12–50 preserves what many scholars believe are ancient traditions. However the significance of the narratives in their final form is that they address the identity and problems of more or less elite communities outside their homeland in terms of a traumatic deportation after the fall of Jerusalem in 587 BCE. Abraham's origins are in Mesopotamia, the very scene of 'Israel's' exile. Many of the stories deal with land disputes concerning the rights to wells or property. In this way they are relevant to the later community outside the land since they establish 'Israel's' right to its property on return. Even more important, the nomad narratives express a hope in a form particularly meaningful to a later community. The stories revolve around the notion of faith in God's promise (Gen. 12; 15).

In similar ways, the stories about Joshua establish the Israelites' right to the land. The books of Joshua and Judges are generally acknowledged to form part of the literary corpus known as the Deuteronomistic History encompassing Deuteronomy to 2 Kings (minus Ruth). In its revised form, Dtr2, this can be seen as an attempt to explain the trauma of 587 BCE, as Noth (1981) proposed for his Deuteronomist. Why has 'Israel' been exiled, and why have Jerusalem, the temple and the monarchy been destroyed? The Deuteronomistic History is not history. It is an extensive—but *extremely selective*—theological interpretation of Israel's supposed past written to demonstrate that the events of 587 BCE are not due to Yahweh's weakness or infidelity but rather to Israel's apostasy. The major themes are apostasy, repentance, obedience and salvation. The book of Judges most clearly illustrates the pattern, while the stories of Joshua, particularly those in Joshua 1-12, illustrate the benefits of obedience and the rejection of all 'foreign' elements. The claim of Israel's right to the land is clearly advanced as well as the underlying promise for the future (see for example Joshua 21.43-45). Israel's final conquest will be the result of faithfulness to the law of Moses as set out in Deuteronomy (Mayes, 1983:56).[2]

These examples ought to suffice to illustrate the fact that whatever the underlying historical core, or first ideological use, of these traditions, they remain important because they correspond to the life of the later communities and, in the words of J.A. Sanders, remained 'adaptable for life' (1976). It is this feature that has made the Bible dynamic and life-affirming for a whole succession of communities of faith.

Questions of historicity are not dependent solely upon the use of specialized tools to identify particular layers within the biblical text. Even if it is possible to show that particular narratives or units are contemporary with a particular period under study, it is important to be aware of the dangers in contemporary descriptions. What we are presented with is a particular perception of certain events and relationships (cf. Whitelam, 1984). Braudel (1972:21) expresses this point most elegantly:

> We must learn to distrust this history with its still burning passions, as it was felt, described, and lived by contemporaries whose lives are as short and as shortsighted as ours. It has the dimensions of their anger, dreams or allusions . . . a world of strong

passions certainly, but blind like any other living world, our own
included, and unconscious of the deeper realities of history . . .

It is this feature over which the historian must stumble. The
adaptation and reformulation of the various traditions mean that it is
extremely difficult if not impossible to get behind or beneath to
anything like an underlying historical core. It is because they have
faced this dilemma squarely that many have understandably
abandoned the historical task. In the context of the present state of
the discipline of biblical studies, with its concern with literature,
structure, final form, and philological minutiae, attempts to reconstruct the history of Israel are often understandably looked upon only
with passing antiquarian interest or seen as the pursuit of the
impossible.[3] Why then venture into this minefield?

The past, in the form of our traditions, our perceptions of the past,
exerts tremendous influence on the present and thereby makes such
a venture of utmost importance. Various political and religious
communities view themselves as heirs to the biblical traditions, and
their perceptions of the emergence of Israel in the distant past have
tremendous repercussions in the modern world. This study is an
attempt to provide a new synthesis of the history of early Israel by
bringing together insights drawn from many disciplines as well as
recent biblical studies. It is not meant as a broad survey of conflicting
opinions, since that role is already well served (Hayes and Miller,
1977; Ramsey, 1982; Chaney, 1983). Instead, we seek to advocate a
particular reconstruction of the emergence of Israel and to indicate
how that reconstruction bears on the ways in which later ideas of
Israel developed and functioned in communities of faith.

The Power of the Past

If, as many believe, the study of history is really a dialogue with the
present, then this task poses an awesome responsibility upon those
who presume to undertake it. George Orwell dramatized the power
of the social function of history writing—in the form of its abuse—in
his novel *1984*. Winston Smith's assignment in Oceania was to
'rectify' previous newspaper reports now out of line with official
reality. The Party had the power to reach into the past and decide
whether or not a particular event ever happened. The Party slogan
decreed that 'who controls the past controls the future; who controls

the present controls the past' (cf. Plumb, 1969; Herion, 1981:32-33). Orwell's nightmare represents an extension and perversion of the important historiographic principle that historians discuss the past using categories and paradigms drawn from the present. J. Sasson (1981) has illustrated how the models of previous biblical scholarship, mainly those associated with American and German historiography, have been fractured by the altered historiographic perceptions of post-war Germany and post-Vietnam America.

These considerations lead to further necessary questions about the nature of history writing in biblical studies. The most immediate for biblical scholars is what type of history is possible or appropriate given the changed perspective of recent years. The struggle with this question, far from being worthless or peripheral, needs to be carried out with the greatest vigilance and determination if the all-important dialogue between present and past is to continue rather than be abandoned to the kind of monologue dictated by the present and conducted in Oceania.

Rewriting the History of Israel

It has become apparent in recent years that the growing body of archaeological evidence from Palestinian sites cannot be fitted into any of the present dominant models of the emergence of Israel in Palestine (Fritz, 1981; Weippert, 1979; 1982). The continued attempts to reconstruct the history of Israel from the starting point of minute literary study of the traditions of the Bible show little sign of real progress.[4] Such studies run the risk of perpetuating the theological inclinations of their sources, whether from the Pentateuch, the Deuteronomistic History, or the prophetic books. As more archaeological evidence becomes available, it raises ever more questions about the nature of our literary sources. The time has come to attempt a synthesis of the history of early Israel from a different perspective. A change in our perspective of history means moreover a change in our view of the history of the biblical literature. Accordingly we shall eventually return in this book to some schematic considerations of the sources, particularly those purporting to deal with the emergence of Israel and therefore playing a particularly influential role in the history of the idea of Israel.

As has been said above, the histories of Noth and Bright have dominated the field, shaping the perceptions of a generation of students and teachers. Despite the considerable differences between their presentations of the so-called patriarchal and conquest periods, these works concentrate on the nature of the literary sources. The picture of much of early Israel's history they share is remarkably one-dimensional. They are indeed concerned to describe what happened but they rarely ask why it happened.[5] They present an odd world, drawn from the biblical traditions, populated by a few leading individuals (cf. Bloch, 1954:59) with a minimal and shadowy supporting cast. These reconstructions, dominated as they are by the events and individuals of the artful narratives of the Bible, are the epitome of Voltaire's complaint about French history: 'It seems that, for fourteen hundred years, there have been none but kings, ministers, and generals in Gaul' (cited by Bloch, 1954:178). As such these standard presentations fail to account for or even investigate the underlying causes of social change (cf. Frick, 1985:14).

A major debate has grown up in recent years concerning the historiographic intent of the biblical narratives themselves. J. Barr's seminal essay (1980) categorizing the narrative complex of the Hebrew Bible as story rather than history allied to the ever-increasing new literary studies raises fundamental questions for the historian.[6] It might be thought that this debate strips the historian of the ability to write any kind of history of early Israel by removing the greatest body of information about its emergence and development that we have at hand (see Miller 1982:215; cf. Thompson, 1978a:20). The result has been for many a retreat into an historiographic scepticism.

But it is by no means the case that the historian cannot or should not investigate periods devoid of usable written sources or should not seek to explore those aspects of society which are not the subject of literary remains (cf. Febvre, 1973:34). The study of historical geography in combination with long-term settlement patterns is the foundation of such a history which transcends the short-term perspective of traditional political histories (cf. Brinkmann, 1984). Settlement pattern is precisely the best historical evidence we are in possession of with respect to the emergence of Israel. The recent developments of a Palestinian archaeology devoted to surface surveys and focussing upon anthropological, sociological and ecological concerns is obviously central to such a venture. The historian is able to build up a network of mutually supporting relationships which make up for the absence of written documents. Such a procedure does not simply consist of making an archaeological inventory but is rather the attempt to analyse and interpret the data provided by the archaeologist's spade to throw light on settlement history, demography, and economic and political relationships, that is, the shifts and strains which are vital for understanding social change. The correlation of evidence independently culled from the biblical traditions is secondary to this task (cf. Thompson, 1980).[7]

This discussion obviously touches upon many of the issues involved in the recent debate over the status of 'biblical archaeology' in relation to Syro-Palestinian archaeology. What is being advocated here is caution against the all too common subjugation of archaeology in the service of biblical studies thereby dictating the aims of excavation and limiting the amount of evidence produced for historical reconstruction. Both sets of evidence, the biblical and the archaeological, possess their own inherent biases. The greatest misunderstandings may arise when different categories of evidence are thought to be readily compatible (cf. Price, 1980:157). The biblical material preserves only the smallest fragment of all possible reminiscences by the social actors themselves. By contrast, archaeological evidence is determined by the research and excavation strategies of the observer and again only represents a fragment of the possible evidence for the material remains of the society under observation. Clarke (1973:18), while discussing the implications of New Archaeology in general, claims that 'the new developments insist that the historical evidence be treated by the best methods of historical criticism and the archaeological evidence by the best archaeological treatment and *not some selective conflation of both sets of evidence and their appropriate disciplines*' (emphasis added).

In order to illuminate a historical, social or political process, the historian often appeals to an analogy from some other society or period of history. But it is not always clear how valuable particular analogies are, especially if they are drawn fron societies that are considerably removed in time and space from the one under consideration.[8] The sea-change in the reception accorded Noth's hypothesis of a premonarchic amphictyony in Israel, which has declined in the last decade from general acceptance to general rejection, demonstrates the inherent risks of analogy. These are compounded by the lack of objective controls that provide a check upon free-ranging eclecticism. The importance of a consciously formulated research strategy or interpretative framework is that it provides some controls over analogical reasoning (cf. Price, 1980:173). Of course a greater knowledge of archaeology, anthropology, sociology, or other disciplines will not automatically produce a more accurate interpretation (Price, 1980:173). Data need to be categorized, organized, and structured, especially when they are as sparse as they are concerning early Israel. Admittedly, as many have observed (Thompson, 1978b:11; Frick and Gottwald, 1975:177), structure is no substitute for data since conclusions need to be drawn from data. Nonetheless 'facts' are meaningless until placed within an interpretative framework. Explanation has to be imposed upon otherwise mute data. As C. Renfrew (1973:5) maintains, the past is not recovered but recreated. One of the essential elements of this recreation is inference based upon comparative material; but such inference can only be carried out in the context of a well-defined research strategy. It is then possible to make logical deductions or informed guesses on the basis of the comparative data.

One of the strongest objections to the use of social scientific categories in the study of early Israel is that it is impossible to use the field worker's notebook and observe Israelite society directly. Yoffee's rejoinder (1982:348) to the same objection made with respect to Mesopotamian studies applies equally to the study of Palestine: 'If certain elements of Mesopotamian social systems will never be directly observable, it obviously does not follow that those unattested elements did not exist in the living culture, nor does it mean we cannot infer their presence in an orderly, rigorous way'. Inference is a dynamic process which allows the formulation of new questions, the investigation of previously unexplored areas and the refinement or reformulation of hypotheses to take account of new discoveries, fresh ideas or greater understanding of available data. It is precisely because of the lack of data, the inability to observe directly, and despite continued advances and refinements in archaeological techniques, that it will remain impossible to offer a definitive reconstruction of the emergence of Israel. But historical nihilism is not the only choice in the face of this residue of uncertainty. Certainty is not a prerequisite to understanding. It is the will to understand rather than simply the will to know for certain that is the driving force for the inquiry to be undertaken here (cf. Loyn, 1980:132).

The distractions of our own specialization within biblical studies need to be balanced by investigating how Israel fits into or differs from the regular and recurrent patterns of Palestinian history which can take centuries to unfold. Thus it is necessary to extend the chronological perspective of biblical history, which spans the period from the thirteenth century BCE to the first century CE, to include the whole of Palestinian history from at least the Early Bronze urban phase to the present day.

The myriad of social and political permutations throughout the kaleidoscopic history of Palestine which presents such a formidable obstacle to any attempt to provide a broad overview of Palestinian history will be dealt with in Chapters 2 and 3. Only after this material has been grappled with will it be possible to achieve the perspective from which to view the emergence of Israel and its transition to statehood as part of complex processes spanning many centuries. These processes are related to the geographical constants which provide the foundations on which the surface events are played out and which in turn affect the range of possibilities open to any community. The domination of this area by non-Palestinian political powers is one of the most important constants of Palestinian history which has had a profound effect upon settlement patterns. The rare periods of serious decline or absence of outside political influence, of which the period under study is partly an example, thus take on much greater significance but still need to be viewed in relation to the whole pattern rather than in isolation.

The works of authors like Braudel, Harris, and the Lenskis have had a particular influence on our thinking in this area. The importance of Braudel (1972; 1980) for our critical sense of periodization, following his important distinction between different levels of time, has already been referred to in the preface. The progression of this study from broad overview to a narrower focus upon a more specific period has been inspired by Braudel's influence on the study of history in the post-war period. The Lenskis are useful to us mainly for their description of the type of 'agrarian society', based on the use of metals for agriculture and warfare. Even so, their distinction between advanced and simple agrarian societies on the basis of the difference between iron and bronze use does not seem significant for the emergence of Israel. This is despite the fact that its emergence occurs approximately on the cusp of the Bronze and Iron Ages and the two events are without doubt related in some way. In addition, although the category agrarian society is based primarily on the history of technology, we do not subscribe to recent attempts to emphasize the significance of technological change in Palestine for the emergence of Israel. Further still, the Lenskis' sharp exclusion of 'nomadic' societies from their category of agrarian society means that the latter must be modified and adapted to the Palestinian setting, with its prevalent and politically significant pastoral nomadic component. Yet theirs is possibly the most astute justification of the socio-historical category, the agrarian society, that allows us to make comparisons between ancient and modern Palestine, at least up to about the middle of the nineteenth century and in some instances even closer to the present. They and others have worked out the basis for ascribing a degree of commonality among all periods of Palestinian history and culture from the early Bronze Age to the beginnings of industrialization. Similarly, Harris's view of infra-structural causation requires considerable modification for certain aspects of Palestinian culture considered in this book, since few aspects of Palestinian culture can be represented in isolation from the heavy influence of non-Palestinian cultures and forces.

Such broad-gauge enterprises are not fashionable within biblical studies (cf. Mendenhall, 1961:38; 1976:15) and certainly run the risk of attack from specialists in many disciplines. Yet there is pressing need to attempt a new synthesis of the history of Israel from this extended chronological perspective. It is an attempt to loose biblical studies from the merely descriptive or chronological histories which concentrate solely upon what happened, particularly in the political area, in order to ask the fundamental question of why it happened. The search for broad patterns and generalizations helps to throw valuable light on periods of social change. Viewed from the perspective of millennia-long processes, the history of Palestine reveals a number of patterns, of which the most significant is the domination of this area by major outside powers and their political economies. Biblical studies in the past have sought to illuminate only a small fraction of the long and complex history of Palestine. There is much to be gained by trying to see how biblical history fits into the tapestry of Palestinian history, a tapestry still being woven with many of the same threads. This is a daunting task. But Palestinian history is so rich that it draws the researcher forward to learn more, ever conscious of the vast array and quantity of material that beckons. The dangers of such an approach are partly offset by the rewards of fresh understanding.[9]

There are many different fields of academic study whose subject is Palestine. For several reasons, including academic specialization, the different languages and ideological contexts of the sources used for Palestinian history, and the varying present-day contexts for the study of Palestinian history, there exists a profusion of different sets of categories and terms used to describe what are probably quite similar phenomena. This is a frustration for anyone who desires to use more general categories in the historiography of any one period or categories derived primarily from any one type of source. This book represents among other things a preliminary attempt to develop comparative categories applicable to most of Palestine's history.

The approach here adopted offers a fresh perspective on the emergence of Israel in Palestine while providing a corrective to a number of misleading assumptions which underlie much of biblical scholarship. As we hope to show in Chapters 2 and 3, it is the regular and recurrent that shape the possibilities open to a particular society but so often escape the awareness of the social actors themselves. Febvre (1973:vii) notes that with regard to the environment 'there are no necessities but everywhere possibilities'. This extended chronological perspective helps to overcome the problem of periodization, that is, the belief that social, economic, political and religious change can be chronologically compartmentalized without distortion. The emergence of Israel, datable to about 1250-920 BCE, is, to use concepts popularized by Braudel, a surface event understandable only in terms of the wider, slower movement of much longer duration, what Braudel styles *la longue durée*. Human beings in history are constrained by climate, topography, vegetation, animal population, agricultural potentialities, and the like. Surface events, primarily those events which are most often the focal point of traditional political histories, are played out around more permanent elements such as urban sites, trade routes, harbours, and climate.[10] The realizations of the various potentialities of Palestine have been governed throughout its agrarian history by the presence (or more rarely absence) of outside powers and the complex interaction of external world events.

We are interested in describing less the cause of the emergence of Israel—though that is not in itself an invalid subject of inquiry—than the set of conditions and circumstances within which Israel emerged, and in terms of which its emergence might most comprehensively be understood. Among other things, this means that the history of changing social groupings needs to take account of the opportunities their various members encounter within a given set of constraints. In other words, our analysis might perhaps be described as a history of opportunism. Furthermore, for most events of the type to be considered in this book, the set of conditions and circumstances within which Israel is understood includes the future of groups, organizations, and societies calling themselves Israel and of their self-identities. In other words, the cultural meanings of Israel are retrospective, formed largely as a consequence of events and experiences that ensued after those events and the interpretation of the experiences.

The theme of this book should not be mistaken for what has properly been called the fallacy of origins, namely that a thing is what it is in origin. Our point is really the opposite: a critique of origins is the basis for a critique of any definition of Israel which assumes—explicitly or implicitly—that Israel corresponds to its origins. Furthermore the critique of Israel's origins does not pretend to be a description of anything more than a mere fragment of the whole history of groups that have regarded themselves as Israel; but as one point of comparison among many, it is a useful starting point. In particular, there could hardly be a better vantage point from which to assess the earliest elaborate versions of the history of Israel, especially the Yahwist's history, which have subsequently had such a profound effect on the history of the idea of Israel, from the beginning of the formation of the Torah to the present.

Another feature of this synthesis is that the emergence of Israel and the development of the monarchy, that is, the transition to the state of David, must be seen as a continuum, rather than as a dialectical conflict, such as is a commonplace framework in other studies whether sociologically oriented or not. The common view, or rather the domain assumption, that the monarchy is some kind of aberration or alien institution foisted upon true Israel is partly due to the self-limiting perspective of specialization. The views of Bright and Noth (alien), Mendenhall (pagan reversion), and Gottwald (dialectically opposed) fall short of explaining how the significant social changes that led to the rule of David came about. Buccellati (1967), in his important study of Syria, has already emphasized the crucial point that such notions deny the internal dynamics of Israelite society. The monarchy is rather an outgrowth, though by no means inevitable (*contra* Mayes, 1977:331), of the particular configuration of circumstances surrounding the emergence of Israel in Palestine.

Past and Present

It is the assumption of the uniqueness of Israel which has had the greatest distorting effect upon the study of Israel.[11] This notion of uniqueness stems from Jewish and Christian ideologies which have developed from at least as early as the Roman era—and probably earlier—to the present day. It is for this reason that it is essential to develop an analytical, inter-disciplinary approach to the history of Israel. It is unreasonable to assume that early Israel's social organization differed in its salient features from all other known human societies. The uniqueness of the Bible in Jewish and Christian culture stems from the developments that occurred well after the emergence of Israel. It is vital to ensure that the all-important dialogue between the past and the present is maintained rather than to abandon the past to the tyranny of the present.

It is inevitable that the historian approaches the past from the perspective of the present (Lewis, 1968:ix). The ever-increasing pace of change over the past few centuries and particularly during the twentieth century means that our view of the past is subject to radical changes of perspective (cf. Renfrew, 1973:5). Comparative studies at least offer some hope that historians need not be imprisoned by their own present. The perspective of *la longue durée* is able to readjust and balance our own view of the emergence of Israel.

The most fundamental question remaining touches ourselves as authors. How far are we as historians reshaping the past to suit our own present, to suit our own political and religious prejudices? Have we in undertaking this study reached back into the past and decreed that particular events did not take place, or at least that particular perceptions of those events are mistaken, because they do not conform to some present official (or unofficial) reality? It ought to be obvious that complete objectivity is not an attainable goal for the historian. That is surely one of the landmark perceptions of twentieth-century historiography. All that is possible is to set out one's presuppositions and methods of working for critical gaze without turning the work into an extended treatise on the philosophy of history. It is hoped that this study will throw fresh light on the emergence of Israel onto the stage of history. The importance of the task is aptly summed up in the dictum of M. Bloch (1954:43): 'Misunderstanding of the present is the inevitable consequence of the ignorance of the past'. The opposite is of course also true, and we are aware that it is our understanding of the present that is to be tested here, as much as anything, as is the case with every other historian. It can only be hoped that the errors we have made will be corrected by others who find this approach of value however incomplete and inadequate the present work might be.

Chapter 2

SETTLEMENT PATTERNS
AND INTERREGIONAL TRADE
IN THE HISTORY OF PALESTINE

Israel emerged in a small but strategically important area of the globe. It would be difficult to imagine a more strategic location, despite its size and lack of natural resources. The meeting place of two oceans and three continents, the hub of elite trade during the entire growth of civilization from the Neolithic to the Renaissance, the importance of this little region's strategic position far outstrips the importance of its physical resources. Because Palestine has no natural harbour, trade by sea can choose to by-pass it. But what goes by land must go by way of Palestine, bounded, as it is, by the desert on the east.[1] For major outside powers, time and again it was important to secure Palestine not for its own sake but as part of a strategy for securing other more productive areas like the Syrian or Egyptian grainlands. This meant, of course, that Palestine was continuously open to invading armies, although as will be seen this openness often affected only certain parts of the region. This region and its history are inextricably bound to the fortunes of larger interregional powers and areas. The patterns and processes of Palestinian history, whether in antiquity or the present day, therefore need to be understood in relation to the fluctuations of world political economy and world history.

In any survey of the history of this region, one of the most noticeable features is the periodic fluctuation between expansion and retraction of settlement. The emergence of Israel must be examined within this dynamic pattern of settlement change. The most commonly agreed datum to mark the emergence of Israel is the extension of village and agricultural settlement in the central highland of Palestine from the thirteenth to the eleventh centuries BCE. Before asking what caused this particular shift, it will be worth while to describe the set of conditions and circumstances in which it occurred and in terms of which it can be most comprehensively understood. This is best done by comparing it as one particular shift with other similar shifts in the settlement pattern of Palestine in order to assess just where it fits into the broader patterns and processes of Palestinian history. The key question of this chapter is: what are the significant characteristics of settlement changes in Palestine in general that will help us to understand the emergence of Israel as part of one settlement change in particular?

Shifts in settlement pattern in Palestine occur locally within a generally arid climate and terrain characterized by a complex mixture of highlands and dry lands and hence by extensive marginal territories. Because shifting settlement patterns have considerable bearing on the total population of the whole region, demography may be regarded as a corollary measure of historical change within it, though it is less directly acccessible. Contrary to the way we usually think of change in population in a given area, as a constant increase in numbers, change in population over the ages in Palestine, as in many areas of the world, involves a constant fluctuation up and down. E.A. Wrigley (1969:77) points out that this is true for traditional societies throughout history:

> In a very broad sweep of history it is true that the secular trend has been upwards, but the sweep must be very broad indeed if the trend is always to be found for, in addition to the frequent ups and downs which so often give a jagged, saw-tooth appearance to a graph of annual totals of births, deaths and marriages, there were periods of centuries during which population totals were lower than before, or when population, though not declining, showed no upward trend.

A glance at a work like the *Atlas of World Population* (McEvedy and Jones) will show how such fluctuations characterize most areas of the world. The figures for Palestine presented there show, for example, that the population of Palestine in the first century CE was higher than at any time prior to 1900 CE. The continuous fluctuation in settlement and population in Palestine provides a way of defining historical change in Palestine so that the emergence of Israel can be placed in the context of such general change and analysed and described in appropriate terms.

Readers who pick up several books about Palestine written at different times and from different points of view are liable to find conflicting statements concerning the quantity and fertility of its soils, the productivity of its agriculture, the suitability of its terrain for various crops, the number of people it is able to support, and similar features. They might well end up wondering whether the soil of Palestine is good or bad, its productivity high or low, and so on. The reason for such conflicting statements is that agriculture and settlement have in fact varied considerably over time. The possibilities for food production and settlement offered by the geography of Palestine are not constant, even if, broadly speaking, its geographical constraints and limitations are.

The conventional manner of dealing with the agricultural variability of Palestine has been in terms of the 'desert' and the 'sown'. The oscillation of these has a venerable history of discussion, and at least one full-length book dealing with Palestine takes these terms as its title (Reifenberg, 1952/1955). Sometimes the desert predominated, sometimes agriculture; or, in terms of the supposed social groupings involved, sometimes the nomad, or *bedu*, held sway, sometimes the peasant, or *fellah*. It was assumed that the main historical dynamic of the land was the struggle between these two, and the history of agriculture and settlement in Palestine was comprehended by the description of this struggle on an internal, local basis. It is understandable that such an opposition should dominate the consciousness of nineteenth- and twentieth-century observers in Palestine, who were witnesses to or participants in the accelerating process of turning what appeared at that time to be a land of agricultural desolation into what is today—quite contrary to the historical norm—the most developed land in the Middle East. In this sense, the history of modern Palestine represents a decisive victory of the sown over the desert, and such are the terms used by many to describe that history.

Those who could achieve a historical perspective on this process knew that it was a refulfilment of a geographical and historical possibility. The land itself declared—in its decrepit monuments and wasted terraces and waterworks—and literature from ages past confirmed the fact that sometime in the past the land had supported a larger population than recently, despite improvements in agricultural technology and the increasing integration of Palestinian agriculture into the markets of the world. Perhaps the classic statement of this view is A. Reifenberg's concise and well-illustrated *The Struggle Between the Desert and the Sown* (1952/1955). Here he demonstrates on the basis of an inspection of the land and an examination of literary sources that the modern development of the land fulfils one inherent possibility that had already previously been realized. He sees a once great civilization being restored, in the author's own time. In other words, something that had gone terribly wrong with agriculture in the region is about to be righted. For Reifenberg writing in Israel in the early 1950s, it was sufficient to present this tale as a single epic wave, from development to decay to redevelopment, without differentiating anything other than one long development from the Early Bronze Age to the Byzantine period and without inquiring more deeply into the reasons for such fluctuations beyond the culture, skill and will of the inhabitants.[2] Thus he was able to state that 'it was after the Arab conquest that the type of agriculture began to change fundamentally' (Reifenberg, 1952/1955:98). As archaeologists of the twentieth century confirmed that early Israelites had settled much land which in that time had been recently unsettled if not unoccupied, this view of the recent history of Palestine may have influenced the archaeologists' view of the earlier period, even when they did not make analytical or even conscious use of the comparison.

The Major Settlement Phases

A simple linear portrayal of the history of isolated periods of settlement and agriculture in Palestine can be misleading. If we take a panoramic view of the history of Palestine, it is possible to identify major phases of the expansion and contraction of settlement. These phases are individually well known to historians and archaeologists of particular periods. In order to understand them as a type, however, and eventually in relation to the emergence of Israel, it is necessary to view them together comparatively. The comparative view then places the conditions and circumstances that influenced any particular phase in the most comprehensive perspective.

Such an approach may appear overly schematic and artificial and runs the risk of crossing the demarcation lines of specialists in particular periods. Different historians have interpreted the degree of fluctuation involved in these phases in quite different ways. In addition, the variations affect the different subregions and micro-areas of Palestine differently depending on detailed circumstances. The following descriptions therefore should be taken as general and suggestive of the variations that are of interest to us rather than as exact analyses of the phases. Such a comparative view of the cyclical nature of expansion, stagnation, decline and then transition before regeneration accords well with Renfrew's study (1979) of systems collapse and social transformation, albeit in state societies, over much wider geographical areas. It is becoming clearer that these periods of settlement expansion in Palestine are intricately linked to the periods of transition and collapse that precede and follow, without recourse to explanations based on cultural change through large-scale invasions of different ethnic groups.

In drawing together the evidence for the settlement phases, it is useful to examine separately the periods of expansion and decline. Throughout the history of Palestine there have been both major and minor cycles of expansion and decline. It is possible to sketch some periods in greater detail because of the scholarly attention paid to these areas, whereas specific information is lacking for other phases due to factors like the lack of scholarly attention and the destruction or erosion of archaeological remains. A further consideration governing the amount of detail presented here is that some periods are considered of greater potential for comparative purposes with the period of the emergence of Israel.

Archaeological and Historical Periods in Agrarian Palestine*

Early Bronze (EB)		
	EBI	3150-2850 BCE
	EBII	2850-2650 BCE
	EBIII	2650-2350 BCE
	EBIV/MB I	2350-2000 BCE
Middle Bronze (MB)		
	MBIIA	2000-1750 BCE
	MBIIB	1750-1550 BCE
	[MBIIC	1650-1550 BCE]
Late Bronze (LB)		
	LBI	1550-1400 BCE
	LBIIA	1400-1300 BCE
	LBIIB	1300-1200 BCE

Iron

IronIA	1200-1150 BCE
IronIB	1150-1000 BCE
IronIIA	1000-900 BCE
IronIIB	900-800 BCE
IronIIC	800-587 BCE

Persian	538-332 BCE
Hellenistic	332-63 BCE
Roman	63 BCE-330 CE
Byzantine	330-636 CE
Early Muslim Caliphs	636-661 CE
Umayyad	661-750 CE
Abbasid	750-972 CE
Fatimid	972-1071 CE
Seljuq	1071-1098 CE
Crusader	1099-1291 CE
Ayyubid	1187-1260 CE
Mamluk	1260-1517 CE
Ottoman	1517-1917 CE
British	1920-1948 CE
Israeli	1948-present

*These are conventional chronological divisions, based on technological and political categories. They do not directly reflect the periods of settlement history in Palestine.

Regeneration and Expansion

1. Early Bronze I-III (3150-2350 BCE)

The Early Bronze period in Palestine developed from many small rural settlements in the Early Bronze I to a truly urban culture in Early Bronze II-III with significant concentrations of population within massive fortifications. Our knowledge of the many small rural unwalled settlements of the Early Bronze I period has been greatly enhanced by the salvage operation carried out at 'En-shadud by Braun and Gibson (1984). This small site located in the fertile Jezreel Valley near an abundant water supply was based on an agricultural-pastoral economy. It is significant that the artifactual and architectural remains attest to trade and close interaction with contemporary sites. Most of the small Early Bronze I sites like 'En-shadud were shortlived, although the reasons for their abandonment are not at all clear. Nevertheless, this period forms the transition to the Early Bronze II-III urban expansion.

The Early Bronze II-III period represents the first urban period in the history of Palestine. By the beginning of the Early Bronze III the settlement pattern of the country had changed significantly. The type of settlement was represented by either very large sites or small and very small sites, with only a very few medium sites. Broshi and Gophna (1984:45-49) have identified more than 160 settlements of less than one hectare; and, as they point out, the number was probably much greater since most of the settlements of this size still remain to be discovered.

Recent studies (Gophna, 1984; Broshi and Gophna, 1984) have also added significantly to our knowledge of the pattern of distribution of sites during this period. Settlement was not simply confined to the fertile plains and valleys but also spread to the Shephelah and hill country. In fact, the Early Bronze Age is the first phase in the history of Palestine which saw major settlement in the highlands. Half of the total settlements investigated by Broshi and Gophna (1984:49) were to be found in Galilee, Samaria and Judaea. Thus forty-five percent of the total area of settlement for the whole country was located in the mountains. The opening up of these more marginal areas, including the Arad plain and the Negev, clearly indicates the growth of population and the competition for land during this period (Broshi and Gophna, 1984:50). The hill country was not to be as densely settled again until the emergence and growth of Israel during the Iron Age.

As Gophna (1984:29) points out, this movement into the hillcountry also has implications for the agricultural landscape, since with many of the sites situated in the uplands it seems reasonable to assume that this must have led to the clearance of scrub. The evidence at 'Ai, Arad and Tel Dalit also suggests that the population were able to solve the problems of water shortage in these more arid areas by the storage of rainwater in cisterns cut into the cretaceous limestone or even by the construction of dams to hold the run off of surface water.

In conjunction with the settlement in the steppes and highlands, there is also evidence that sites in southern Sinai had close interconnections with the Negev sites such as Arad (Amiran, Beit-Arieh, and Glass, 1973). Beit-Arieh (1983) has identified 50 very small sites from the Early Bronze II period in central and southern Sinai. Oren's study (1973) of sites in northern Sinai shows that settlement was spread over a wide area and dependent in the main on an agricultural-pastoral economy. Clearly the Early Bronze period represents a major expansion of settlement and agriculture even into the most marginal areas of the country.

Middle Bronze II (2000-1550 BCE)

Following the transitional, mostly non-urban Early Bronze IV/ Middle Bronze I period,[3] the succeeding Middle Bronze II period in Palestine again witnessed a major settlement expansion. Mabry (1984) describes how large numbers of walled and unwalled cities, towns and villages reappeared after several centuries of non-urban settlement. The archaeological evidence suggests a significant expansion of settlement and rise in population. The greatest expansion took place in the coastal plain with the greatest concentrations of population in the urban centres on the main trade routes (Broshi and Gophna, 1986). Mabry also refers to an expansion of smaller medium-sized sites.

Even allowing for the unevenness of settlement surveys it is evident that many settlements were established in the fertile and well-watered coastal plain, as in the Huleh, Jordan, Jezreel and Beth-shean valleys (Mabry, 1984:3). The Shephelah and central hill country became more densely populated in the later Middle Bronze IIB and C phases. There is also evidence of settlement at this later time in the more peripheral Arad and Beersheba valleys. As most commentators recognize, the development of this urban period seems to have been peaceful, since there is no evidence of destruction at any of the preceding Middle Bronze I sites. Furthermore, the urban centres at the beginning of the Middle Bronze II lack fortifications, a feature to be contrasted with the development of massive fortifications during the Middle Bronze II period (Dever, 1976:15).

Mabry (1984:4) shows how the initial phase of the Middle Bronze II settlement was divided between many small rural sites and a few large urban centres, with the overwhelming majority of the population living within the cities. The recent study by Broshi and Gophna (1986) of settlement distribution and site size confirms that demographic growth during this period was urban based. They estimate (1986:88, n.1) that 80 per cent of the total area of Middle Bronze IIA occupation and 66 per cent of Middle Bronze IIB occupation was accounted for by large rampart settlements. The division of settlement between small rural villages and large urban centres is reminiscent of the pattern of settlement during the Early Bronze II-III period. The further development and diffusion of medium-sized sites during the Middle Bronze IIB and C periods indicates an increasing complexity of regional and interregional economic and communication links as well as a significant increase in population. Mabry's study (1984:5) shows that:

> While the number and combined occupational areas of very large sites remained about the same in the MBIIB and C periods, the total area of intermediate-sized sites rose significantly. The per centage of the total occupational area represented by very large sites therefore decreased more than 15%, while the percentage of total area represented by medium and large sites increased by almost the same amount (12%). This shift suggests that by the MBIIB and C, large villages and towns had become important local centers of population in the countryside, perhaps the centers of rural networks of communications within regional urban-rural hierarchies.

The expansion of settlement was evidently not uniform throughout the country, with the pickup much slower in the Shephelah and hill country (Gophna, 1984:25; see also Broshi and Gophna, 1986). The Early Bronze IV/Middle Bronze I culture seems to have persisted for a greater period of time in Transjordan (de Geus, 1971:46). The fact that the urban development at the beginning of the Middle Bronze II phase took place in the coastal areas and plains (see Broshi and Gophna, 1986) at the time of the revival of Egypt under the 12th Dynasty indicates that trade was a major factor in the regeneration of Palestine. The evidence for Egyptian trade throughout the Levant and beyond is to be found in the many Hyksos scarabs scattered throughout every region and including Anatolia and Cyprus (Aharoni, 1982:106). Gophna (1984:31; see also Tubb, 1983) believes that this economic activity was caused by the beginning of maritime trade which led to the establishment of Akko, Dor, Yavneh-Yam and Ashqelon as harbour cities along the Mediterranean littoral. The prosperity of this period is well attested in the material remains at many of the sites. Wright (1971:293) describes this as the greatest period of prosperity in the country's history, which was not to be surpassed until the phenomenal economic and demographic expansion of the Roman-Byzantine period. According to Dever (1976:8), the pottery of the Middle Bronze IIA period represents 'the finest locally made pottery in the history of the country, both in its aesthetic pleasing forms and its exquisite workmanship and finish'.

The Iron I-IIC (1200-587 BCE)

The Iron I period experienced a dramatic increase in small agricultural settlements throughout Galilee (Aharoni, 1957), the central hill country (Kochavi, 1972) and the Negev (Aharoni, 1976;1982). This expansion of settlement both in the highlands and on the southern steppe border is the primary feature of this period. Stager (1985:3), based on the work of Kochavi (1972), illustrates the dramatic increase in settlement in the highland. Small rural settlements increased from 23 in the Late Bronze Age to 114 in Iron I, of which 97 were new foundations. Weippert (1979) refers to a corresponding expansion of settlement in Transjordan, where similar ceramic forms, architectural features, and agricultural practices have been discovered (Ibrahim, 1978). The reasons for this expansion of agriculture into the highlands and steppes, usually associated with the emergence of Israel, will be the subject of Chapters 4 and 5.

The end of the Iron I and beginning of the Iron II periods, roughly corresponding to the Israelite and Judaean kingdoms, witnessed an increase in urban settlement and fortification. Surveys have shown that this was a period of centralization and expansion of urban settlement, which would suggest a corresponding increase in population. The development of monumental architecture during the Solomonic period is well known from the casemate walls and gate structures at Hazor, Megiddo and Gezer (see Dever, 1982a). However, recent studies (R. Cohen, 1979; A. Mazar, 1982) have shown that the Judaean hills and Negev were densely settled with a whole complex of fortifications throughout from the ninth through the seventh centuries BCE. Aharoni (1976) has already described the important Iron Age fortifications at Beersheba, Tel Malhata, Tel Ira and Arad. There is also evidence of extensive farming during the Iron Age in the Negev (Stager, 1976b). The evidence clearly points to a period of settlement expansion, although the concentration upon urban tells means that there is little information on the nature of rural settlement during this period.

The Roman-Byzantine Period (63 BCE–636 CE)
A glance at a map of Palestine during the Roman-Byzantine period immediately reveals the extraordinary expansion of settlement in the early centuries of this era (see, for example, Avi-Yonah, 1976; Broshi, 1980). This period represents the greatest density of population in the history of Palestine before the 1900 CE. 'The partial archaeological surveys carried out in the various sectors of Palestine both west and east of the Jordan give a proportion of four to one for the Roman Byzantine period, as compared to the number of villages extant in 1900' (Avi-Yonah, 1974:109-10). Palestine had enjoyed a general economic improvement throughout the preceding Hellenistic period despite the struggle for control of the area between the Seleucids and the Ptolemies. Once again the focus had shifted to the Mediterranean coast with the coastal ports handling wheat, wine and olive oil for export. The Nabateans benefited greatly from their involvement in the transit of spices and other luxuries between southern Arabia and the Mediterranean through the Negev (Orni and Efrat, 1966:157). Palestine experienced even greater economic benefit under the stability of Roman and Byzantine rule, particularly after the traumas of the post-70 CE period, which encouraged the further increase of international trade and the import of valuable technology into the area. An elaborate paved road network was developed throughout the country, including some of the more difficult or peripheral areas such as the Negev (Karmon, 1971:47). The Romans also invested heavily in the improvement of harbour facilities on the Palestinian coastline. Caesarea, built by Herod as a client of Rome, represents a major feat of engineering. All this was necessary to aid the flow of troops and goods throughout the empire, especially as Syria had become the major supplier of grain. The security of the area was guaranteed by the construction of the defensive network, the *limes arabicus*, skirting the edge of the Arabian desert.

The transfer of power to Byzantium and the state adoption of Christianity had even greater repercussions for the material prosperity and settlement patterns of Palestine. Economic and technological investment along with the influx of settlers and pilgrims resulted in flourishing trade and the greatest density of population Palestine and Transjordan had ever achieved. The most important mark of this expansion of settlement and population is to be found in the more arid marginal zones such as the Negev where sophisticated technology was employed to harness scarce water supplies from over very large areas to support intensive agriculture, a feat that has not been emulated until the heavy financial and technological investment of the present day. The recent survey work of Dauphin and Schonfield (1983) confirms that the Golan heights were densely settled in the Roman-Byzantine period. The Negev sites thrived in the vicinity of trade routes that crossed this area from Egypt and the Red Sea.

The Modern Period

The cyclical pattern of decline and regeneration continued and culminated in a long period of depopulation up until 1900 CE. The effects of industrialization in other parts of the world reached Palestine after some delay during the second half of the nineteenth century, gradually at first and then at an accelerating pace (Owen, 1981; 1982; Issawi, 1982). This development stimulated the most recent expansion in population growth and agricultural settlement. By the time of the founding of the state of Israel, Palestine had achieved essentially Western standards of industrial development, and its population was increasing, partly again through immigration, at a rate greater than any other Middle Eastern country, and possibly greater than any other comparable area in the world. Wilson (1979:54) describes Israel as the only developed economy in the Middle East. Its agricultural production rose by more than 650 per cent between 1950-70, while *per capita* production trebled. This represents the highest growth rate in agricultural production world-wide (Wilson, 1979:56).

Decline and Transition

Prior to the periods of expansion, with the possible exception of the first, there occurred definable periods of significant decline in settlement and agriculture. At times we see quite dramatic collapses and at other times noticeable periods of decline from what had preceded linked to periods of transition before the phase of regeneration and expansion began again. As before, some of the more dramatic evidence will be described for the specific periods of decline without trying to cover every major and minor cycle.

Early Bronze III (2650-2350 BCE)

As we have seen there was a general expansion in population and settlement throughout the Early Bronze period. One of the major features of the archaeological record is the development of massive fortifications as the period progressed, especially during the Early Bronze III. It has long been held that the end of the Early Bronze period saw the total destruction of Early Bronze III cities (cf. Aharoni, 1982:79-80). However, Richard (1980:12) has recently questioned this by arguing that although a number of urban sites were destroyed at this time, like Jericho, Bab edh-Dhra' and 'Ai, many more seem to have been abandoned, for instance Bethshan, Lachish, Tell el-Hesi, Tell Beit Mirsim, Hazor, Dothan, Megiddo, among others. However this debate is resolved, it is clear that the end of the Early Bronze III phase witnessed a sharp decline in urban-based settlement. It should also be noted that this urban decline had begun to a certain extent at the end of Early Bronze II with the destruction of Arad, Dan, Ashdod, Tell el-Far'ah (N), Gezer, and others (see Richard, 1980:9; Dever, 1980:38; Prag, 1984:61).

The alteration in settlement pattern towards the end of the Early Bronze period is again striking. Dever (1980:38) speaks of a massive shift of population from the fortified tell sites of central Palestine to the more marginal areas in the south and Transjordan. Thus it would appear that the fertile coastal plain and valleys experienced serious depopulation while the focus of population switched to the marginal and peripheral zones where small settlements were dependent upon intensive agriculture and herding (Richard, 1980:25). This would suggest that the general upheaval had led to a dramatic decline in trade upon which the coastal cities had been heavily dependent. The movement of settlement to the more marginal hill country and peripheral areas indicates a need to seek refuge from the vulnerable lowlands on the international trade routes while developing subsistence agriculture in order to survive. The exact causes of the collapse are not easy to determine, although Richard (1980:10-11) attributes it to the combination of climatic change and a weakened economy after the cessation of trade with Egypt following the decline of the Old Kingdom (cf. Prag, 1984:67).[4]

Early Bronze IV/Middle Bronze I (2350-2000 BCE)
This period forms the transition between the collapse of Early Bronze III urban culture and the Middle Bronze II expansion. The shift in settlement pattern which followed the Early Bronze III collapse becomes standard for the next 350 years. Recent research has confirmed the view that the Early Bronze IV/Middle Bronze I

period was largely non-urban, with an overwhelming majority of small agricultural villages (Prag, 1974; 1984; Dever, 1980; Richard, 1980; Falconer and Magnes-Gardiner, 1984). Dever (1980:58) has characterized the Early Bronze IV/Middle Bronze I as 'the brief triumph of the 'desert' over the 'sown''. It is most important to recognise, as Dever has already pointed out, that the move to a largely non-sedentary, pastoral-nomadic way of life was the result not the cause of the Early Bronze III collapse. It has become increasingly recognized in recent years that the developments which took place were largely due to internal conditions in response to political and economic factors rather than the result of a major Amorite, or some other, invasion (de Geus, 1971; Liverani, 1973; Dever, 1980; Tubb, 1983; Prag, 1984).[5]

The spread of settlement into the more marginal and more arid zones of the country was not the result of population pressure in search of further agricultural land (cf. Aharoni, 1982:83-85) but a withdrawal from the more vulnerable lowlands at a time of political instability. Dever (1980:42-44) refers to over 400 sites in the Negev during the later Early Bronze IV/Middle Bronze I period which had a diversified economy based on herding, dry farming and, possibly, some trade. He does not rule out the possibility of finding such sites in the central and northern Palestinian countryside, but emphasizes the problems of discovering such sites due to the shallowness of surface deposits and poor preservation (1980:45). The change of settlement to the marginal areas of the Negev and Transjordan away from the urban sites is reminiscent of the change which occurred at the beginning of the Iron I period.

Late Bronze Age (1550-1200 BCE)
The whole of the Late Bronze Age is a period of settlement and demographic fluctuation which culminated in the spectacular collapse of eastern Mediterranean civilization at the end of Late Bronze IIB. Gonen (1984) draws attention to the disparity between the picture of urban wealth and strength presented in various texts and the archaeological evidence for destruction, abandonment and poverty. Her analysis emphasizes the decrease in number and size of Late Bronze Age settlement compared with the Middle Bronze II. Surface surveys reveal that in the Late Bronze Age the number of settlements was only 37 per cent of the number in the Middle Bronze period (Gonen, 1984:65). There seems to have been a decline in

settlement in the first two centuries of this period (Kenyon, 1973:555; Gonen, 1984:63), followed by a period of regeneration, before the well-documented collapse of the late-thirteenth century BCE.

The Late Bronze Age experienced both a decline in settlement size and the total settlement area occupied. According to Gonen (1984:68), small or very small sites eventually constituted 88-95 per cent of the total number of settlements, whereas the area of settlement shrank to only 45 per cent of that of the Middle Bronze II. At the very end of the period a dramatic economic recession accompanied a contraction of settlement and general depopulation following widespread destruction at most of the major tells in Palestine as well as throughout the whole of the Eastern Mediterranean. It is this situation which precedes the emergence of Israel at the beginning of the Iron Age.

The Persian Period (538-332 BCE)
It has long been assumed that following the destruction of Jerusalem by the Babylonians in 587 BCE, the Persian period in Palestine represented a decline in settlement and population. This period has not received anything like the attention that the periods preceding have benefited from, and it is this fact along with the general paucity of remains that has largely contributed to the conclusion that this was a period of decline. This is a view that can be found expressed in numerous works from Albright and Kenyon onwards. However, the recent detailed work of Stern (1982; 1984a; 1984b) in examining the surveys and excavation reports available for this period led to a reappraisal of previously held views. He has shown (1982:48) that the destruction, depopulation and only gradual resettlement took place in the southern and central hill country. By contrast, the coastal area and Galilee seem to have been densely populated and to have prospered. Surprisingly, given the prevailing views of destruction and decline, the survey of the Beth-shean plain and its surroundings revealed that the area was densely settled. Once again the prosperity of the coastal cities was dependent on the flourishing international trade with the rest of the Persian empire. Therefore rather than a general destruction and decline it is now clear that the decline was limited to certain areas, namely the southern hill country. Thus once again a familiar pattern in the history of Palestinian settlement emerges with contraction in the hill country and urban-centred growth in the coast and lowlands.

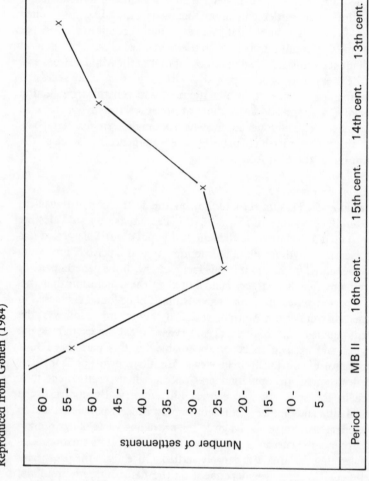

Figure 1 Fluctuations in number of settlements

Reproduced from Gonen (1984)

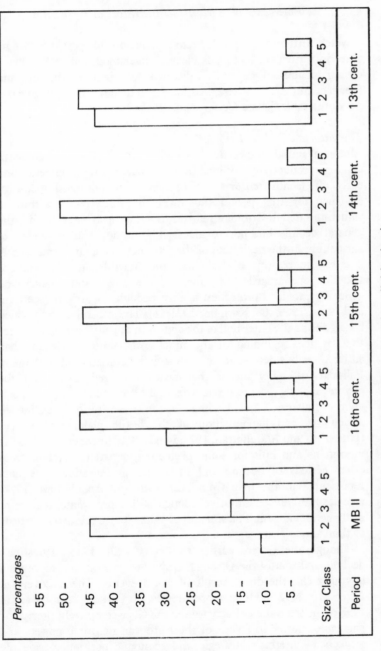

Figure 2   Size of settlements (in percentage of total available data)

Much further work will have to be done on this period before its place in settlement history is clearly understood. It may be that a clearer picture will depend on distinguishing between the fifth and fourth centuries BCE where possible. Until then it is liable to give rise to considerable debate (Avi-Yonah, 1977:19).

The Ottoman Period (1517-1917 CE)

After an initial resurgence of agriculture during the sixteenth century, productivity declined until the nadir of the eighteenth and early nineteenth century was reached. The improved historical evidence for this period illustrates the fluctuations within it, sometimes tied to Ottoman reforms; these were able to influence the general decline but not to arrest it for long. The expansion of agriculture at the beginning of the Ottoman occupation was largely due to the reforms of Suleiman the Magnificent who reduced taxation, encouraged trade, fortified the towns and villages and generally provided protection against bedouin incursions (see Orni and Efrat, 1966:167; Karmon, 1971:51). The general decline which began during the latter half of the sixteenth century became so severe that by the beginning of the nineteenth century Palestine had suffered serious demographic decline and contraction of settlement. Political instability meant that bedouin ranged throughout the country making most routes unsafe, as the numerous visitors' reports vividly illustrate, and leading to the most serious decline in agriculture and depopulation of the fertile plains and valleys (Hütteroth and Abdulfattah, 1977:54-63). Settlement reverted to the mountains and hills for some protection, a pattern familiar from other periods of decline and instability in Palestine. The data represented in the map from Hütteroth and Abdulfattah (1977) provide the only quantitative, though still approximate, picture of settlement change in Palestine other than site surveys over a period of time.

Though there were earlier factors (Curtin, 1984), Palestine's decline, and that of the Ottoman empire in general, was more than anything else the direct result of world events. The discovery of America in 1492 and then, more directly, the Portuguese discovery in 1498 of the sea route to India around the Cape completely altered the balance of power in favour of the European maritime powers and weakened Palestine's strategic and economic position astride the trade routes to the east and west. It was now left on the periphery of

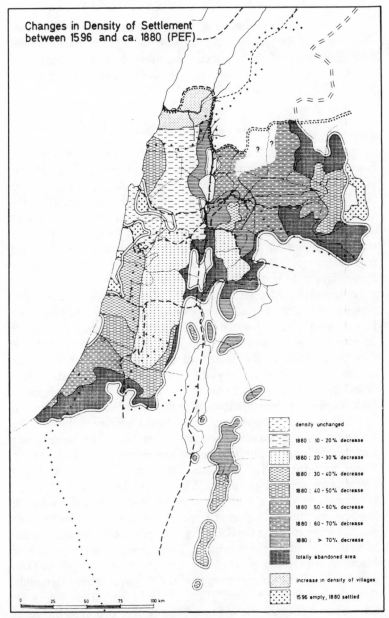

Map 1 Changes in density of settlement between 1596/97 and ca. 1880 A.D.
Reproduced from Hütteroth and Abdulfattah (1977)

the economic and later industrial boom that was enjoyed in Europe. The dramatic decline in trade through the Middle East and the mismanagement of the Ottomans contributed to the recession in infrastructural and political investment in Palestine which gave rise to instability and spiralling decline.

Minor phases of Expansion and Decline

Several minor phases as well as innumerable smaller fluctuations, apart from the more major phases outlined above, can also be identified. These minor phases are worth outlining briefly since they tend to confirm the patterns of settlement we have already seen. They are also helpful in highlighting the importance of interregional economic factors for the settlement history of Palestine. Indeed, in the next chapter we will consider some similar developments on a regional basis and the ways in which they interact with interregional factors identified in the present chapter.

Looked at in the long term, the spread of settlement and density of population in Palestine achieved during the Roman and Byzantine periods were apparently not duplicated until this century. During the intervening twelve to thirteen hundred years, periods of relative expansion included the Umayyad caliphate, the first Crusader century, and the first century of Ottoman control in Palestine. The failure of the Umayyads to match the previous era was related to their inability to chase the Byzantine fleet out of the Mediterranean. The political capital was moved inland from Caesarea to Ramlah, the only major new urban centre founded by the Umayyads, as sea trade was curtailed. Agricultural expansion into marginal drylands like the Negev subsided, and it is possible that at the same time many highland terraces fell into disuse. The relative decline under Muslim sovereignty continued with the removal of the Abassid capital to Baghdad and the setting up of European trade connections through Russian waterways and the Baltic in partial place of the Mediterranean. With the Crusades Palestine once again experienced the expansion of Mediterranean trade particularly through the Italian ports. The population of the coastal towns seems to have increased mainly through the influx of settlers. The situation in the hill country is not clear since nearly all the information available concerns the main urban centres such as Jerusalem (see Edbury, 1985). The Seljuq 'empire' based on the unification of Egypt with Palestine saw an initial period of expansion before it yielded to the comparative decline of prosperity and population during the succession of Mamluk rulers. This period suffered the devastation of the Black Death in the fourteenth century in addition to political fragmentation. As we have seen, a brief resurgence in the first half of the sixteenth century eventually gave way to the severe late Ottoman decline which continued virtually to the beginning of the present century.

Summary
The preceding discussion clearly shows that the expansion of settlement and accompanying growth in population were not unilinear in any period of Palestine's history. The complex cycle of expansion, contraction and regeneration means that no periodization may be regarded as rigid or absolute since it is impossible to assign precise dates to the various phases of settlement. Further refinement in the description of fluctuations in settlement will be possible only with further archaeological research, especially for some of the later periods. Despite the limitations in our knowledge of specific periods, the above sketch at least makes clear some of the more important recurrent patterns in the settlement and population history of Palestine. Its value for the present study is that the emergence of Israel during the early Iron Age, a detailed discussion of which is reserved for Chapters 4 and 5, can no longer be viewed as an isolated or unique episode in the history of this region. The broad overview of settlement patterns from the Early Bronze Age to the present enables the emergence of Israel to be understood in its proper historical perspective.

The comparative perspective has highlighted significant patterns in the periodic fluctuations of Palestinian settlement which deserve more careful study. Although it is clear that the regional distribution of settlement, the total area occupied, the type of settlement and population size varied from period to period, it is also evident that patterns of settlement can be identified and compared. In particular, there are a number of periods of expansion, such as the Early Bronze II-III, the Middle Bronze II, the Roman-Byzantine, and the modern period, which were urban-based and where the focus of settlement was to be found in the coastal plain and lowlands. However, we have already noted that such periods of expansion were by no means uniform or unilinear in their development. The various phases of expanded settlement eventually gave way to increasing insecurity, as seen in the development of massive fortifications, and social conflict resulting in the destruction or abandonment of once prosperous urban centres. The reasons for the stagnation and decline, sometimes dramatic collapse, of these urban economies are not always clear, although traditional explanations based upon external invasions and population change no longer satisfy the available data. The subsequent periods of decline and transition illustrate a perceivable shift in settlement away from the exposed lowlands to smaller dispersed settlements in the more marginal areas of the highlands or arid zones. The shift in settlement which accompanied the emergence of Israel following the Late Bronze Age collapse can now be seen as comparable to similar shifts during the Early Bronze IV/Middle Bronze I after the urban-based Early Bronze III decline, or the later Ottoman decline which led to serious depopulation, particularly in the lowlands.

Agriculture in the highlands and margins of Palestine therefore developed in response to differing political and economic circumstances. During periods of general political stability and flourishing international trade through the lowland urban centres, economic growth often led to demographic growth and an expansion of settlement throughout the whole region. The opportunities offered by outside investment, along with the pressures of demographic growth, allowed the highlands and steppes to be exploited more fully. However, the emergence of Israel at the beginning of the Early Iron Age does not fit this pattern of settlement expansion. It must be compared with shifts which occur in response to urban decline rather than urban prosperity. The settlement shift at the beginning of the Early Iron Age was rather a response to the disruption of international trade and urban decline at the end of the Late Bronze Age. Therefore it needs to be set within the general cycle of decline and transition along with the Early Bronze III urban collapse and settlement shift to the highlands and margins during the Early Bronze IV/Middle Bronze I period, or the similar shift away from the lowlands during the later Ottoman period. The potential of this comparative perspective to illuminate important factors in the emergence of Israel at the end of the Late Bronze and beginning of the early Iron Age will be explored in Chapters 4 and 5.

The discussion of the phases of expansion, decline and transition also indicates that various scholars have offered a variety of explanations for the shifts in settlement during particular periods.

We turn now to a closer consideration of the question why such variation occurs. Why has Palestine not produced an ever-expanding population and border of settlement? Is it possible to identify circumstances which most or all of these phases of settlement expansion or retraction might have in common that might help to explain the fluctuations? What factors appear to have had the greatest influence on the demographic and settlement changes in Palestine? The following discussion will attempt to assess some of the factors which have been put forward to account for social changes in Palestinian history. The important difference in the present study, however, is that our discussion will look at a number of factors from a comparative perspective rather than in isolation, with reference to only a particular phase of settlement history. Once again the strategy adopted here is to use such comparative findings to suggest fresh questions and thereby stimulate research into the particular social transformation which accompanied the emergence of Israel.

Major Factors in the Cyclical Variability of Agriculture and Settlement

The phases in settlement and agriculture can be related to a number of factors that influence change and process in the history of Palestine. Several factors have figured prominently in the discussion of these phases, considered individually or together, and merit attention because of their correlation over the entire historical period. These are demographic variability, climate, technology, peasant unrest, changes in sovereignty and interregional economic exchange. All these have a significant infrastructural component—a direct link with reproduction and basic production—and it may be assumed that they all therefore play some role in historical change in Palestine. They are of course interrelated, although this is particularly true of suzerainity and interregional economic exchange. The last is especially important, as it more than any other factor looks beyond the essentially local, internal or indigenous effects in Palestine, which is after all a region of relatively low population and production under the constant influence of outside regions, to take adequate account of interregional relations. Though the other factors are important, interregional economic exchange will require the fullest treatment because it correlates best with the phases described. It bears closest coincidence with, and thus apparently the closest relation to, the *set* of historical changes in comparative perspective. Although it is appropriate for us to give thorough attention to interregional economic exchange, it is not our purpose to prove its causal priority. Its relative explanatory significance in any particular instance will and should always be a matter for assessment.

Demographic Variability
Mendenhall (1973:216-26) claimed that the major archaeological phases Early Bronze I-IV, Middle Bronze I-II, Late Bronze and Iron I-III were all demarcated by ash layers. These destruction layers appeared with rhythmic frequency every 250-300 years or so. He thus developed the view that every tenth generation was characterized by wealth and a high density of population followed by destruction and abandonment of many cities. This theory of a rhythmic pattern to history, like many ostensible predecessors, has not been well received. Some have ridiculed it by association, while others have dismissed it as Hegelian or determinist (Hauser, 1978). It is clear, however, that in the past the density of population in a given area or region did in fact often rise and fall in a rhythmic cycle, often marked by quite dramatic fluctuations. Braudel (1974) has demonstrated such cycles on a world-wide scale in his study of population fluctuations for Europe in the period 1400-1800 CE. Many other studies could be adduced to confirm this basic perspective on demography (Wrigley, 1969; McEvedy and Jones, 1978).

Demographic increase is a prime aspect of the comprehensive historical cycle of intensification and depletion, as schematized and illustrated by Harris (1980) among others. An increase in population was typically accompanied by an increase in production and trade. The efforts of community or society were harnessed to the use of all available space by means of the most intensive technology, in order to accommodate the growing number of mouths to feed. The search for agricultural land forced cultivators out towards more marginal areas of woodland, swamp, dryland and highland. Technological breakthroughs could result from such population pressure, particularly breakthroughs in the use and spread of previously known technologies (Boserup, 1965; 1981). On the debit side, banditry became more profitable, while more serious disputes and even outbreaks of war could increase proportionately. The inevitable consequence was that the ever increasing numbers eventually outpaced the capacity of the land or the society to provide food (Braudel, 1974:2). The result was a dramatic decrease in population through war, epidemic, famine, or some combination of these. The phase of depletion could assume catastrophic proportions. In this way a balance between numbers and the land's or the society's capacity was restored. Space became available so that, once the surviving population had stabilized, living standards could rise, numbers again increase, and the cycle begin to repeat itself.[6]

One of the major factors contributing to periods of depletion and decline was disease, whose effects could be particularly catastrophic. The increase in population in conjunction especially with increased urbanization provided substantial human repositories for disease that could remain dormant for long periods before striking with deadly ferocity. The density of urban population, crowded in close proximity under conditions of primitive sanitation, meant increased contact with stagnant pools, rotting waste, and human faeces, as well as increased danger from infested water supplies. Palestine—particularly its lowlands —was perennially vulnerable to fatal outbreaks of disease accompanying the constant march of foreign armies, whose numbers, often small, were out of all proportion to the deadly effect of the diseases they carried, to which the indigenous population might have little or no immunity. Trade followed the same routes as the armies. The routes of lowland Palestine provided an easy passage for bacteria and virus in the company of travellers, merchants and their merchandise. The hazard of the lowlands was compounded during less developed periods when drainage was less extensive, by areas of swamp lands, breeding grounds of malaria, an affliction that the highlands of Palestine have escaped. The devastating effect possible from the spread of disease from one population to another in earlier times can well be imagined when it is recalled how virulent was the influenza that spread around the globe in 1956-58, despite the discoveries of modern medicine.[7]

Meyers (1981:107) has already stressed the significance of large-scale outbreaks of fatal disease contributing to the collapse of Late Bronze civilizations around the Mediterranean. The cause of the collapse of the Mycenaean empire evidenced in the destructions of Mycenaean IIIB and the onset of the Greek Dark Age has long been sought in the influx of new populations. When it proved impossible to locate the presence of these supposed new groups in the archaeological record, some resorted to the view that the invaders withdrew immediately they appeared. It is now widely held that the quest for these groups has failed. A different explanation might be indicated by the evidence for the adoption of cremation and individual cist tombs. The cist tombs are often associated with the renewal of settlement after a break along with a change in the location of the cemeteries (Snodgrass, 1971:179). This suggests some concern with the problem of contagion. Snodgrass rejects the view of Desborough (1972) and others that these cist tombs indicate new populations: the cist tombs are not new but a resurgent phenomenon of the pre-Mycenaean period. The spread of cremation throughout the Aegean, particularly as the Dark Age drew closer, might also point, through the associative logic of magic, to problems of contagion, although the indications that cremation was not used for child burial are puzzling. Cremation is also known from Hittite cemeteries at Osmankayasi and Ilica from 1600 BCE. The fact that many of the areas of the Aegean—the Argolid, Dodecanese, and Messenia—reverted to the more traditional practice of inhumation at a later date suggests that cremation was a short-term expedient to deal with outbreaks of disease that had devastated the communities.

McNeill's study (1976) of the tremendous, though often unrecognized, effects of disease throughout history leads to the conclusion that for later periods where there is more evidence something like 120-150 years are needed for human populations to stabilize their recovery from catastrophic infections. This is an important area of study for the history of early Israel that has not been accorded sufficient attention (see Mendenhall, 1973:105-21; Meyers, 1981). Biblical curses refer to disease frequently, and in particular the *herem* may indicate a wish to avoid contagion. The narrative of the exodus makes stylized reference to plague in Egypt, while the narrative concerning the the ark in I Samuel refers to a plague that affected the Philistines. The rhythm of the past with its periodic waves of disease and demographic fluctuations represents one of the several indicators of periodic depletion, which itself has long-term and far-reaching economic effects. This is an important area of historical research that Mendenhall has identified but that has not yet been followed up in biblical studies.[8]

Climate

Climatic change is a perennially popular but elusive explanation of significant historical change. In the early part of this century, Elsworth Huntington of Yale suggested what is now a discredited form of this explanation, and it has not often been applied to Palestine since.

Recently Horowitz has restudied the question in relation to Palestine (1974) for the period of the last 6000 years. He identifies two periods of more humid climate (presumed to be conducive to an expansion in agriculture) during which, to name his criteria, 'vegetation belts moved southwards and the share of olives in the natural maquis increased: until about 2400 B.C. and from 2100 until 1100 B.C. Dry phases have been recorded around 2250 and 950 B.C.' The first phase correlates well with the onset of Early Bronze IV, and the succeeding humid phase tolerably well with the onset of Middle Bronze IIA about 2000 BCE. The second dry phase however comes at the height of the Israelite revival of agriculture in the highland and does not produce a recognizable lull, even if some might wish to identify its effects with the droughts of the Elijah and Elisha narratives. Furthermore, this explanation cannot be applied on the available evidence to other later phases of agricultural expansion and decline, and the phases it does seem to pertain to can be explained equally well in other terms. Recent work based on weathering patterns in stones has not been able to detect the fluctuations reported by Horowitz (Danin, 1985).

A growing number of archaeologists and historians are beginning to investigate the effects of climate on historical change, in particular the change in settlement patterns. Tubb (1983) has combined climate with political and economic causes to explain the emergence of the Middle Bronze II urban expansion. Similarly Richard (1980) follows the same procedure in attempting to account for the abandonment of sites at the end of the Early Bronze III period. She actually goes further and argues that although the collapse of Early Bronze urban sites was due to the interaction of socio-economic and political factors, probably the major cause was the shift to a much more arid climate. She cites (1980:25) a growing body of environmental evidence from both Egypt and Palestine to substantiate her argument for a period of greater aridity c. 2350 BCE. As studies of this type multiply and the analysis of pollen, tree rings, and other factors becomes more sophisticated, our knowledge of the climate of Palestine and its effect upon particular periods of change will increase. Certainly climate should have an effect, but probably not directly on an interregional scale, given the subordination of Palestine to more powerful external influences.[9]

Rhys Carpenter (1966:63-75) has argued that the Mycenaean collapse was the result of a sharp climatic change which led to a prolonged period of drought and famine (see also Stiebing, 1980).

Despite criticisms of this hypothesis (H.E. Wright, 1968:123-27), it has been suggested by Bryson, Lamb and Donley (1974) that although it is not possible to prove a drought of major proportions at the time of the Mycenaean collapse, there is sufficient evidence to justify that such a hypothesis is consistent with available evidence for weather patterns. More scientific studies of long-term climatic change mean that this type of speculation can be set upon a much firmer footing. The failure of previous explanations of this type has been due to the fact that change is more easily accounted for by other more tangible means. Nevertheless in recent years, through greater scientific rigour in the analysis of pollen counts and tree rings, the study of the history of climate has become a legitimate and illuminating area of research (see especially Ladurie, 1970; 1972). It is now less concerned with theories assuming the unvarying duration of climate and more with fluctuations that occur over periods of varying lengths. Recent detailed research by historians and meteorologists indicate the consequences of fluctuations in temperature and rainfall on agriculture.

In a marginal agrarian economy like that of Palestine, the lack of rainfall or its dramatic decline would be devastating. Two consecutive bad harvests would result in famine and expose the undernourished population to the ever-present danger of epidemic. A glance at the alarming variations in rainfall that characterize present-day Palestine indicates how real a threat this must have been throughout the history of the region. This is especially true in the areas around the 200 mm isohyet which forms the critical divide between agriculture and pastoralism. The peasant population, forced to give its surplus to the land-owning class and dependent upon the towns for seed and the means of production, had little protection against the vagaries of an unpredictable climate. Conversely, a number of good harvests following favourable conditions could provide the basis for expansion and growing numbers. Climate obviously has an important effect upon historical change, but it must be viewed in light of and in conjunction with many other factors. At present our information is much too imprecise to be able to do justice to the analysis of the effects of climate or its interconnections with social and political factors (cf. Hopkins, 1985:99-108).

Technology
Technological change has long been recognized as one of the most

significant factors in historical change. It plays an obvious role in at least two of the major phases of agricultural expansion in Palestine. The vastly increased capacity of the modern period is unquestionably a result of industrial technology. A similar connection might be drawn from the great advance in administrative integration and control in the Roman Republic and Empire, and hence in Palestine during Roman hegemony there.[10]

For the two earlier phases of extension of agriculture and settlement, technological innovation was less likely to bear direct responsibility. Aharoni (1982:97) and others connect the MBIIA with the beginning of bronze use in Palestine. This correlation does not mean, however, that the significance of this innovation to Palestine derived simply from its use there alone. More likely, bronze influenced the pattern of settlement in Palestine as a result of the economic shifts and advantages enjoyed by neighbouring states linked to their dominant role in the trade of copper, tin and bronze.

A case has been made by several authors for at least the possibility that the introduction of iron played a role in the emergence of Israel, along with the development of slaked lime plaster cisterns, pit silos and terracing (Thompson, 1978a; Gottwald, 1978; 1979; Chaney, 1983). However, there is now ample evidence that terracing and the art of storing water in cisterns was known in the region well before the inception of the Iron Age.[11] Waldbaum's studies (1978; 1980) in particular have shown that the general use of iron for agriculture in the highland towns and villages does not appear until the tenth century BCE. Thus it has become increasingly difficult to argue for the significant use of iron by the Palestinian highland villager prior to the monarchic period.

The significance of technological change for Palestine depends, furthermore, on several theoretical issues that widen the scope for consideration well beyond Palestine. One of these issues is presented in its recent guise most pointedly by the work of Boserup (1965; 1981). A good deal of evidence has been arranged to suggest that the use of new technology often lags behind its discovery or invention, and that use, as opposed to invention, is frequently demand-induced by a prior increase in population. Though of little value apart from the evidence for specific regions and periods, such a theory should be carefully considered when it comes to Palestine, whose demography has proven, over the ages, to be so sensitive to external economic and political influences.

A second theoretical issue concerns whether or how a given technology comes to be applied in Palestine, and by whom. Pacey's work (1983) has perhaps the most recent discussion of the general point that different groups benefit from technology differently. Most often the cost of a new or newly-introduced technology is quite high and drops only after a period of development and widening use. This characteristic, familiar from new technologies in industrial and computerized societies and adaptable to agrarian technological improvements, suggests that new technology will be affordable only by the better off at first. Unless strong evidence exists to the contrary, it is unlikely that peasant technology was of leading significance among the conditions attending the major shifts in settlement and agriculture in the history of Palestine.

The clearest instance of technological significance mentioned above, industrialization in modern Palestine, is particularly instructive in this regard. Under Ottoman auspices, industrial technology entered Palestine relatively gradually, and then mostly to the economic advantage of the town and city elites. Yet over the decades during the nineteenth century it did make a steady rise in population possible. Then in the twentieth century, the British along with the Zionists transformed Palestine dramatically with Western industrial technology, applied to all areas of life, but especially to agriculture, policing and administration. As already pointed out, Palestine has become in this century the most industrially-advanced country in the Middle East. Why technology was introduced so heavily in this way is always the prior question, given the economic marginality of Palestine over the ages and in so many regards. One cannot ignore the effect of the influx of capital, first from the British state and European Jews, who provided the means of development and comparative political stability, and then, following the Second World War and the creation of the modern state of Israel, from the USA. In other words, technology is a factor in the history of agriculture, settlement, and demography in Palestine, but the focus in its application should not be so much on the region itself, from which very little if any new and significant technology originates, but rather on the external factors for its coming to be applied in Palestine.

A specific modern example of this principle involves the railroad and motor car. Both of these developments had a profound positive effect on agriculture in Palestine and negative effects on the traditional camel-centered bedouin economy. They may thus be said to have significantly affected the relationship between the desert and the sown. Yet these entered Palestine when and how they did largely due to European—especially German and British—interest in securing European affairs in Palestine. Indeed it could be argued that the primary historical matrix for the emergence of the technologically advanced Palestine of this century was the run up to and the course of the First World War. It is a virtual axiom that the history of the Middle East since Napoleon is manifestly tied to world history. There is no reason to believe that the axiom did not apply to technological innovation as well.

A third and very important theoretical issue concerns the relative constancy of basic *agrarian* technology over preceding millennia, at least since the introduction of iron 3000 years ago, if not longer. The basic farming culture of biblical times did indeed pass as recently as two generations or so ago—as attested by numerous Victorian and Edwardian tracts—despite millennia of technological innovation. During nearly the entire period under consideration in this book, technological innovation made little or no difference in the economic and social relations of the village peasant, and little to the nomad, except as it invited greater impositions of greater productivity by sovereign powers and their local proxies. To repeat, clearly changes in technology have contributed to historical change in Palestine at all levels. To mention just one example of interest, the availability of iron and improvements in its manufacture played a role in the eventual political consolidation of Israelite society and in the shift in hegemony over Palestine in the first millennium BCE from Egypt to Mesopotamia. However, for a technological innovation itself to be of leading significance for the extension of settlement and agriculture in Palestine, it would have to be shown that the innovation came into use quite apart from wider economic and political relations, or that a technologically based change in agricultural productivity could affect the pattern of settlement apart from such relations. It is difficult to think of a single example of such an innovation.[12]

Peasant Unrest

Peasant unrest, in the sense of tension, hostility, and open conflict of peasants against individuals and groups that dominate them economically and politically, is endemic to agrarian Palestine as to any agrarian society. The existence of the 'class struggle' as interpreted for example by Ste. Croix (1981) can easily be shown for Palestine, and like the other factors already discussed had an obvious effect on historical processes. The description of most significant historical events in Palestine would not be complete without some notice of the role played by workers and poor.

The evidence for unrest among the great majority of the population of Palestine with little or no wealth suggests however that peasant unrest is typically—and perhaps always—to be considered together with similar unrest among the urban masses, expressed through the activities of gangs and mobs of towns and cities. These tend to have larger numbers than rural gangs because of the cities' larger concentrated population, the closer social contact with the many in the city, and the proximity to the sources of payment and bribery that induce the mob to action. There are exceptions to this rule, but by and large it holds (Lapidus, 1984:143-84). It is doubtful, however, whether active unrest among the workers and poor of Palestine ever had a significant effect on the settlement of Palestine, despite the fact that they in part *were* the villagers.

It is important to consider peasant unrest for two reasons. First, peasant withdrawal from cultivation, particularly in the lowland, during periods of the decline of economic and political stability is an important factor in the settlement history of Palestine. This is particularly true of those periods outlined above when the focus of settlement switched from the urban-centred lowlands to the rural highlands or more peripheral regions to the south. Second, the topic is of particular interest in relation to the hypothesis of Mendenhall and Gottwald that early Israel originated in a peasant revolt or withdrawal to a highland frontier. Clearly since the peasants were the cultivators they only planted when the conditions were right. But the important question is whether such behaviour is an expression of class interest and solidarity or the result of individual household strategies in response to growing instability. Active unrest on a class basis tended to occur in the form of political action which was not closely linked with changes in settlement but tended to occur as a 'peaceable' consequence of agglomerated economic strategies. It is probable that many of the peasants of early Israel were lowland villagers who had withdrawn to the highlands, where they found conditions more conducive to cultivation. It is doubtful, however, that active unrest on a class basis played a leading role in creating those conditions in the highlands in the first place. It would appear to be rather a response to the dramatic economic decline of the Late

Bronze Age rather than a major cause of that decline. How Israel did emerge is the subject of later consideration, for now we need only consider in general what placed limitations on the effect of mass (rural *and* urban) unrest (see Kautsky, 1982:293-319).

Mass unrest is endemic in the history of Palestine as in any agrarian society, and the hostility and marauding of groups of workers and poor extremely common occurrences. These, therefore, hardly constitute a distinctive explanation for periodic fluctuations in settlement whose wavelength, as it were, extended over centuries. The same must be said for the element of frontier added by Lenski (1981) and Chaney (1983) in refinement of the revolt model of Israel's origins. The frontier is present throughout the history of Palestine, even to the present day. Indeed if one had to choose one word to sum up Palestine over the ages, one might, despite its hub-like centrality in many periods, choose the word frontier.

References to peasant revolt *per se*, as distinct from endemic unrest, tend to limit themselves to periods of expanded rather than expanding agriculture and population. If anything, this suggests that such revolts are more a result than a cause of such expansion, and are part of the cycle of depletion described previously when demographic pressures reach their height. Such a case could be made for the clearest examples of Solomonic, Omrid, Herodian, early Ottoman, and twentieth century revolts. There may be exceptions to this pattern, but it seems to set the norm (see Baer, 1982).

This correlation, furthermore, exposes the infrastructural component of what is otherwise essentially a political explanation. For it is increased population that distinguishes the periods of active peasant revolt from others. This increased population results from greater agricultural output, even when much of agriculture is in commercial crops because the added security of such periods induces greater productivity. Rather than setting in motion an expansion of agriculture and population, peasant revolt is a consequence of the combination of high population and a high degree of political control, which invariably go together. In a land like Palestine, peasants usually have alternative escape routes from endemic and perennial pressures: shifting to an increase in pastoralism and moving towards the margins of settlement along the frontiers of the land, either highland or steppe. Under expanded conditions, the pressure is greatest and the way to escape least open. Thus revolt becomes increasingly likely under such conditions. It may not be simply an accident of our sources that we know more about peasant revolt in Palestine in the first century CE than at any other period prior to the twentieth century.[13]

The reciprocity between peasant unrest and peasant pastoralism means not only that peasant revolt is a less compelling political solution to rural unrest, but also that the consequence is more likely to be the contraction rather than extension of agricultural settlement. Typically, to the *villager* the frontier is a *pastoral* frontier. A related consideration adds to the unlikelihood that peasant unrest ever led to the extension of settlement. As some peasant cultivators shifted their subsistence strategy in the direction of pastoralism and became increasingly nomadic so as eventually to adopt the social and political roles of the nomadic tribe, they concurrently assumed other political roles. That is, the two strategies as types, the peasant and the nomad, led to distinctive socio-political roles in the wider society. Nomads, though in many ways more independent from the urban elite, were at the same time more closely related to them than the peasants. In other words, as some peasants shifted to a nomadic strategy, they were able to take advantage of a social mobility made possible by the pastoral option in Palestine's frontier that is not always present in other agrarian societies.

Perhaps the most important limitation on mass unrest as an explanation for historical change in general in Palestine is the prevalence of vertical instead of horizontal socio-economic cleavage for the expression of economic discontent. In other words, it is questionable whether the lines of unrest were ever drawn primarily on the basis of class. Local conflict fed by mass unrest invariably, it seems from the evidence, pitted faction against faction, party against party, in a perpetual mirroring of the conflicts among urban notables (Lapidus, 1984:143-84). Urban factions and parties typically drew the rural masses in their train, and just as the urban mobs had no will of their own (Lapidus, 1984:165), but supported the cause of the notable who could offer the greatest economic promise, so neither did the rural masses. Lapidus' summary (1984:165) for the Mamluk period applies to other periods as well: 'The populace behaved as an amorphous mass seeking only the most immediate monetary gains, having no deep attachments to any party'. This kind of behaviour follows, of course, from the extremely short-term perspective produced by poverty; but the existence of poverty is not at issue, only its effects. As an expression of class interest, mass unrest was typically and perhaps always in Palestine subordinated to the interests of urban factions. In addition, the hostility between rural and urban masses and the bedouin overrode any solidarity these groups might have shared against the urban elite (Lapidus, 1984:169).

Chaney (1983) analyzes the *apiru* of the Amarna texts, a category of the Palestinian population that may have played a significant role in the emergence of Israel, in terms of Hobsbawm's description (1972) of 'social bandits'. Chaney's analysis is compelling and sheds fresh light on much of this well known data. He conceives of the *apiru* bandits as basically transformed peasants, although he is careful to insist that the class distinction between peasant and urban elite was only one of the possible cleavages that played a part in the socioeconomic dynamics of that period. Yet the comparative evidence for alternative cleavages strongly suggests that the class distinction was invariably overridden (cf. Blok, 1972). The features of the *apiru* in the Amarna documents might be elucidated even better by comparison with the pre-Mamluk *'ahdath* and Mamluk *zu'ar* described by Lapidus (1984:157-58, 176-77), urban gangs easily induced behind this party or that, paid by one faction then another in the squabbles and civil wars of urban notables, in order to be utilized as 'paramilitary reserves'. The more complete evidence for the Qayis and Yaman factions in the eighteenth and nineteenth centuries CE confirms this pattern in considerable detail.[14]

Changes in Suzerainty

A series of over a score of maps on facing pages of the *Atlas of Israel* dramatizes one of the most important regularities in the history of Palestine. This region is nearly always dominated, more or less, by outside suzerainties. There is scarcely a time when this is not so. Changes in suzerainty serve perhaps as the commonest hooks on which to drape the history of Palestine.

Scholars of the Middle East have found it useful to follow a distinction popularized by Coon (1951) between suzerainty and sovereignty (Fisher, 1961). Sovereignty is real political or military control, whereas suzerainty is nominal sovereignty. Clearly this distinction is a matter of degree, but it has been found to be widely applicable to the entire Middle East over long periods. Maps like the ones just mentioned, which emphasise suzerain territories with distinct boundaries, can be misleading. They suggest that the great suzerainties, or empires, of Middle Eastern history exercised uniform sovereignty over sharply bounded territories. Uniform sovereignty can indeed prevail in many modern states, but in agrarian states, especially in the Middle East, this was far from usual. Normally sovereignty was strongest near political centres and in areas under most intensive cultivation or agricultural development. It then diminished with distance as one moved into the hills or out into the steppe and it is this pastoral frontier that plays an important role in the history of settlement in Palestine. For a wider region with a geography like the Near East's, sovereignty was widely curtailed or, more accurately, held by a local ruler on behalf of the more distant suzerain.

Thus, although it is appropriate to speak of Egyptian, Assyrian, Persian, Macedonian, Ptolemaic, Roman, Islamic, Abbasid, Ottoman, and British suzerainty in Palestine—and many more could be named—these represent a considerable variety of actual local control. In most instances, real local control, or sovereignty, was exercised by local rulers, some of whose names are preserved, as well as innumerable unrecorded officers, sheikhs, priests, dignitaries, notables and the like in a complex hierarchy of authorities.

Because Palestine is a small and poor area, it is normally dominated by outside powers. Furthermore, because it is a border and transit zone, control changes frequently. These changes are too frequent to correlate consistently with the major settlement phases, and changes in suzerainty do not fit well with many of the cusps of the settlement phases. Certainly there is some correlation, such as the beginning of MBIIA which corresponds with the emergence of the Middle Kingdom in Egypt and might well represent a marked increase in Egyptian sovereignty in Palestine. The Hellenistic and Ottoman conquests, the latter only briefly, seem to have brought a similar increase in control. American suzerainty at present makes a crucial difference in modern Palestine. Economic changes were sometimes favoured by changes in suzerainty. The nature of economic change and development in Palestine was heavily influenced by the nature of the suzerain interests in Palestine, as will be seen.

The issue of suzerainty furthermore leads to the very important idea of ever-widening circles of political and economic influence from outside on local Palestinian conditions, and brings us to an investigation of the economic aspects of suzerainty in Palestine.

Trade

General Considerations

Trade, as a form of economic exchange, is the most wide ranging of all the factors previously discussed since it acts upon and in turn is influenced by most of the factors hitherto considered. The main interest in trade for this study of changes in settlement and agricultural patterns in Palestine is in interregional economic exchange or extraregional economic input. All the explanations considered so far are partial explanations and ought always to be considered in any general treatment of the conditions and circumstances of significant historical change. The point here is that trade cycles correlate best with the major phases and might be described as a leading if not determinative circumstance. This should occasion little surprise since as Curtin (1984:1) points out, 'Trade and exchange across cultural lines have played a crucial role in human history, being perhaps the most important external stimuli to change, leaving aside the unmeasurable and less-benign influence of military conquest.' It is important to discuss a number of general considerations before going on to define trade more closely and its importance in relation to changing settlement patterns in Palestine.

Interregional trade is best thought of as world-wide in scope, or at least Eurasian prior to the integration of the New World into Old World trade. The history of Palestine necessarily involves the histories of major interregional areas such as the Near East, the Mediterranean, and—even when the lack of evidence prevents specific conclusions—the entire Asian-European trade axis. Palestine, due to its position as a strategic and trade bridge between East and West, has almost always participated in a world economy. Braudel (1984:22) defines a world economy—as opposed to *the* world economy—as 'a fragment of the world, an economically autonomous section of the planet able to provide for most of its needs, a section to which its internal links and exchanges give a certain organic unity'.[15] For Palestine this concept can be applied to periods of Egyptian and Mesopotamian dominance, as well as to the vast terrritorial expanses of the Persian, Hellenistic, Roman, Byzantine, Arab, and Ottoman conquests. Thus we can agree with Braudel (1984:24) that 'there have been world-economies if not always, at least for a very long time . . . ' The strategic position of the overland routes traversing Palestine means that it has often found itself very near the centre of world economies and benefited greatly from its privileged position.

At other times in its history, it has been pushed to the peripheries of such economies. These changes in its relation to the centre of a particular world economy have been reflected in its material prosperity and settlement patterns. Although the precise connections will not always be known, the greater historical error usually turns out to be the disregard of these far-reaching economic bonds and dynamics. Interregional trade thus offers the most panoramic vantage point from which to view and compare particular moments in the settlement history of Palestine.

Palestine is only rarely an interregional trade centre or focus—as it was perhaps in Solomonic and Ayyubid times—precisely because of its infrastructural minority. Because prior to the industrial era production was labour intensive, regions with the greatest local agricultural resource and labour pool had the greatest production and hence the largest base for supremacy. Thus Egypt and Mesopotamia tended to dominate Palestine, followed by Anatolia and the Persian plateau, and eventually Europe, at first in combination with North African bread baskets.[16] Depending on the openness of trade routes, India and China have periodically played significant roles in the history of the Middle East and of Palestine. Simply to mention 'the Great Game' of the nineteenth century is to recall that the influence of outside suzerainties on Palestine is essentially a function of their infrastructural superiority—in this case Britain's lead in industrialization and Russia's vast territorial and demographic advantage. The primacy of agriculture is indicated by the relative poverty of such areas as Egypt and Mesopotamia in such basic resources as wood and most metals.

'The fact from which Middle Eastern history starts (or started before the technological revolution of our age) is the fragility of settled life...scarcity of water or the threat of the nomadic pastor made agriculture precarious...' (Hourani, 1981:26). This fragility coupled with the nearness of pastoral areas means that political control and stability are necessary for extensive agriculture—as distinct from sporadic pastoral agriculture—to occur and expand. Such control and stability, given Palestine's infrastructural inferiority, depends on the influx of outside resources. Palestine as a region cannot support a high level of agriculture for any length of time on the basis of a simple 'balance of payments', because this would only serve to expose its inherent inferiority in relation to neighbouring regions. For agriculture to prosper, those regions end up making an 'investment' in Palestine for the sake of 'development'. A high level of agriculture in Palestine is invariably subsidized, and this is true even of the present day. The subsidy is often not immediately visible because it usually takes the form of military or police support rather than direct capital input. As will be elaborated shortly, trade and military support and control are two sides of the same coin.

It is for this reason that a growth in agriculture without such a subsidy or an attempt to hold local suzerainty over the terms of that subsidy are inherently unstable situations for Palestine. This is a significant point because the emergence of Israel was such an expansion of agricultural settlement in the highlands without outside subsidy due to the power vacuum created by the collapse of Late Bronze Age interregional powers, whereas the formation of the state under David and Solomon was an attempt to hold local suzerainty over the expanding agricultural community. Trade thus can have a significant influence on Palestinian settlement in its absence as well as its presence. When lowland economic arrangements collapse, the highlands or marginal frontiers tend to become more extensively settled. This can be illustrated from the Early Bronze IV/Middle Bronze I period, the time of the emergence of Israel, as well as in Greece following the Mycenaean collapse.

Disease also can have a particularly drastic and sudden effect on lowland economic arrangements. Lowland populations have a greater susceptibility to disease because of their location on trade routes and the problems of drainage. The greater concentration of lowland populations in the urban centres gives rise to relatively crowded and adverse conditions which are often excacerbated by the contamination of water and the curtailment of food supplies. In this way disease can be seen as a particularly potent cause of the disruption of lowland and suzerain economic arrangements.

Although the interregional trade economy is interlinked with the local subsistence economy, it is possible to distinguish them for the purposes of analysis. The subsistence economy is local and rural involving primarily food production for the local workforce. It also involves production for taxes, rents, and other payments to creditors and elites, as well as efforts to produce in return for cash which peasants need for purchasing or bartering what they themselves do not produce. The trade economy is urban, interregional, and involves commodities, strategic military items, and luxuries. The second is indeed based on the first, but in the case of Palestine, given its infrastructural inferiority, its trade economy is based on the infrastructure of other regions in addition to its own.

The distinction between these two economies is important because they involve two distinguishable demographies of historical significance. It is an important distinction because it crosscuts the usual categories based on national, suzerainty, ethnic, regional, genealogical (actual or fictional), and other less significant categories. The distinction is not often made in ancient and medieval sources because it is not of use to writers who are either drawn from or supported by the urban elite. It is also true that the distinction cannot be applied rigidly since, for example, enclosed nomads do not fit easily within such a binary scheme. The subsistence economy of nomads tends to give them greater political independence than village peasants, although they are more a part of and dependent upon interregional trade than are peasants.

The interregional trade which passed through Palestine up to the industrial era was controlled by the urban and bedouin elite. It was the ruling family, or 'house', whether the imperial or state ruling house, which conducted and benefited from the commercial activities conducted through the urban centres. The benefits of this elite trade were in turn passed on to the royal retainers and allies. Sovereignty was exercised through the ownership of land and drew its economic advantage from the imposition of land tax, poll tax, customs and duties and the movement of goods. Interregional trade, therefore, involved the exchange or movement of goods and workers for the mutually advantageous maintainance of power and privilege of the urban elite. Control was primarily military, but also social and ideological, all based ultimately on the threat or use of force. The manipulation of power required military arms, luxury goods for maintaining class differentiation and goods and land for rewarding retainers. Despite political and ideological hostility among urban elites, trade enhanced and represented the mutual benefit they enjoyed. This is seen in the fact that such trade often disregarded political boundaries: during the Crusades, for example, the Italian ports were happy to trade with Middle Eastern traders across the political and religious divide. The same was true during the Late Bronze Age (Merrillees, 1986:50). The interconnections of this complex nexus of trade routes through the urban centres also meant that disruptions at any point could have profound effects over wide geographical areas. The various centres dependent upon transit trade were forced to adjust to any interruptions in the flow of goods. The whole system was inherently fragile, so that a break at any point in the chain might lead to general collapse (cf. Adams, 1974:247; Hodges and Whitehouse, 1983:160-61).

The Main Forms of Trade
It is possible to identify five main forms of trade relevant to Palestine. However in order to understand the significance of these different forms of trade it is worthwhile reiterating the two basic elements of any suzerain's interest in Palestinian trade. These can be labeled as strategic (geographic) and productive (infrastructural). Typically Palestine has had a high strategic but low productive value. The interconnection of these two elements produces, as will become clear, the basic pattern of regional political economy in Palestine. We have already discussed the strategic value of Palestine standing as it does at the crossroads and so at the focal point of elite trade of the hemisphere.

In comparison with most regions of the Middle East that are well settled and support dense populations, Palestine produces little. With the exception perhaps of olive oil, there is nothing it produces in quantity that cannot be gotten without too much effort elsewhere. There are no local products of such outstandingly high trade value as to justify continuous large-scale investment by an outside power for their sake alone. This is not to say that under certain economic conditions a product of Palestine cannot be extraordinarily valuable on the market, or otherwise in high demand. A suzerain power might find it advantageous to develop Palestine's commercial production in order to reinforce political bonds by means of economic links; in other words, its high strategic value can modify and influence its low productive value.

These two main elements of suzerainty interest in Palestine can be seen operating in the five main forms of trade: military investment, transit trade (including customs), local production, labour extraction, and pilgrimage.

A. *Military investment for strategic purposes*
Suzerain powers are unable to secure their political interests in Palestine on the basis of local production alone and so invest in, or subsidize, its military control. The clearest form of such investment is the direct garrisoning of the land, which occurs particularly during

periods of intensive production, as much a result as a cause of such production. There are many obvious examples: the Egyptian garrison at Beth-shan; the Roman investment at Caesarea and in total garrisoning, paid in part by local production and labour which increased under Roman security, all in the service of securing Rome's eastern borders; Crusade investment, again paid for in part by local production and labour; and British investment, for which there was too little direct return to justify its continuation, especially after Britain's leaving India.[17]

Military investment has often taken the form of providing funds for paying mercenaries and partisans in the strategy of keeping Palestine in the suzerain's camp through local fragmentation. Invading armies can recoup some of their expenses through booty and tribute, but these are not usually the main reasons for an invasion in the first place.

B. *Transit Trade*

The story of the caravan that transported Joseph to Egypt is paradigmatic for the biblical period and can be repeated for every period down to the twentieth century. Although there is no limit to what has been brought across the land, the most significant items have been high in value and low in weight or volume due to the much higher cost of land transport. Items of transit trade include gold, silver, copper, tin, bronze, iron, gum, balm, myrrh, frankincense, spices, silks, fine linen, precious stones, ivory, ivory work, finished weapons, woods and woodwork, both military and luxury, and livestock, especially horses. Much of the product that transits Palestine can remain there; its rulers have traditionally enjoyed the material and social advantages of the best in strategic and luxury item productive technology. The income from transit fees, tolls, customs, and trade profits for intermediaries can support local rulers as well as the suzerain economy.

C. *Local Production*

Commercial products from Palestine have tended to have lower unit value than items in transit, and higher weight and volume. Local products depend on seaports more than transit trade, and so tend to be economically more significant when an outside power is able to fund the outfitting of a suitable local port. The Roman construction of Caesarea for the export of grain is perhaps the outstanding example. Local agricultural commodities include, grains, wine, oil, fruits and vegetables, dates, cotton and tobacco, whereas animal products consist of livestock such as sheep, goats, asses, camels and horses, as well as wool and skins. Horses were a strategic commodity, especially during the Israelite period (1 Kgs 10.28-29), and may have been raised, or partly raised, in Palestine. Local natural resources such as wood, salt, bitumen, honey, and possibly some iron were produced for interregional exchange. Palestine has traditionally manufactured woollens, skins, soap and glass. All of these products pertain of course to the pre-industrial period. The industrial development of Palestine in some ways has partly removed its local production from the constraints of geography and history, though the inherent stability of this situation remains to be proven.

D. *Labour Extraction*

A major segment of the interregional economy involves the transit and local recruitment or impressment of labour, of which the military draft is only one facet. Labour is forced into service for agriculture, mining, and construction, both locally and externally, to the direct benefit of the interregional economy and the detriment of subsistence labour and production. The most important factor to bear in mind is that the maintenance of control over labour varies at different times depending on the degree of state control, but is especially affected by the nature of the terrain. The marginal areas of Palestine, particularly the highlands, have often provided a refuge resistant to state control.

E. *Pilgrimage*

Pilgrimage has been a constant feature of Palestine's interregional economy from its earliest development, but especially since the spread of the ethnic Judaean population during the Persian and Hellenistic periods. In fact, given the prevalence of expatriate Palestinian elites and others throughout history, there may not be a period when there was not an expatriate Palestinian population. As an ideologically motivated activity, pilgrimage bears roughly the same relation to the interregional transit economy and its strategic corollaries as temple building and repair bear to the local economy of commodity and surplus production. That pilgrimage and the maintenance of local holy places have economic significance occasionally becomes quite clear, for example in the Palestinian pretext for the Crimean episode in the Great Game—in which ideological pretext is not to be minimized as in the usual assessment—or, more comprehensively and significantly, in the European protection of local religious communities: France and the Catholics and Maronites; Britain and the Druzes and Jews; Russia and the Orthodox; America and the local Protestants. The Lebanese borders are essentially based on French and British spheres of influence as patrons of religious minorities. This is all quite apart from the major Christian and Muslim shrines in Jerusalem and their relation to interregional political economy and trade over the ages.

Patterns of Sovereignty Influenced by Trade Interests and Conditions

A surprising feature, and yet arguably the most characteristic feature, of sovereignty in Palestine is that although the region has been continuously under the suzerainty of an outside power, for the comparative infrastructural reasons already discussed, nevertheless its rulers are almost always locally autonomous. There have been few periods when Palestine has been, for example, a direct part or province of Egypt, as one might expect from its location. The normal pattern is usually interregional suzerainty combined with regional or subregional sovereignty. Whether suzerainty is exercised through trade advantage, taxation, tribute, theft, other means, or some combination of these, the result is essentially the same, economically speaking. The variations have mostly political and ideological significance, having to do particularly with the local credibility and authority of local elites.

Thus throughout Palestinian history it is important to identify the suzerain overlord of the local ruler, since it is a rare moment when one does not exist. Local sovereigns are surrogates for suzerains who to one degree or another supervise or at least partly share sovereignty. The numerous examples that could be cited include Late Bronze Age local governors and kings, most kings of Judah and Israel, Nehemiah, the Maccabees, Herod the Great, the Crusaders, heads of cities in the Mamluk period, Fakhr al-Din, Dahir al-Umar, Ibrahim, Aqiili Agha (Zenner, 1972) and others.

The reason for the pattern of interregional suzerainty with regional or subregional sovereignty lies precisely in the two elements of suzerain interest in Palestinian trade, i.e. high strategic value and low productive value. From the suzerain's point of view—the view that makes the final difference—the costs of full sovereignty over local production outweigh the few benefits. High control means high investment, so the suzerain power normally settles for a lower degree of control concentrated in the urban centres, along trade routes, and on the military and transit forms of trade. As the latter sometimes concentrate in marginal areas, the cost of alliance with pastoral nomads is added on.

Adequate control of trade does not require territorial control. The territory is open to invasion, but it is not *per se* particularly valuable to the invader. The invader will attempt to control, within available means, only as much as is necessary for the protection of trade routes and lines. In this sense Palestine has been relatively 'easy' to conquer, because it is only necessary to capture centres and lines rather than territory. This leads to the relatively regular feature of separate garrison depots: Hellenistic cities, Roman Caesarea, Crusader castles, and so forth.

Suzerains are able to exercise sovereignty in Palestine normally through two partially distinct elites: urban and nomad. The urban elite are able to control trade routes through the urban centres, while nomads control trade routes and more marginal terrain over which they range. Because territorial control *per se* is of relatively less importance to suzerains, they will play nomad and urban elite off against each other. The interrelationships and demarcations of the whole social spectrum in Palestine will be discussed in more detail in the following chapter; for now it is sufficient to stress the point that the settlement patterns of the region are influenced by the degree and nature of suzerain control and investment.

Trade and the Major Settlement Phases

We can now review what is known of trade in relation to the major settlement phases outlined earlier in the chapter. Given that information about preindustrial economy is sketchy at best, only for the final phase is anything like a full account possible, and that of course will not be given here. We must limit ourselves to some general comments in proportion with the comments made on the other suggested causes.

Early Bronze I–III

It has already been seen that the Early Bronze period represents a major expansion of settlement in Palestine. The work of Braun and Gibson (1984) at 'En-shadud shows that the many small agricultural settlements which sprang up during the Early Bronze I period were open to trade and outside influence. The development of a major urban culture as the Early Bronze period progressed also indicates the importance of trade, particularly long-distance trade. Richard (1980:25) speaks of a 'healthy trading economy' during Early Bronze I-II reflected in the amount of Egyptian material discovered at different sites (see in particular Hennesey, 1967). The interrelationships between sites in southern Sinai and the south of Palestine, particularly Arad, also indicate developing regional trade networks with special interest in the copper deposits of the Sinai (Amiran, Beit-Arieh and Glass, 1973; Beit Arieh, 1983). The primary location of the urban culture in the lowlands suggests that the cities here owed much to the development of trade along the interregional routes.

The decline set in with the destruction of a number of Early Bronze II urban sites and became most acute at the end of the Early Bronze III period with the destruction and abandonment of most of the Palestinian cities. The precise mechanism which triggered the decline is not clear, yet the evidence suggests that the change in settlement pattern to the periphery was closely linked to the disruption and decline of interregional trade. Richard (1980:25) has already pointed out that the paucity of Egyptian objects at Early Bronze III sites indicates that overland trade through Palestine ceased or was severely curtailed. She attributes the deurbanization to several factors which include, as we have seen, a change in climate in combination with a weakened economy brought about by changes in regional and interregional trade systems. The results of this are most evident in the following period.

Early Bronze IV/Middle Bronze I

This period corresponds apparently to the Egyptian First Intermediate which led to a decline in Egyptian suzerainty in Palestine and an apparent reduction in political stability at least in parts of Palestine. As mentioned above, Egyptian goods seem to have come to a halt in Palestine by the end of the Fifth Dynasty, indicating severe disruption of interregional trade. Archaeological evidence tends to disprove the theory of a full-scale nomadic invasion from outside during this period, the so-called 'Amorite' invasion. The striking shift in settlement pattern and economic strategy away from an urban based culture on the lowland international trade routes to an agricultural-pastoral economy in the more marginal regions of Palestine is now explained in different ways. Richard (1980:25) and Tubb (1983:56) both speak in terms of a decline of urban trade and culture from a combination of changes in trade and climate. Tubb (1983:57) goes on to add that '. . . despite many internal complexities which still require elucidation, the Early Bronze IV culture of Palestine must be seen as a result of an indigenously based alteration in life-style in response to changed economic circumstances.' Both Prag (1974) and Dever (1980) describe in some detail the agricultural-pastoral economy of Palestine during this period. The development of such an economy in the more marginal and arid areas of Palestine suggests a wish to avoid the more vulnerable lowlands, despite their relative fertility, in order to develop a subsistence economy in response to the collapse of the urban economy based on trade. The influence of trade upon settlement pattern and demography is further suggested by the fact that when the relative isolation of Palestine comes to an end with the emergence of the Middle Kingdom in Egypt, urban culture re-emerges first in the lowlands on the main international routes, whereas the Early Bronze IV/Middle Bronze I culture persists longer in the hill country, the Negev and Transjordan (de Geus, 1971:52).

Middle Bronze IIA

As we have already noted, most commentators agree that the Middle Bronze IIA expansion in Palestine coincides with the re-emergence of Egyptian imperial power under the Twelfth Dynasty. The reunification under Mentuhotpe II, the founder of the Middle Kingdom, once again meant centralization and the reopening of trade routes (Tubb, 1983:57). The fact that there is no evidence of destruction at any of the Middle Bronze I sites suggests that the growth of an urban culture and economy was an indigenous response to a change in the economic cycle. Gerstenblith (1980:75) believes that the opening of interregional trade and communications between Palestine, Syria, Anatolia and Mesopotamia is the possible mechanism for the innovations that characterize the Middle Bronze II period and lay the foundations for the urban culture. The distribution of Hyksos scarabs over wide areas, including Anatolia and Cyprus, is a further indication of the expanding trade networks throughout the region (Aharoni, 1982:106). Gophna (1984:31) thinks that economic stimulation resulting from the beginnings of maritime trade led to the establishment of Akko, Dor, Yavneh-Yam and Ashqelon as harbour cities on the Mediterannean littoral. This upturn in the regional and interregional economy would appear to be borne out by Mabry's study (1984) of the Middle Bronze II period where he demonstrates that in later phases the number of intermediate sites increased significantly from the beginning of the period when the settlement distribution was clearly between a few large urban sites and many small rural agricultural villages. This change in settlement pattern during Middle Bronze IIB and C suggests, as Mabry points out, the development of complex regional and interregional economic and communication links.

Late Bronze Age/Early Iron I

The social upheaval and population displacements around the East Mediterranean Basin during the Late Bronze Age disrupted normal trading patterns so severely that three major trading states in the region collapsed, in two cases quite suddenly, and in the case of Egypt by the middle of the twelfth century BCE (Weinstein, 1981). The collapse of Mycenaean trade is a crucial feature of this disruption, as is the spread of the 'Sea Peoples' referred to in Egyptian sources. The causes of the dramatic decline are not at all clear. The reasons for the movement of the Sea Peoples are equally obscure, as is their failure to assume a trading function rather than in some cases piracy. In any case, the decline in trade at the end of the Late Bronze Age is widely regarded as a well-nigh disastrous occurrence for an entire network of urban centres in the eastern Mediterranean.

The shift in settlement pattern away from the urban centres of the lowlands to small agricultural villages in the highlands and other marginal zones of Palestine is strikingly reminiscent of the shift which takes place at the end of the Early Bronze III, following major urban development during the Early Bronze II period, to the characteristic agricultural-pastoral Early Bronze IV/Middle Bronze I culture in similar marginal areas. Palestine highland settlement began to expand during the early Iron I period not simply as an accompaniment of restored trade a century or two later, even though one can properly speak of Israel's rise from origin to greatest sovereignty as having ridden the crest of an upswing in interregional trade. This is one of the main arguments for not separating the analysis of Israelite origins from the rise of the monarchic state. The settlement associated with the emergence of Israel was trade related, but was triggered by depression in trade rather than expansion. This special circumstance, a measure of the extremity of this decline phase, will be discussed in greater detail in Chapter 4.

For now it is necessary to note that the pattern of the expansion of agriculture in the highlands and other regions at times of political stability is prevalent enough for Thompson (1978a:25) to want it to hold for Israel also: 'The character of these [Israelite] settlements (judging from the analogy of the Middle Bronze II period) suggests that they were undertaken during a period of political and military stability; that is, that centralizing, peace-keeping forces were effectively involved in the settlement of Iron Age Palestine.' Thompson is not able to distinguish between early and later pre-monarchic Israelite settlements and so does not distinguish in theoretical terms between the triggering mechanism of highland village expansion at the end of the Late Bronze Age and the positive feed-back loop of expansion when emergent Israel caught the crest of the trade growth that eventually led to the formation of an Israelite state under David and Solomon. The study of settlement patterns throughout the history of Palestine indicates that the development of agricultural-pastoral villages in the highlands or steppe zones is usually a response to two very different circumstances. On the one hand, agricultural settlements expand to the peripheries and marginal zones at times of strong urban cultures in response to growing demographic and political pressures for land and foodstuffs. On the other hand, the focus of settlement shifts to the highland or steppeland villages at times of decline or collapse in interregional urban trade as a means of risk reduction when an agricultural-pastoral subsistence economy offers the greatest hope of survival away from the more vulnerable lowlands. The emergence of Israel appears to fit this second pattern, though the first certainly warrants further consideration.

Iron II

The restoration of Mediterranean and Middle Eastern trade assisted the emergence of two strong Israelite states, the house of David in the south and a century later the house of Omri in the north. Each seems to have enjoyed a special relationship and advantage with

Tyre, which had been the first of the Levantine ports to profit from the upturn in interregional trade, especially benefiting from its purple died woollens of such high value throughout the ancient period. The western trade routes and colonies of Tyre stretching from Carthage and Utica in North Africa, Malta, Sicily, and southern Spain are well known (e.g. Curtin, 1984:76-77). Interestingly Oppenheim (1967) has revealed extensive trade routes and relations to the east. The Israelite monarchies it would seem were able to benefit from this extensive Phoenician trade network.

The Persian Period

The wide variation in regional settlement in Palestine during the Persian period has recently been demonstrated by Stern (1982; 1984a; 1984b). Rather than a general decline throughout the whole of Palestine, it appears that the coastal lowlands and Galilee enjoyed prosperity and settlement expansion whereas the southern highlands suffered destruction and decline. Once again the pattern seems to have been a return to settlement on the lowland trade routes which were oriented to the rest of the Persian empire, while the highlands became something of an economic backwater under the control of local strongmen. This pattern would appear to correlate with the increased caravan trade during the Persian period on the southern trade routes which by-passed the hill country (see Wapnish, 1981).

The Roman-Byzantine Period

The late Roman Republic and early Empire achieved an unprecedented degree of military, communication, and administrative integration over the bulk of the Mediterranean basin and what later became Europe. Rome took special interest in Palestine with the rise of the Parthian threat, against which Palestine could serve as a regional buffer, and with Rome's growing need for grain from north Africa and the Levant. A concomitant of Roman control in the East was the development of Idumaean and Nabataean agriculture in the desert on a garrison and trade base. This is one of the fixed points of Palestinian economic history, leaving its mark on the Negeb to the present day. The Idumaean urban elite were accepted into Roman service to integrate the Jewish state into the empire, thereby establishing the Herodian Kingdom.

The reign of Herod the Great under Roman auspices was one of the high points of settlement expansion in the millennia-long history of Palestine. The construction of the harbour at Caesarea had a profound effect upon trade routes, acting as the port of southern Syria and rerouting Transjordanian trade from Gaza or Akko (Isaac and Roll, 1982:6). During the last century BCE and the first CE, the decapolis was developed along the eastern trade routes. Nabataea became a Roman province in 106 CE, and the high point of the whole development of expansion and control came possibly just a few years later during the reign of Hadrian. The network of Roman roads throughout the area (see Isaac and Roll, 1982) also contributed greatly to the security and so expansion of regional and interregional trade. The tremendous expansion of settlement and demographic growth is linked to the development of trade that the Romans were able to stimulate.

The Middle Ottoman Period
The capture of Constantinople gave the house of Osmanli control of the Byzantine network of trade, which subsequent generations of rulers were able to revive and thrive upon. The highwater mark for this prosperity came with the reigns of Selim, who conquered Jerusalem in 1517, and his son Suleiman, who ruled c. 1520-1566 and built the present walls of Jerusalem. The Ottoman empire has been described by Braudel (1984:467) as of 'planetary dimension ... a jigsaw of interlocking land masses in which potentially divisive stretches of water were held prisoner'. Yet the shift of trade routes in the world's great oceans under the lead of the Portuguese, Spanish, English and Dutch during the sixteenth and seventeenth centuries led eventually to an Ottoman decline that continued with Europe's dominance of the Middle East until close to the present (Steensgaard, 1974). Despite whatever nuances need to be added to such an observation, the decline of the Ottoman state over three centuries can be rooted in the Portuguese and Castilian drive to find new routes for acquiring spices and gold during the latter half of the fifteenth century. The eventual effects on Palestine were so great that the infrastructure was seriously weakened leading to severe depopulation and economic decline throughout the region. This spiral of decline was not to be halted until the present century (cf. Lewis, 1966; Hütteroth and Abdulfattah, 1977:54-63).

The Modern Period
The interpretation of the introduction of industrial technology into

Palestine depends on its modern economic history. The history of modern Palestine grows out of an on-going struggle over the spheres of economic influence that can be considered as centring in Western Asia. The Great Game is perhaps the epitome of this struggle, though by no means its only manifestation. The Game incorporated among other things Britain's interest in its trade routes to India, especially after the opening of the Suez Canal, and Russia's age-long desire for warm-water ocean ports. The Ottoman empire was the focus of their struggle during most of the nineteenth century and the first decades of the twentieth.

The gradual formation of the modern state of Israel is in part a continuation of this struggle, even though at least one significant event, the Balfour Declaration and its outcome, occurred mainly within the framework of the relation of the great powers during World War I (with Britain and Russia on the same side) to dispersed Jewry. The Zionist movement eventually gained momentum in a region where already in the nineteenth century the greatest incentive to agricultural development was the market for cotton—England and Europe's industrial technology lies behind their interest—and tobacco, especially during and just after the American Civil War. The expansion of agriculture achieved in the modern state has been heavily subsidized from outside, particularly from the USA. The importance of the Suez Canal and Middle Eastern oil for world trade ensure a continued investment and involvement in the region by the superpowers.

We have already seen that the minor phases of settlement outlined above were also intricately linked to trade cycles or patterns. The shift of settlement inland away from the coastal areas during the Umayyad period was a response to the continued dominance of Mediterranean shipping by the Byzantines. Prosperity and settlement expansion returned to some of these areas under the Crusaders when the Palestinian ports benefited from expanding Genoan and Venetian trade. The period of growth under the Seljuqs followed Saladin's unification of Egypt with Palestine. The following decline during the Mamluk period was greatly affected by the Mongol advance, only halted in 1260 CE, which spoiled trade routes and led to political instability, a situation reminiscent of the earlier movement of the Sea Peoples.[18]

Conclusion

The wide-ranging review of major settlement phases and the various factors involved in periodic shifts in settlement over a long period of time has been important for the comparative perspective it offers on any particular phase. It has become evident in the course of the discussion that changes in trade patterns and cycles are associated with many of the major and minor phases of settlement shift. This is not to suggest any causal priority but simply to identify an important correlation between the changes in interregional trade and fluctuations in the settlement patterns of Palestine. Clearly the factors which trigger the upturns and declines in trade cycles need further detailed study if these processes are to be better understood. The vast array of material which could be brought to bear on this problem is outside our competence to control and would require a multi-volume study to do justice to the subject. Only further research and additional data from archaeological surveys will refine or refute the arguments we have presented.

We have crossed many specialist boundaries, not with any pretension to settle particular problems outside our competence, but rather to offer as wide as possible a perspective from which to view the emergence and development of Israel. The vast sweep we have taken is often generalized and impressionistic with many questions remaining to be answered about the nature of trade and demographic cycles. Yet the most significant point is that there do seem to be important correlations between these various cycles and particular patterns of settlement. In making these identifications, however generally, we are able to see that the emergence of Israel and the later formation of the state of David is not an isolated occurrence but part of a complex cycle of growth, stagnation and depletion. As trade increases under the aegis of outside powers and numbers rise, pressures build up on the carrying capacity of the land until a crisis point is reached and decline sets in. We have seen that settlement patterns respond in particular ways at different points in the cycle. The typology developed here, albeit rather imprecise, provides a vital comparative perspective and much needed information to aid our understanding of the processes involved in Israel's emergence onto the stage of world history.

Agricultural settlement seems to expand in the hill country and marginal steppe zones, or at least the focus of settlement returns to these areas, in response to two specific stimuli. The first is on the basis of outside sudsidy during times of political stability which is conducive to increased trade, such as during Early Bronze II-III, Middle Bronze II, Iron II, and the Roman-Byzantine periods. The opening of these more marginal frontiers is a response to growing demographic and political pressures which can only be controlled by the acquisition of more land and its produce. The second, quite different stimulus comes from the need for the population of Palestine to develop a subsistence pastoral-agricultural economy in these marginal areas following the disruption of lowland long-distance trade, as can be seen from the Early Bronze IV/Middle Bronze I, Iron I, and late Ottoman periods. This pastoral frontier offers a refuge from the ravages of armies and disease which frequently devastate the lowlands of Palestine. Before going on to draw out the full implications of the results of the present Chapter for the emergence of Israel, it is necessary to draw attention to some other regular patterns and constraints of the local Palestinian environment and society which have an important bearing on reconstructing the history of early Israel. Thus the following Chapter will again attempt to provide a comparative, long-term perspective from which to view the complex interrelationships between the environment of Palestine and its various social groups in order to illustrate that the emergence of Israel is part of recurrent patterns that have been played out over the centuries in this region.

Chapter 3

GEOGRAPHY AND SOCIAL RELATIONS
IN THE HISTORY OF PALESTINE

Introduction

The previous Chapter has demonstrated how the history of Palestine
can be understood in terms of the control exerted by outside powers
through direct sovereignty or more often through local rulers. Baly
(1984:1-2) asserts that

> for the whole of the long period under review Palestine may be said
> to have had, properly speaking, no internal history; everything that
> happened there was in some sense conditioned by the fact that it
> was the prisoner of its position at this crossroads. There was in
> theory an independent state for less than ten per cent of the time,
> and even much of that independence was illusory.

Although we would agree with the last point about the dominance
of Palestine by outside powers, to say that the region has no internal
history or that its history is 'geographically determined' (1984:3) is
perhaps to overstate the point. The present Chapter seeks to consider
how the factors discussed in the previous Chapter interact with
internal socio-economic patterns in relation with the geography of
Palestine. In this Chapter the longer perspective leads us to ask, are
there features of Palestinian society that persist over the centuries
and that characteristically channel interregional economic change
into regional settlement change?

Geographical constraints have a profound effect upon the history
of Palestine, particularly by setting certain limitations on the history
of settlement expansion and decline. It is the combination of outside
powers with other internal factors that defines which possibilities
will be realised. As our focus narrows to concentrate on the search
for the constants on which the settlement patterns were formed and

social groupings which populated those settlements, it is important to bear in mind the significance of interregional factors discussed above. This approach is once again an attempt to sharpen the perspective from which to view the origin and development of Israel as part of complex processes spanning many centuries.

For the purposes of comparative analysis, it remains useful to think in terms of three basic social groupings, the urban elite, pastoral nomads, and peasantry.[1] These basic or major groupings must be seen, moreover, in relation to the geographical constants which provide the foundations on which the surface events are played out and which limit the range of possibilities open to any community. The typical interrelationships of the broad social groups interacting with the geography of Palestine and with outside powers are essential to understanding the emergence of Israel.

The present Chapter will consider a number of features which act as constants in the general relations between people and their environment. Terrain, climate and rock type determine soil type and structure which in turn determine agricultural strategies, while the factors discussed in the previous chapter have the main influence on which possibilities are realized. The different agricultural strategies suited to particular geographical regions play a significant role in the history of Palestine and especially the emergence of Israel.The way in which these long-term features combine with particular social and geographical constants and fluctuations to provide discernible patterns in the history of Palestine will be the subject of this chapter.

Geography and Environment

Despite Palestine's small size, comparable to the area of Sardinia or Vermont, it contains a wide array of micro-climates and subregions. Nevertheless it is still possible to generalize about some of the overall dominant features which play a significant role in the history of Israel.[2]

The main climatic feature of Palestine is the border of aridity. This governs which areas receive sufficient rainfall to sustain agriculture. The marginal nature of the climate along with slight changes in altitude gives rise to a variety of climatic zones, often sharply distinguished, within a comparatively small area. This variety in conjunction with interregional influences has a pronounced effect upon the distinctive settlement patterns of the region (Sapin, 1981/82).

The two main geographical features of the region, terrain and aridity, combine to produce three kinds of areas: highlands, lowlands and steppelands. Their relative advantages and disadvantages shed significant light upon the origins and centralisation of early Israel. Although it is necessary to simplify details for comparative purposes, it is important to avoid oversimplifying the dichotomy between highlands and lowlands. Throughout Palestinian history cultivators have readily shifted from the lowlands to uplands for pasturage, highland villages often establish temporary settlements in the lowlands for seasonal crops, and generally agriculture and pastoralism form a symbiotic relationship spanning all three areas. Nonetheless particular agricultural strategies adapted to highland or lowland conditions involving long-term versus short-term investment and different types of land tenure, with herding in all three areas, are integral to the emergence of Israel, its subsequent history as well as the history of Palestine in general.

The Highlands
Most discussions of early Israelite history either assume or imply that the hill-countries of Judah, Ephraim, and Galilee, the scene of Israel's emergence, were underpopulated, or even empty, marginal areas greatly disadvantaged in relation to the lowlands, the primary focus of urban Canaan. As often stated, the lowlands do possess the benefits of deeper, richer, and more easily ploughed soils, and they are easier for the elites to control. The study of settlement prior to the Iron Age, however, shows that the hill country was not uninhabited before the Israelite expansion. As we have seen, the highlands often provided a refuge for many groups from the vulnerability of the lowlands during times of political upheaval. The focus of settlement often returned to these areas for protection even if the pickup in trade was slower to reach the highland enclaves.

It is significant that the greater rainfall enjoyed by the highlands with its longer wet season, reducing the risk of severe drought, provides better opportunities for grazing while helping to sustain agriculture on the terraced slopes. The many perennial springs rising in the highlands and the possibility of storing rain or spring water in stone cisterns provide potentially a better water supply. Yet the vagaries of climate in the highlands pose a constant threat to sustained agriculture. Frick (1985:103-109) has gathered together data illustrating the alarming deviations in annual rainfall that can occur in Palestine, especially in the highlands and steppe. He shows how a negative deviation of 30 per cent or more can occur in annual rainfall quite frequently, often in consecutive years, which would prove disastrous for agriculture in such marginal areas.

The very nature of the terrain provides natural defences. This is particularly true of the compact rock plateau which forms the Judaean hill country. Rocks cleared for ploughing provide plentiful building material, although the stony nature of Palestine means that no area is devoid of such material. Again terracing, a strategy to overcome the shallowness of soils and erosion, is an important technique for the conservation of terra-rossa and rendzina soils; the rocks cleared for ploughing can be used for terrace walls. The highlands also possess the major advantage of natural drainage. This alleviates the severe problem of stagnation and swamps thereby reducing the spawning grounds for such debilitating diseases as malaria to which the lowlands are vulnerable.

The highlands are capable of producing a range of agricultural produce. Wheat and barley are grown on all suitable soils and slopes, even in marginal climatic regions. Seasonal fruit and vegetables can be grown, partly by irrigation, close to the springs. The pastoral sector, with the grazing of sheep and goats, particularly on more marginal lands, provides milk products, meat, wool, other raw materials for cloth and manure for fertilization and fuel.

The outstanding feature of highland agriculture is the cultivation of tree crops, chiefly olive, vine and fig, which often figure in commerce. The olive has been pre-eminent as a commercial crop because the climate does not readily allow the preservation of animal fat. Olive oil is used for consumption, light and cosmetics. The great riverine civilizations of Egypt and Mesopotamia, with their dense concentrations of population, were unsuitable for olive cultivation and thus provided a significant export market.

Terracing and commercial tree cultivation require residential stability (see Marfoe, 1979). The terrace walls, the very foundations of highland agriculture, have to be permanently maintained to prevent rapid deterioration. Similarly, commercial tree crops are a long-term investment since, for example, olive trees need ten years before they produce and only reach full capacity after fifteen to twenty years. Highland farming systems demand long-term investment and residential stability.

This is clearly seen in the permanence of settlement patterns in the highlands when compared with the fluctuation of lowland settlement. The major highland towns of Hebron, Jerusalem, and Shechem have a long history of uninterrupted settlement. This is equally true of rural sites which have frequently continued *in loco* while retaining their biblical names. This residential stability, a result of highland farming strategies and natural defences, provides the key to understanding why it was the hill country which was the scene of the Israelite centralization that eventually extended to and dominated the lowlands.

The Lowlands
The lowlands of Palestine, set astride the major international trade routes of the Middle East and beside the Mediterranean littoral, possess seemingly tremendous natural advantages. The flow of wealth and innovative ideas along the Via Maris and through the few Palestinian ports makes this a cultural melting pot. The great urban concentration of the plains grew up in response to these natural advantages. As we have already seen, it was the coastal sites that were usually the quickest to revive once regeneration had begun in Palestine. However, it is precisely this strategic military and trade position as a land bridge between Africa, Europe, and Asia and the ease of communication which have led to continual fragmentation and destruction. In a sense the greatest strengths of the lowland sites were also their greatest weaknesses since they provided rich and easy pickings for outside powers.

The agricultural hinterland is given over to grains, vegetables and grazing. Grains are grown on the heavy and semi-heavy soils of the eastern and southern coastal plains and the Jezreel and Harod valleys. Wind erosion is a significant problem, but probably the greatest problem is the lack of natural drainage. Large areas of the plains tend towards bogs and swamps, which spawn disease and pose a serious threat to the rural community. Disease produces a debilitated and demoralized population. The Huleh valley was a breeding ground for malaria until it was drained in recent times. Attempts to drain these areas were prohibited for long periods of Palestine's history due to the heavy requirements of capital and labour.

It is not surprising that the same degree of residential stability as the highlands is lacking. Devastation in the wake of foreign armies, the high cost of urban defence, local urban warfare, disease and famine gave rise to a chequered settlement history. The agricultural population were able to place significant amounts of capital in highly movable herds which in order to avoid taxation or conscription or to escape the dangers inherent in the political instability of the lowlands could be moved to pasturage in the highlands or steppes away from lowland urban control. Residential instability in the lowlands is thus also determined by the agricultural strategies and the lack of defence. The archaeological record clearly shows that although the urban sites have a long history of settlement they have suffered frequent destructions and rebuildings. It is also illuminating that both urban and rural sites have not retained their biblical names, unlike the highlands.[3]

The Steppelands
The steppe regions illustrate most clearly the wide variety of climatic zones in close geographical proximity. It seems paradoxical that this often inhospitable landscape should provide refuge for pastoral and peasant groups after the collapse of lowland urban centres as in the Early Bronze IV/Middle Bronze I and early Iron I periods. Once again, just like the highlands, these marginal zones provided a means of hasty retreat but were often the last to benefit from the revival of interregional trade.

The arid wilderness of Judah begins just a few kilometres from the gates of Jerusalem and Hebron. Although it was never an area of permanent settlement, it is equally important to realize that it was never the empty wasteland it is often portrayed as. The Judaean wilderness is a series of ever declining steps on the eastern side of the Judaean hill country falling steeply to the Dead Sea and the Jordan valley. In no more than 20 km it sinks from 800-1000m above sea level down to 400m below sea level. This varied landscape, undulating hills to steep cliffs, allows the cultivation of grains on the higher terraces with an average of 650mm of rainfall per annum, with villagers and bedouin using the lower steps for grazing.

This was by no means an empty, even if inhospitable, landscape. It has been the site of important villages east and north-east of Jerusalem: Michmash (Mukhmas), Geva (Jaba), Azmavet (Hisma) and Anatot (Anata) with Teqoa further south. A series of springs at the very foot of the wilderness provided an important oasis which was the site of the important urban centre of Jericho (Tel-es-Sultan near the largest spring Ein-es-Sultan). Its extremely lengthy settlement history is also punctuated by destruction and abandonment. These sites provided important markets where peasants and nomads, not mutually exclusive categories as we shall see, met and exchanged goods. According to A. Shmueli (1984:19) the road network between the Dead Sea and Jerusalem provided an important economic link between the producing areas of the Judean wilderness and the main urban centres in the highlands and an important trade route with Edom and Moab.

Equally important, the wilderness was populated by bedouin and bandits, with the bedouin in close proximity to Jerusalem especially at the end of the rainy season when flocks were moved back to the higher areas. The extent of settlement and nomadic movement in this area was heavily dependent on the political situation. In particular the steep slopes on the west of the Dead Sea have long been a traditional refuge of bandits (cf. 1 Samuel 20–26) or those seeking isolation, such as the Essene community at Qumran or the later monasteries. Such areas of refuge as borders between settled agriculture and grazing have an important role to play in the emergence of Israel.

The Negev (or Drylands) is an extensive arid zone (see Aharoni, 1976:55ff.; 1982:162ff.). The degree of aridity decreases from south to north, where a marginal annual rainfall (200-350mm) allows the cultivation of grains in rainy years. This is an area of sheep nomadism and agriculture, with agriculture becoming more precarious the nearer the 200mm isohyet approaches. Even in the north conditions are unstable for sustained agricultural settlement. The characteristic windblown loess soil forms an impermeable crust preventing the absorption of water which causes deep wadis and sharp run off during later rains. Nonetheless four important sites have been established in the region in early biblical times—Beersheba, Arad, Tel Malhata and Tel Masos, and many more during the Roman and Byzantine periods. Once again this is an important area of bedouin influence with grazing in the more marginal areas supplemented by the dry farming of barley.

The importance of the Negev is that it acts as a kind of political barometer for the whole of the region. During periods of state control and stability the agricultural and settled boundary is pushed further south. The boundary recedes northwards with the growth of bedouin influence as state control weakens and declines. The extensive agricultural development of this region during the Roman and

Byzantine period is, as we have seen, one of the landmarks of Palestinian history, unsurpassed until recent times.

Once again this region has an important part to play in the emergence of Israel. It is worthy of note that both the Judaean wilderness and the Negev are areas where urban centres, villages and bedouin find themselves in close proximity. The importance of this three-way relationship will be developed in the following sections.

The Social Actors

When we turn our attention to the social actors who populated these landscapes, it is not a search for the individuals and leading figures of our standard histories but for broader socio-economic groups. One of the striking features of Palestinian history throughout the ages is the constancy of such groups within the region. The broad analytical categories of urban elite, nomads, and peasantry should not obscure the fact that there is an important three-way relationship throughout the social spectrum. It is clear that there are important distinctions and often hostility between these groups as well as merging and co-operation between them. The urban elite, from the ruling house down, are employed in the service of the state. This bestows ownership of large resources in both land and livestock, and this group tends to play the most important role in the interregional or trade economy. The basic resource of pastoral nomads is invested in more movable capital, their flocks. The peasantry are involved with less movable capital since their basic resource is agricultural land. Nevertheless these categories are not rigid since nomads use land for agriculture, and often live in cities and participate in trade, while peasants own flocks. Thus the boundaries among the groups become blurred. There are also groups which fall in between. Nonetheless the analytical categories are still useful for the purposes of our discussion. These groups will be introduced in the order in which they are most directly influenced by the interregional factors discussed in the previous chapter.

It is appropriate to mention at this point the urban bias of our sources. Our secondary literature is often heavily dependent upon literary sources originating from the urban elite who emphasized their superiority or benign attitude to the peasantry and their hostility to the bedouin and bandits who were a threat to their political influence. There is little or no first-hand evidence stemming from the rural community, a lack only partly offset by travellers' reports of earlier centuries or more recent field studies. This is of particular concern when assessing the Hebrew Bible as evidence for the emergence and development of Israel.

The City and the Urban Elite
The location of Palestinian cities has been governed throughout history by the constancy of centuries old trade routes. The network of trade routes from Asia to Africa and the West crossed the Palestinian lowlands and ensured that the greatest concentration of urban sites formed in this area. The previous Chapter has already demonstrated the sensitivity of such sites to the fluctuations of interregional trade. The cities naturally enough had to be guaranteed a plentiful supply of water, proximity to agricultural lands, as well as adequate defence. These determined their final position in relation to the trade routes (Aharoni, 1966:95-96). No one city has dominated the whole of Palestinian history, although Gaza situated at the confluence of major caravan routes has remained perhaps most constant. Yet the annals of Palestinian history are littered with the sudden demise of major urban centres such as Jericho, Arad, Hazor, Lachish, Megiddo, Eglon, Caesarea, Acre, and many others. The influence of outside powers on the urban topography of Palestine is illustrated with the creation of such centres as Samaria by the Omrids, Caesarea by the Romans, Ramlah by the Arabs, and Tel Aviv by the modern state of Israel in response to world-wide trade and economic inputs. The shifting fortunes of lowland Palestinian cities, as a response to interregional trade, is in contrast to the persistence of the three main highland cities of Hebron, Shechem and Jerusalem.

The nature of Palestinian cities, especially their size, is frequently misunderstood, particularly by students of biblical studies, who naturally enough base their conceptions upon their own realm of experience of modern Western cities. Most Palestinian cities have been relatively small, possibly only five to ten acres (Yadin, 1963:18-19: Frick, 1977:79), administrative and trade centres with little room for private dwellings. They were mostly given over to monumental and administrative buildings. A major difference from modern Western cities is the lack of middlemen as in Europe, who played such a pivotal role in the rise of capitalism and who through their position and wealth were able to exert great power. In Palestine it was the urban elite who controlled trade, local and international, and retained all major forms of political power, which was at most delegated to retainers.[4]

The cities play a vital role in the economy of Palestine as commercial, administrative, and more recently, industrial centres. Apart from their prominent position in relation to the major trade routes, the urban centres have also stood at the very centre of the agricultural life of the region. In fact they could not survive without the agricultural surplus from the hinterland they control. Most of the good agricultural land is under the ownership of the cities and devoted to cash crops, mostly perennials. City lands are usually farmed by hired labour, debt slaves or villagers. The urban elite are able to command the agricultural surplus of the rural hinterland through taxation or acting as a market as well as providing the lifeline of credit for the use of village lands. As centres of local trade, the cities functioned as distribution points for the buying and selling of cash crops, livestock, textiles, pottery and even some furniture. The urban elite were thereby involved in close economic relationships with peasantry, bedouin and even bandits.

The urban elite held power mainly at the behest of and as representatives of the suzerain's power. Their political power was out of all proportion to their demographic size since they formed often no more than a few per cent of the population. These small royal, military, administrative, bureaucratic, and religious groups were installed as the representatives of outside imperial powers, whether Egyptians, Assyrians, Persians, Hellenistic sovereigns, Romans, Crusaders, or Turks. It is clearly possible to distinguish between foreign and indigenous elites, since the presence of foreign urban elites, placed by the suzerain, is a constant of Palestinian history.[5]

The ability of these groups to dictate the categories of history through the written output of bureaucratic specialists has been exaggerated further by the concentration of archaeologists on the more commercially rewarding urban tells. The local interests of even indigenous elites were governed by the pull of interregional factors. Ideologically their role is presented as that of the peacemaker, guaranteeing stability and protection from internal or external threat to the rural community. It was in their self-interest to maintain conditions conducive to economic growth and stability through trade and agricultural development. In return for their protective role, they received taxation in the form of agricultural surplus or livestock from the hinterland. Since the cities were the focal point of local trade, the ruling elite were able to control the peasantry through market forces operating on cash crops, receive interest on capital investment in the villages, make debt slaves of those unable to repay, take the profits of commercial trade, and draw on labour from the villages through conscription into the army to protect the status quo and for prestigious building projects designed to emphasize and maintain their position and power.

There are also urban commoners, who are of considerable political significance. Because of vertical socio-political segmentation, i.e. the formation of social factions along other than class lines, indigenous elites, because of their local connections, have political opportunities and advantages foreigners often do not. Nomads are also a significant urban political force. Urban politics tend very much to be less class conflicts and more local versus foreign or one indigenous segment versus another. The discussion of the Mamluk period by Lapidus (1984:7) is equally applicable to much of Palestinian urban history: 'The question of the relation between notables and masses must then be rephrased in terms of a triple interaction between alien military elites, local notables, and urban commoners'. The urban conflict at the time of Antiochus IV Epiphanes would appear to be a useful example of this (see Schäfer, 1977:576-85; Tcherikover, 1979:110-74).

Expatriate Palestinian elites are also a significant political force in the history of Palestine. These are the kin of local elites with wide-flung travel and political connections, often at the very heart of foreign empires where they are able to lobby effectively for their Palestinian factions. Ezra and Nehemiah at the Persian court or the Herodians in Rome are good examples. This pattern is very common throughout the history of Palestine. The story of Joseph and traditions about Abraham are paradigms of the importance of expatriate Palestinian elites. The opportunity and incentive to leave the country, often under foreign domination, provides valuable contacts at the centres of power where there is much wealth to be acquired.

Although we have noted that trade revivals usually branch out from the coastal regions, highland geography in no way ensures that highland regions will not participate in interregional trade. One good example nowadays is the opium and heroin trade that concentrated recently in the highlands of south-east Asia and presently in the highlands on the Pakistan-Afghanistan border. It has often been the case that the highland routes have played an important role in interregional trade during times of the dislocation of lowland and sea routes. The highland urban elite benefit from this trade, but then so do the nomad elite. Indeed, when they are present in numbers, so do the villagers themselves. One might compare the difficulty in getting highland farmers in Pakistan today to give up poppy production. This is a very significant feature not only of the economy and location of Jerusalem, but of the economy of highland groups, in the Late Bronze and Iron I Ages.

Bandits

Bandits are very much like the urban elite since economically they are dependant upon a combination of peasant produce and inter-regional trade. It is for this reason that it is most useful to discuss the influence of bandits at this point rather than later after peasants or nomads. They represent an indigenous military force as opposed to foreign military elements, although they provide their services usually as mercenaries. They might be considered 'the rural military elite', although nomads also contend for this title, as their livelihood also includes some combination of peasant produce and interregional trade. The parallel with the urban *zu'ar* of Mamluk Palestine has already been suggested.

The varied topography of Palestine with its steppes, woodlands, and mountain enclaves offers plentiful refuge for bandit groups, the displaced of urban, village and tribal society. Hobsbawm's discussion (1972) of European social banditry is broadly applicable to Palestine, as Chaney (1983) has demonstrated. Banditry plays a significant role in Palestinian history during periods of social and political upheaval. It can become rampant during periods of crisis in agrarian societies, whether from famine, excessive pressure by urban land owners and taxation by the state, or the upheaval of war with subsequent loss of the means of livelihood. Hobsbawm describes how on certain occasions banditry can play a significant role in major social movements such as peasant rebellion, particularly during the disruption of traditional society by the imposition of new political or socio-economic systems (see also Wolf, 1969). Horsley and Hanson (1981:409-32; Horsley and Hanson, 1985) provide one striking example of this with the role of bandits in the revolt against Roman imperialism. Reports of travellers in Palestine in the nineteenth century provide ample testimony to and illustration of the extent of banditry in the region. Most instances of widespread banditry pertain to periods of increasing imperial impositions, as these provide both the economic incentives and the economic means conducive to banditry.

Bandit groups in Palestine have usually been composed of detribalized elements, that is, those forced to leave the tribe through famine when the loss of livestock means the family can no longer be supported, the mobile elements of the peasantry forced out by famine or state demands, and urban cast-offs. Chaney's analysis of the Amarna *apiru* illustrates the socio-political complexity of social banditry in the period prior to the emergence of Israel.[6] The complexities of the nature of banditry is illustrated in the wide range of relationships they enjoy with peasants. It is often the case that peasant groups will protect bandits from the central authorities. Yet at the opposite extreme bandits often replace the exploitative functions of the urban elite by appropriating peasant agricultural produce for themselves.

The political influence of bandits, which is similar to that of nomads, stems from their raiding and military activities, usually as mercenaries. The state is forced to come to terms with such local power groups where its own control is remote or ineffective. Josephus reveals that he was forced to enter an uneasy alliance with Galilean bandits or employ them as mercenaries (Horsley, 1981:427). During periods of state weakness or where central control was ineffective, bandits were able to control larger rural tracts of land. Landowners and herders in areas remote from state control often had to pay protection to bandit leaders. The story about David's request for protection money from Nabal (1 Samuel 25) is paradigmatic of such a situation. One of Herod's most immediate problems was to eliminate bandit groups operating relatively freely along the Syrian border area (Horsley, 1981:412-414). The extent of social banditry in Judaea at the time of Roman attempts (67-68 CE) to pacify the region (Horsley, 1981:428-430), and the evidence of social unrest from the Amarna letters, show that the central highlands were particularly conducive to this way of life.

Bandits also have had an important role to play in the local economy (see Hobsbawm, 1972:83-97). They appropriate peasant produce, receive protection payments from local landowners and raid the caravan trade. John of Giscala seized imperial stores of grain in upper Galilee and profiteered in olive oil at the expense of Jewish communities in Syria (Horsley, 1981:431). Since they often possess greater wealth, especially cash, than the peasantry, they play a significant role in the local economy. There is also the case of bandits and pirates as well as nomads using the cities of Dahir al-Umar to trade their spoils in the eighteenth century (Orni and Efrat, 1966:168).

Thus it can be seen that the bandit is intimately linked to local markets and the wider economy, and any significant decline in either will have a dramatic effect upon the livelihood of such bandit groups. This is the most important point regarding banditry that needs to be borne in mind when considering the emergence of Israel in response to the severe curtailment of Late Bronze trade.

Nomads

1. *The Ecology of Pastoralism*

The border of aridity, as a major characteristic of the geography of Palestine, has a profound effect on the social make-up of the region. The basic means of extracting food and other economic value from lands that are too arid, infertile, or insecure for settled agriculture is sheep and goats. In essence, sheep and goats are a means for converting the inedible vegetation of uncultivated land into useful products. Although for any given time the relationship between pastoralism and agriculture is therefore ecological, the determination of what lands cannot support agriculture—in other words are not being cultivated—at a particular time is primarily political and economic. Under the right political and economic conditions there is little land other than absolutely rainless desert that cannot support some form of agriculture. The usual situation can however be described as follows. The 400-350 mm isohyet defines the limit of permanent agriculture in Palestine with sheep nomadism predominant in the region between 200-100 mm isohyets of the steppes. It is the areas between 400-200 mm where rain agriculture and sheep nomadism are constantly and closely interwoven.

For most periods in Palestine's history the pastoral lands for the region as a whole have been extensive. Agriculturally marginal lands include not only the steppe and desert, but land within what could be called settled zones that is too rocky, hilly, marshy, sandy, covered with trees, or otherwise unsuited for settled agriculture under prevailing political and economic conditions. Thus although such marginal lands support only a fraction of the population that settled agricultural lands can support, because of the size of the marginal area the pastoral population has usually been a significant percentage of the whole population. The usual estimate is that the pastoral population accounts for 10-20 per cent of the total population of the area, although even these limits probably fluctuated with demographic extremes.

2. *Mixed Subsistence Strategies*

The prevailing subsistence strategy for most residential groupings involves a mixture of agriculture and pastoralism, perhaps along with some other form or forms of economic activity like hunting, village manufacture, or trade. Viewed in terms of this mixture and quite apart from any other parameters, the various combinations line the full spectrum from nearly exclusive agriculture to exclusive pastoralism. Thompson (1978a:22) catalogues the forms of this mixture to include farmers in villages with small flocks, some of whom might leave their village seasonally; farmers or villagers who hire shepherds to care for their flocks locally or at a distance; cave-dwellers subsisting primarily on agriculture; steppe-dwellers for whom agriculture is subsidiary to pastoralism in various degrees; bonded or hired servants of the royal house in charge of the state flocks; predominantly pastoral groups having the use of good agricultural land in return for state service; predominantly pastoral groups who force other pastoral or village groups to cultivate land they control for them; and predominantly pastoral groups who also engage in caravaneering, mining, raiding and the like.

In addition to this continuum of strategies, there is a symbiosis between most combinations of agriculture and pastoralism which means that, except possibly in rare instances, neither is carried on in isolation from the other. In the summer dry season, when the drylands tend to be entirely devoid of vegetation, shepherds must have access to field stubble in settled regions for grazing. The droppings from the flocks provide valuable manure for the fields. The limited springs and wells throughout the land must be shared between farmer and shepherd if both are to survive. Thus because of the continuous nature of the mixing of subsistence strategies, it is possible for groups engaged in one form of economic activity to shift to another, all along the spectrum.

3. *Social Groups and Distinctiveness*

Despite the economic continuum along which the farmer and pastoralist exploit the productive potential of nearly the entire region, the people of the region themselves have long recognized distinctive types within this continuum. The most important of these have been the peasant (*fellah*) as distinguished from the nomad (*bedu*).

In other words, even though groups engaged primarily in agriculture and those engaged primarily in pastoralism overlap considerably in economic activity, in general they distinguish themselves from each other, and usually quite sharply. Finn (1879:72) records the following sayings:

> The Bedaween have a saying—'The townsman is the table of the world, the peasant is the donkey of the world, the Bedawy is the sultan of the world.' But the Fellahheen give a different version, and retort, saying—'What is the townsman? The sultan of the world. What is the Fellahh? The donkey of the world. What is the Bedawy? The dog of the world, for he snatches from everybody, but nobody dares to snatch from him.'

This socio-economic and socio-political distinction seems to arise from some mutually conflicting requirements of the two main emphases of agriculture and pastoralism. The primary distinction appears to be whether a group holds mainly immovable or movable property. Villagers are primarily tied to houses within a fixed settlement, with social relations with other individuals and families equally fixed. Groups in possession of extensive flocks are not so fixed to one place, but move with the flocks from place to place. This is not just a matter of the movability of the main form of wealth in the group. Precisely because the flocks are held in order to exploit marginal lands, the pastoral group must be more movable because the marginal lands are generally less predictable and require greater flexibility in their exploitation. Because one type of wealth is more movable, the two groups have quite different relations with the state where it exists, which can impose demands on settled and village groups that it cannot impose on moving groups.

It may seem gratuitous to emphasize such a simple distinction, but in the context of the current discussion both among anthropologists and biblical critics it can be obscured by so many important details. The recent work of Gottwald (1974; 1979), following on from Mendenhall (1962), has been concerned with overturning the 'nomadic mirage' underlying much earlier Old Testament study. Gottwald has decisively rejected the notion that Israel had its origin in some form of external nomadic invasion and by using some recent anthropological studies has attacked the domain assumption that nomadism is the evolutionary forerunner of settled agriculture. They have demonstrated that pastoral nomadism is a specialized offshoot of agriculture with seasonal migration for pasturage. As such it is a form of risk reduction to cope with the threat of crop failure as well as a strategy to escape the excessive demands of the state. This conclusion is one of the landmarks of recent biblical scholarship that has undermined the conquest and infiltration models of the origins of Israel.

However, the 'nomadic mirage' has more substance than has recently been allowed. Gottwald was concerned with a particular intractable problem and thus focused on one important element in the whole complexity of Near Eastern nomadism. However, the distinction between peasant and nomad needs to take full recognition of the fact that pastoralism in Palestine has been highly territorial in all its manifestations. Thus there is a basic difference between the necessity of cultivating a defined body of agricultural land associated with the village and the opportunism and variability in the pastoralists' cultivation within their territory. The complexities of this relationship need to be investigated in some detail since they have important implications for trying to reconstruct the emergence of Israel.

Groups identifiable as peasant or nomad are conservative groups, cohesive and parochial as such, even if they can change economic behaviour over years and generations. The socio-economic distinction is reinforced by a whole set of further distinctions that grow out of this basic one. For example, villagers typically enter into economic relationships with wealthier persons and groups, including the urban elite, from the need to shift the short-term risks of cultivating a given piece of land, whether the risks be ecological, political or both, on to someone else, in order to avoid short-term economic catastrophe. Nomadic individuals and groups, on the other hand, typically enter into economic relationships with the commercial elite more as equals, and less out of necessity. Nomadic groups can often dominate villages in their territory, and so there is often a hostility between nomad and peasant that can be expressed in the basic social distinction. Mendenhall (1978:33) has been quite clear and definite about the existence of pastoral nomadism as a distinct cultural type: 'steppe nomadic groups . . . by [the thirteenth century BCE] did exist as distinct *cultural* entities'. Gottwald (1979:889-94) also warns against the over-reaction that followed the publication of his and Mendenhall's conclusions which seemed to deny the existence of pastoral nomadism in early Israel:

> Pastoral nomadism had a relatively small role to play in the total Israelite social structure on all levels, but it did have a role (especially in the eastern and southern frontier regions), and it can be understood properly only if the gaps and indeterminations in our knowledge—not simply about specifically Israelite data but about the ancient nomadic forms themselves—are securely held in mind at the same time we work systematically to reduce them (1979:892; cf. Gilbert, 1975).

The image of the nomad wandering aimlessly or unattached to the land has been relegated to romantic fiction. Enclosed nomadism includes both village tribesmen who spend a few months each year with the flocks in the steppes or the highland pastures, as well as nomads who live the whole year in camp.[7] Included in all this is a continual process of sedentarization and its opposite. The upper and lower socio-economic extremes of nomadic tribes are continually in the process of settlement. The richer nomads, forced to settle when the size of their flocks exceeds the availability of grazing land for the tribe, maintain expensive town properties. Nonetheless they still belong to the same tribe as those nomads who spend their time in the steppes. The poorest nomads are forced to settle as labourers when their livestock holdings diminish to such an extent that they are unable to support the family. Nevertheless, there is a strong attachment to territory and fellow tribe members (Rowton, 1973a:254; Bates, 1971:114).[8]

The nomad is an ever-present feature of the Palestinian scene particularly concentrated along trade routes. Nomad and peasant are in constant contact since the physical environment places agriculture and grazing land in close proximity. Sometimes they are the same land, and often the peasant and nomad compete for the same piece of ground. Mutual hostility and mutual need characterize this complex relationship. Bates (1971:129-30) notes that this mutuality is riddled with hostility and is very sensitive to shifts of power within it. The interaction is governed by outside forces reinforcing mutualism with the threat of outside interference or resulting in open hostility where state control is least effective, particularly in the outer regions. The tendency towards symbiosis for the fullest exploitation of the land inherent in the physical environment is offset by shifting power relations between the triad of state, nomad and peasant at a local level.

Although it is true that agriculture becomes an increasing risk the nearer settlement proceeds to the 200 mm isohyet, the inherent symbiotic relationship with sheep nomadism, as a means of risk reduction in the event of crop failure, is in reality more a function of the balance of power. It is important to bear in mind the tripartite nature of Palestinian politics and society. The political attitudes and links of nomad, urban elite and peasant range from the extremes of open hostility to mutual co-operation with many subtle shades in between. Thus we have a spectrum of mixing, specialization and exclusion. Nomads often have a vested interest in protecting agriculture, as for example with the Bani-Sakhr tribesmen, who acted as suzerains in the highlands protecting their vassals who produced cereals (LaBianca, 1982:11-12; see also Rowton, 1976:27). Similarly there is often a strong link between the tribe and the town which is reflected in tribal names as a form of gentilic (Rowton, 1973a:256). On other occasions the state may force or encourage the tribe to settle. Thus we should not lose sight of the warning of Bates (1971:109) that this complex relationship between nomads and other groups represents a balance of power rather than intrinsically non-competitive niches. In other words, the state, rather than local ecology, is often the critical factor in determining land use relations.

It might be useful to illustrate the relationship between economic behaviour and socio-political designation by means of an imaginary chart. Consider a two-dimensional chart in which dots are used to designate numbers of persons, so that more dots mean more persons. The chart covers the Palestinian region as a whole. Let us say the horizontal axis measures increasing percentage of movable property over fixed land. The vertical axis measures increasing wealth and power. We can use red dots to represent the peasantry and blue the nomads. The peasantry cluster in the most densely dotted sector of the chart, the lower left corner. The nomads cluster to the right of the chart, more sparsely dotted, with more however rising higher in the chart toward greater wealth and power than is the case with the peasantry. The far upper right section of the chart is vacant: as nomads become wealthier, they acquire more fixed property and move into the area toward the upper left of the chart occupied by the urban elite. If the urban elite are represented by green dots, a few green and blue dots will mix toward the very top of the chart.

In such a chart, the red and blue dots intermingle, particularly in the middle third section of the lowest part of the chart. Some nomad groups settle into villages. Many nomads with little or no wealth move into village society as workers or slaves, while disenfranchised peasants have an option, with difficulties, of moving their entire village into pastoralism or individually joining with pastoral groups.

Nevertheless, because villagers and pastoralists for the most part exist in distinctive domestic, economic, and social contexts, and relate to each other in a delicate blend of aid and hostility, they tend to identify strongly with their own social kind. It is this sense of socio-economic identification that we can represent with different coloured dots.

As we have noted above, in recent Old Testament criticism, the issue of the distinctiveness of peasantry and nomadism has been handled in terms of the evolutionary priority of one or the other. The work of Mendenhall and Gottwald has thoroughly altered the preconceptions of many biblical scholars, particularly in America. Nonetheless there is still a tendency in introductory studies to assume that the early Israelites were nomads because nomadism supposedly precedes agriculture and civilization. The evolutionary issue, however, is not really germane to the description and specification of the relationship among various mixed subsistence strategies and their socio-economic and socio-political designations important for considering the emergence of Israel in marginal areas at the end of the Late Bronze Age.

4. *An Issue of Terminology*

Because of the many ambiguities involved in describing pastoralism, there exists a considerable confusion of terminology. 'Bedouin', 'nomad', 'semi-nomad', 'sheep nomad', 'camel nomad', 'enclosed nomadism', and still other terms are used extensively in the literature, sometimes quite loosely. In particular the terms 'bedouin' and 'nomad' seem interchangeable. In recent biblical studies, there has arisen a powerful resistance to the use of 'bedouin' because of the unreflective supposition that this term refers to exclusive pastoralism based on camels and located deep in the desert. But this is not a good reason to throw out the term. 'Bedouin', with 'Arab', has been the groups' own term (emic term) for nomadism in Palestine for many hundreds of years, and it is arguable that this socio-political category has in fact existed (had etic reality) since long before the biblical period.[9] It is a good term to use.

The Palestinian bedouin are all of the type described by Rowton under the rubric of 'enclosed nomadism' as contrasted with 'external nomadism'. Enclosed nomadism refers to nomads in close and constant contact with settled state societies and cannot be described apart from that relationship. However, it is important to consider the justifications for retaining the term 'bedouin' before going on to describe the exact features of the bedouin and their role in the history of Palestine.

5. *Did Bedouin Exist in Palestine Prior to the Emergence of Israel?*

Traditions preserved in biblical literature refer to bedouin-like groups who supposedly existed in the time during and just after the emergence of Israel. These include the Amalekites, Midianites, Qenites and the eponymous ancestors of the Israelites themselves as portrayed in the Pentateuch. Some of these traditions, such as references to Abraham's camels or to the Amalekites in Exodus 17, are assumed, perhaps correctly, to be anachronistic. The precise dating of these texts, which in itself does not lead to historical conclusions, is not at issue here. The more important question is whether or not bedouin existed in Palestine prior to the emergence of Israel.

This question has been given a resounding negative answer in Gottwald's decade-old treatment (1974; 1979:435-63). The earlier study has been incorporated essentially unchanged into the later *Tribes of Yahweh*, and in this form has been perhaps the most convincing and widely received part of that opus. It is fully in line with the view of Albright and his students in America that the ancestors of the Israelites were not camel nomads, but 'ass nomads', because the camel was not domesticated until the twelfth century BCE at the earliest. Gottwald (1979:458) believes that the term 'bedouin' ought to be reserved for camel nomads. For many in the field now, if there were no camel nomads prior to the existence of Israel, then there were no 'nomads', a point that Mendenhall and Gottwald deny, as we noted earlier. The question which must be considered, however, is whether groups in Bronze Age Palestine that concentrated in pastoralism were socio-economically and therefore socio-politically distinct. If they were, there might have been distinctive terms for them reflecting an etic category in the culture itself. There is ample evidence that such was the case and there are important reasons for continuing the distinction in our own analysis.

There are three bodies of evidence that bear on this issue in general. The first is the evidence that indicates the domestication of the camel came much earlier than has generally been thought. The second and third concern the nomads around Mari in the Middle Bronze Age and the *shasu* of Palestine known from Late Bronze Age Egyptian sources. There have been excellent studies of the latter two bodies of evidence which support the argument that they have much in common, socio-economically and socio-politically, with bedouin of more recent periods. These studies have not carried much weight with those who wish to limit the distinctiveness of pastoralism in Palestine, but they ought not to be so neglected. We will look at each of the bodies of evidence, the first only briefly.

6. *The Domestication of the Camel*

As is now clear, the issue of when the camel was domesticated does not really bear on our discussion of nomadism and so need not detain us long. Although the matter is still susceptible to debate (Gauthier-Pilters and Dagg, 1981:115-22), the latest clear evidence is that the first domesticated varieties of camel appeared in Egypt before 3100 BCE. 'By 1300 BC camels were established as domesticated beasts of burden, at least in Upper Egypt... Fluctuations in use of the camel may account for its recurring absence from the ancient Near Eastern archaeological record, but Albright's date of 1100 BC for the first camel domestication needs revision' (Ripinsky, 1983:21-27). Furthermore, the camel really does not make a difference in the socio-political distinctiveness of early nomads. Their distinctiveness comes from having, on the basis of their socio-economic and socio-political roles deriving from their nomadism, access to the best technology in means of power—the best weaponry—and the social and political practice in their use. In all periods, the urban elite and the elite among the bedouin control the same means of force. Whatever advantage a particular means of force or transport gave the urban elite or one group of pastoralists, the same means were available to others. It was not the camel *per se* that gave pastoralists some decisive political advantage, but the nature of their social and political economy all along. The Mari and Egyptian evidence shows this well by depicting the pastoralists with distinctive designations having very much the same roles as many later pastoral groups. A third reason for camels not making a difference can be seen by noting that more recent nomad groups in Palestine varied considerably in their possession of camels, but that the designation 'bedu' applied to them irrespective of this variation (cf. Rowton, 1974:3-4).

7. *Nomads at Mari*

Ancient Mari was situated on the Middle Euphrates at about the point where today Syria borders Iraq. In the nineteenth and eighteenth centuries BCE it was the capital of a prosperous state stretching along the Euphrates and inland, involved in active diplomatic and trade relations with other similar states in Upper Mesopotamia and northern Syria. The political influence of the ruling house of Mari extended into the surrounding steppe, where their rule depended on regulating and manipulating relations with several more or less powerful nomadic groups. Texts from this period of Mari's history reveal more about court-nomad relations than any other documents from the ancient world. It is possible to deduce from them a great deal about the behaviour of the nomads themselves, bearing in mind, of course, their urban bias.

The Mari texts have been of great interest to biblical historians ever since their discovery. For decades they were used to illustrate what was assumed to be the life of proto-Israelite nomads of the steppe. The work of Mendenhall and especially Gottwald, however, introduced a different emphasis into the discussion: the nomads really did not have a separate existence, and therefore the category 'nomad' was historically much less significant. The basic analysis which gave rise to this view was done by T. Luke (1965). As already indicated, the reaction to these seminal studies was too extreme: *if* previous studies had proceeded on too simple a view of nomadism, or as apparently with Kupper (1957) had confused the issue of nomad relations with other groups with the issue of the evolution of nomadism, the point should have been to revise the category, not throw it out altogether. In fact Luke's work, along with the later study of Matthews (1978), can be interpreted to show that the nomads in and around Mari acted just the way enclosed nomads do in all later periods. There is no reason to consider Mari—or any other pre-Israelite evidence for that matter—a significant departure from the norm.

Thompson (1978a:23) rejects any analogy between Middle Bronze Age Mari and Late Bronze Age Palestine on the grounds that there is no comparison between the interpenetration of grain lands and steppe in the Euphrates valley on the one hand and Palestine on the other. 'In Palestine, almost all of the agricultural regions which are settled during the Bronze Age lie apart from the steppe, and in most cases isolated from it.' Thompson assumes that there were 'very few' pastoralists in the Negev and eastern Transjordan in the Late Bronze Age, and assumes further that those pastoralists who did live in these areas were independent of and isolated from the Late Bronze Age city-states. He seems to overestimate the differences in size and otherwise between the Middle Euphrates and greater Palestine, and gives no reason for assuming that urban-nomad relations in Palestine were different from the norm for enclosed nomad societies. Thompson seems to subsume what should be classified as 'nomad' behaviour under the rubric of urban-village agricultural life. In other words, he appears to share the assumption that 'nomad' should be limited to some ideal absolute which allows no contact with non-nomads. In the light of these assumptions, his complaint that 'a half millennium separates the two periods' is beside the point.

What is seen at Mari is basically what would be expected from the analysis of later forms of enclosed nomadism. Nomads in the region of Mari and its environs were engaged in a mixture of pastoralism and agriculture to varying degrees, and expressed an autonomy in relation to the state in different ways. The Haneans were apparently the most closely integrated with the ruling house of Mari. In return for some guarantee of the security both of pasturage and agricultural land, the Haneans were active in the Mari military as mercenaries and agreed to reduce their raiding activities against the ruling house, its closest supporters and allies, and the populace of their state. The DUMU.MES-Iaminites were less closely integrated. The kingdom was engaged in a continuous attempt to subdue them and bring them more under the control of the court. The Suteans were least under the court's control. They submitted to a very slight tax of their flocks for the sake of peaceful passage to grazing, but were a constant threat through raiding or joining Mari's enemies in hostilities against the state.

Luke's dissertation is an excellent treatment of the relations between the state and nomad in Mari. However, because of its polemical purpose, some of its emphases are misleading. Luke clearly shows that the major nomadic groups 'cannot be adequately described by the traditional theory that all Semites evolved from original nomadism' to sedentarization. The theory creates a sharp contrast between the pastoralist and the villager which is untenable. Luke removes himself therefore from a position in which to analyze the situation at Mari using socio-economic and socio-political categories in terms of which the distinction between peasant and nomad, *fellah* and *bedu*, has always been made. The nomads clearly have political privileges and possibilities that set them off from villagers who are not members of socio-political groups with a large pastoral component. Luke assumes that when nomads are associated with villages they are the primary cultivators of those villages. It is equally possible that the nomads, especially the Haneans in this case, are assigned the overlordship of particular villages for the purpose of seeing to it that the resident peasants of those villages supply the assigned quota of produce to overlords and court. Luke considerably overestimates the control exercised by the Mari court over the nomads across the board. It needs to be remembered that these documents all come from the urban court and so reflect that limited view. By overestimating the control of the court over pastoralists, the differences among tribes become undervalued. For example, his conclusion that 'the economies of these groups were essentially identical; the tribal groups cannot be differentiated according to different degrees of sedentarization' (1965:278) seems to contradict an earlier description of the Suteans which surmised that they probably possessed villages outside the territory of Mari, though this cannot be demonstrated (1965:123).

Most importantly, by making all pastoralists alike and not differentiating them from the resident population of Mari, Luke is less able to recognize the distinctiveness of the nomad economies he does describe, namely that they are not so much a combination of pastoralism and agriculture as of pastoralism and palace income and privileges. Luke (1965:162) describes the Haneans thus:

> The extensive evidence of Haneans serving in the armies of Shamshi-Adad and Zimri-Lim requires one to consider military service as a facet of the Hanean economy, although the tribal troops were certainly not mercenaries ... [They served as] common soldiers, elite corps, police forces, caravan escorts or guards, and messengers.

It is not clear why Luke does not regard the Haneans as

mercenaries. He also notes that 'Suteans were especially valuable as royal courtiers' (1965:129). Luke correctly observes that while military service sets the Haneans apart from the less integrated DUMU.MES-Iaminites, it does not indicate any primary contrast in the culture of the two groups. But of course it does represent a primary distinction between their culture and the culture of the village peasant. The court had to deal with nomad groups in a way that it did not have to deal with peasant villages, which accounts for why the court records and correspondence are preoccupied with the nomads.

It seems reasonable to conclude that the Mari texts show, therefore, that bedouin, in the sense that we are using the term, existed in Syria prior to the emergence of Israel.

8. *The shasu of Palestine in Egyptian Sources*

Egyptian sources use several terms to refer to the various peoples of greater Palestine in the Late Bronze and early Iron Ages. One of these, *shasu*, is most often translated as 'bedouin', though the translation has been disputed.[10] The *shasu* have been the subject of several recent studies, particularly because of the interest surrounding nomads in the discussion of the emergence of Israel (Giveon, 1971; Weippert, 1971; Ward, 1972; Dever, 1977; Gottwald, 1979). It is surprising and noteworthy, however, how often they do not appear in the discussion. They are not mentioned in the histories of Noth or Bright, nor in the most recent essays of Gottwald (1983) and Chaney (1983).[11] In view of the constancy of nomad culture in Palestinian history and the paucity of evidence for the early period, it is important not to neglect this potentially significant designation.

The Egyptian textual references to *shasu* cover the period 1500-1150 BCE, supplemented with a number of graphic representations on reliefs.[12] As with the limitations of the Mari evidence, it is important to heed Ward's warning that the only picture we have of the *shasu* is seen through Egyptian scribal and artistic eyes (1972:50). From the extant evidence, it appears that the *shasu* ranged over a wide area: from the Palestinian highlands and steppes, to Libya and the eastern Egyptian desert. The expression *t3-š3sw*, 'the land of the *shasu*,' is usually taken as referring to Transjordan, which seems to be confirmed by references to places in 'the land of the *shasu*' listed in a text of Amenhotep III (Ward, 1972:50). An obelisk of Ramses II connects 'the land of the *shasu*' with Mount Seir, probably the highlands of Edom, while other sources identify *shasu* with Edom, Mount Seir and Moab (Giveon, 1971:131, 134; Ward, 1972:51). The Egyptians also encountered *shasu* west of Transjordan from southern Syria to the Negev (Ward, 1972:51; Gottwald, 1979:457).

However, it is the socio-economic mode of life of *shasu* that is more important than their geographical location, although obviously this has an important bearing on their mode of life. Giveon, Ward and Gottwald are extremely hesitant to identify the *shasu* as bedouin. Yet there seems to be little, if anything, in the evidence they cite which is not compatible with such an identification. The vast majority of the references to *shasu* are found in military contexts, where they seem to operate as mercenaries fighting with or against the Egyptian armies in Syria-Palestine, or appear as robber-bands operating on their own (Ward, 1972:50; Gottwald, 1979:457). In Pap. Anastasi I (19, 1–4; 23, 7–8) the *shasu* are described as infesting the mountain passes and trails of Canaan. The Egyptian view of *shasu* as mercenaries or freebooters in the employ of the Canaanite urban centres and the caravan trade, but also found preying on the caravans in remote areas or in open hostilities with the towns, is perfectly consistent with bedouin activities. Ward (1972:53) notes that the Karnak reliefs of Seti I describe the *shasu* precisely as the same king's Beth-shan stela describes the *habiru*, implying that to the Egyptian mind both terms referred to the same kind of people. It would appear from this that the term *shasu* represented a social rather than ethnic group.[13] The view of Ward that references to the *shasu* as herders living in tents and dwelling in towns is inconsistent with bedouin character indicates that he is working with a restricted and less accurate definition of bedouin.

The various arguments about the precise etymology of the term *š3sw* are by no means decisive in determining whether or not this group of people are to be identified as bedouin.[14] Gottwald affirms Giveon's own hesitancy in identifying the *shasu* as bedouin by accepting the Semitic etymology, 'to plunder'. He prefers to interpret the evidence in terms of militarized agriculturalists, appearing in Egyptian texts chiefly as marauders and brigands (1980:457-59). He concludes (1979:458) that

> the usual English translation of Shosu as 'Bedouin' in the Egyptian texts gives an unjustified socio-economic skewing of the term, not only because Bedouin is generally reserved for camel nomads but because the primary reference is to 'pillagers' or 'plunderers' rather than to pastoral nomads of any sort.

It was the 'warlike' tendencies of the *shasu* that were probably of most interest to the Egyptian scribes and rulers, and these tendencies do not necessarily indicate the total range of activities of these people. Even so, the military prowess of bedouin, their activities as mercenaries or in raiding urban centres and caravans, fits very well the descriptions of the *shasu*. The detailed references to *shasu*, which can best be studied in Giveon, seem to us consistent with the view that bedouin existed in Syria-Palestine prior to the emergence of Israel at the end of the Late Bronze Age. Their warlike qualities, urban links, raiding of caravan routes, cattle-rearing, the possession of plunderable goods unlike the peasant population, as well as indications that their social organization was putatively kin-based are all in line with the identification of such groups with bedouin.[15]

The Egyptian texts, which themselves mention the *apiru* quite often, together with the Amarna texts, present the problem of the relation of *apiru* and *shasu*.[16] Clearly there are broad similarities between the two groups, well presented in Ward's discussion; but just as clearly there are differences, and there are in the end two distinct terms that occur often enough in the same document, so they cannot be absolute synonyms (Albright, 1975:111).

Gottwald's discussion (1979:458-59) is perhaps the most helpful on this issue, despite his limitation of the term bedouin. Unlike Ward, Gottwald sees that Helck's geographic distinction between *apiru* and *shasu* will not hold, given that both groups are attested throughout Palestine. Gottwald nevertheless would like to make a geographical distinction a secondary distinction, related to the primary socio-economic distinction. He argues (1979:58) that the distinction may have been that

> *apiru* were believed to have been groups composed of outlaw or refugee elements from politically centralized communities who did not have a native region of their own, whereas the Shosu were perceived as having a continuous tribal—i.e. politically centralized— social organization, with a known or supposed land base.

Gottwald (1979:478) does not accept that pastoral nomads can be militarized to the extent suggested of the *shasu*. However the distinction he draws between *apiru* and *shasu* would be the same as our distinction between bandit and nomad, if he had not imposed such a restriction on his interpretation.

The consideration of the evidence from Mari and Egyptian references to *shasu*, allowing for the urban bias of the texts and the incomplete picture they present, suggests that the complex relationship between urban elite, bandit, nomad and peasant also needs to be applied to the situation in Palestine prior to the emergence of Israel. These shifting relationships represent one of the most important constants throughout the span of Palestinian history (cf. C. Nelson, 1973).

9. *The Political and Economic Significance of Nomadism in Palestine*
The nomad comes before peasant in our presentation because the nomad is more responsive to and influenced by the interregional economy. There are four interrelated aspects to this responsiveness: (1) they are more closely tied to the interurban economy than the peasantry; (2) they possess military importance; (3) tribal leaders are much closer to the urban elite; (4) they control most of the marginal areas which form communication and transportation bridges where local production is variable and changes can be initiated, changes which are usually a response to extraregional economic prompting.

The relationship of the nomads to interregional trade and their reliance upon such trade is graphically illustrated in the locations in which they are found. Although nomads are located in the marginal regions of Palestine, their greatest concentration is usually found on or near the trade routes which traverse the region. The maps of Palestine produced under the auspices of the Palestine Exploration Fund (Conder, 1880) illustrate how nomads cluster along the trade routes in Galilee, the Plain of Sharon, and all up and down the coast, but are much more scarce in the hill country proper. This explains their clustering at city gates, which is not simply due to the wealthiest nomads owning land in the city. Thus the nomad economy is often heavily dependent upon interregional trade. In the area of southern Judah and the Negev, nomads played a significant role in state-level trade, as transporters, guardians or violators of a route's security, producers of pastoral commodities for trade, particularly wool, hair, cheese, water skins, and hides for tanning.

It is essential to realize that these nomadic groups are not isolated economic entities but form an integral part of the regional and interregional economies. Economic functions tie the nomad as well as the villager closely to urban elite. The nomad is involved in and dependent upon regional and interregional trade through caravaneering and raiding. Trade is conducted with the cities and towns through exchange of wool, butter, cheese, skins, and other articles for clothing, dyes, and other items. Animals are often sold and the cash used for purchasing goods. In such cases the nomad must participate in and be influenced by market forces.

The demographic insignificance of nomads in Palestine, at most only 10-20 per cent of the population, must not be allowed to obscure their often considerable political influence, any more than the paucity of the elite obscures their influence. It is because of their military expertise (cf. Rowton, 1973a:254) that bedouin possess political power far outweighing their numbers. It is this military role of the pastoral tribe which is important for its relation with the state as well as an important factor in tribal autonomy. During periods of declining state power, often the result of continual warfare, the military expertise of some tribes allows them to gain control of extensive settled areas often incorporating urban areas.[17]

Nomads are less dependent on the urban elite because they have their own power base stemming from their pastoral economy and expertise in warfare which the peasants do not possess. Their activities include raiding, policing, accompanying caravans, and acting as mercenaries. The hierarchical social structure of nomads means that a single sheikh can command a very large force, as the example of Dahir al-Umar in the eighteenth century indicates. This military prowess makes them a potential surrogate or proxy military of importance to the dominant urban elite and often affords them a significant role in the politics of the region. The nomad support of the state can be dramatized for the fifteenth century BCE by juxtaposing the comment in Pap. Anastasi I concerning the *shasu* in the pass of Megiddo with a reference in the inscriptions of Thutmosis III to the king of Megiddo supplying sheep and goats to his Egyptian suzerain in the ratio of 10:1. It is difficult to see how such a ratio would be possible under such political conditions without the assistance of local bedouin groups as the protectors of the flocks.

The interdependence between the tribe and the state is important to both (Matthews, 1978). The nomad can be politically neutral towards or opposed to the state and still be dependent upon the interregional state economy. Nomadic culture is intrinsically far less anti-statist than peasant culture, even if its dominant political feature is the guarding of the tribe's autonomy in relation to the state.

The wealthy nomad sheikhs, who often maintain urban residences, possess great political influence in their roles as the link between the tribe and the state. Even in times of state control, especially the Roman period, persons from nomadic background were able to assume high government office. Antipater, the father of Herod the Great, is a probable example. Nomads have played an extremely important role in the history of Palestine, and not just from the time of the Islamic invasion of the seventh century to the family of Hussein in the twentieth. It is difficult to imagine a time when nomads have not been important in Palestinian politics since the inception of the agrarian era, unless finally at the very present—and even that is questionable.

Peasants

The peasantry of Palestine, as in any agrarian society, occupy the largest segment of the population but exert the least political influence. The near total lack of peasant sources for village life in Palestine is in complete contrast to the urban elite's documentation of their own world view (M. Halpern, 1963:87 and n.25). Our picture of peasant life is therefore heavily dependent upon cross-cultural studies and evidence from later periods in the history of Palestine.

The basic units of production within the peasant economy were the extended family household and possibly in some cases the village. It is clear that the village population lived at subsistence level with the family household growing crops for its own use through the efforts of its members. Agricultural production was labour-intensive rather than capital-intensive, and inefficient, being heavily dependent upon the maintainance of a stable adult workforce sufficient to carry out the laborious tasks of ploughing and harvesting. The two basic resources of the peasantry were therefore land and labour. However both' basic economic resources were only infrequently under the control of the peasants themselves.

Most peasants were firmly locked into what Shanin (cited by Owen, 1981:41) has called a 'centralized network of domination'. The continual struggle of the family household to provide for its own subsistence was by no means its only concern. The peasantry were under extreme pressure to provide for the needs of the exploitative urban elite, militarily superior bedouin and bandits. Thornier (1971:206) points out that it is quite common for peasant families to grow two crops: the first being cereal on which their own subsistence and that of others depend, and the second often being some kind of non-food grain, such as fruit, fibre or oilseed. The peasantry were thus able to participate in the local trade economy to only a limited extent. Owen (1981:28) notes that in the mountains it is only profitable to transport cereals and other foodcrops more than 20-30 miles in times of exceptionally high prices. Villages were unlikely to be completely self-sufficient and needed to exchange on a local basis. In fact a great deal of peasant exchange took place outside the local market. In order to provide for their needs it was necessary for village households to participate in some form of reciprocal exchange in order to overcome the lack of specialization within the village.

Taxation was the most important form of redistribution in relation to the peasant economy. Lenski's study (1966:266) of agrarian societies highlights the tremendous burden this could place upon the village communities who could be forced to part with anything between 30-70 percent of their crops.[18] Conscription of the labour force, for duty in the army or to complete the grandiose building projects which symbolised the power of the urban elite, was also a regular burden on the rural community. Even the residue that was left for the family's subsistence and for seed for the following year was prey to avaricious local agents of the state, powerful local sheikhs and bandits. Under certain circumstances, taxation might also include cash and so force the peasantry into growing cash crops and coming even further under the influence of market forces. This almost certainly meant that the peasants would have to seek credit from wealthy families in the towns, either to pay off taxes or to procure capital in order to work the land. This inevitably led to debt and the loss of land. Thus the two basic resources of labour and land were subject to the control of those elements of society, such as the urban elite or powerful nomads, who had access to a greater resource base and were able to control the means of force. The peasant's most basic economic resource was likely to be in someone else's credit.

The peasant economy was based therefore upon three main forms of exchange: reciprocity, redistribution through the appropriation of peasant produce by urban elite and nomads, and marketing to a very limited extent. They are the least effected by interregional trade of all the groups considered. But this is not to say that dramatic fluctuations in interregional trade did not have a marked effect upon the rural communities. In the periods of transition and regeneration following disaster or disease, conditions usually improved due to the increased need for labour after demographic decline or with the opportunity for peasants to retain a greater share of their produce with the weakening of state control. This is an important factor to bear in mind in the subsequent discussion of the expansion of hillcountry agricultural settlements at the beginning of the Iron Age.

However, given the constant exploitation by elite, bedouin and bandit, and the ever present danger of drought, famine and epidemic, which are often merely functions of socio-political relations, it is not surprising that village life could be characterized by residential mobility. Pastoralism, with a major form of wealth in highly movable livestock, can be seen as both a specialized offshoot of subsistence agriculture as a form of risk reduction against crop failure, but also a strategy to escape insecurity and exploitation. At times of instability, heavy taxation, or the presence of powerful bedouin, villagers tend to become nomadic. There are examples of villages paying bedouin for protection or taking refuge with local bedouin tribes to escape demands of the state.

Such village mobility is more a feature of the lowlands given the different agricultural strategies and greater protection of the highlands. Agricultural production was heavily dependent upon the adequate provision of water along with security. The location of many villages in Palestine indicates that security was often the prime consideration with arable land some distance from the village. Highland farming systems, as we have already seen, apart from affording greater security also demanded a greater degree of residential stability. Cohen (1965:9) indicates that the Arab border villages of the Triangle were originally seasonal settlements for villagers from the mountains which became branch villages and still retain strong links with their parent villages. Presumably under extreme pressure from social and political upheaval and the threat of famine and disease that such conditions bring, such communities could move back for protection into the mountains. The previous chapter has highlighted the periodic expansion and contraction of agricultural settlement throughout Palestinian history. It would appear from the examples of Early Bronze IV/Middle Bronze I and the Early Iron Ages that agricultural settlements often withdrew to the more marginal areas following the collapse of interurban trade. The full exploitation of the agricultural potential of Palestine was, however, only realised under conditions of political stability with the aid of interregional economic, technological, and political input.

Village unity, so often stressed in the secondary literature, stemmed from the need for protection against external threat, particularly from bedouin and bandits. With life expectancy so low and the problem of maintaining a stable workforce, the major area of co-operation was in agricultural tasks, especially the planting, care and harvesting of seasonal produce. In order for villages to remain relatively self-sufficient, they would need to produce some handicrafts, such as clothes and pottery. There seems to have been little social differentiation in terms of wealth between village households. Village arable was probably held jointly, with periodic redistribution, and worked at subsistence level. Village power was diffused and in the hands of the heads of households or patronymic groups.

This emphasis upon village solidarity, particularly evident in times of crisis, should not be taken to imply that agricultural village communities were entirely egalitarian, despite the levelling and recriprocal mechanisms in operation (Gamst, 1974:53). Social stratification is evident within villages, particularly with the growth of wealthier and more powerful families who often assume the roles of secular and religious leaders within the village. The ploughman, for example, seems to have been accorded no social status (Cohen, 1965:11). Similarly shepherding was regarded until recently as the lowest occupation in village society. It was a phase through which every youth had to pass on the way to maturity and possessed no social stigma unless it became a permanent occupation (Cohen, 1965:36-37). Cohen's picture of *hamula* factions in Arab border villages testifies to the intrinsic socio-economic inequalities of village life with the development of powerful families in competition with one another but held in some form of equilibrium unless circumstances radically change. He gives a good description of intergroup conflict in Arab border villages where non-affiliated groups, i.e. non-affiliated to the *hamula*, often play a significant political role when they shift allegiance between equal political factions. Similarly, the emphasis upon village solidarity should not obscure group conflict within villages or between villages—particularly over land and grazing rights.

Peasant factionalism shaped according to patterns of elite patronage, at both village and urban levels, appears to be endemic in Palestine. Once this feature has been examined in materials dating from the seventeenth to the early twentieth centuries, it becomes quite noticeable whenever historical sources for rural life in Palestine exist in any detail. It is a significant factor that regularly crosscuts cleavages based on wealth or the sociopolitical categories discussed here (Haddad, 1920; Tamari, 1982).

This discussion of the peasantry has concentrated upon certain very broad aspects of village life in Palestine that are important for the following treatment of the emergence of Israel. However, it is also important to bear in mind what has already been said about the complex relationship of mutualism and hostility that exists between peasant, nomad and bandit. There are certain circumstances when these three groups are closely interrelated, particularly in their opposition to state control. The more mobile elements of the peasant population often revert to social banditry in more marginal areas or as a form of risk reduction move to greater pastoralism with the movement of village herds to more protected areas. This is inherent in the residential mobility of village life, particularly in the history of lowland Palestine. It is equally important to note that the greater the military expertise and importance of the peasant, the greater his political and economic importance, since the state often had to come to terms with such military power at times of weak state control (cf. Lenski, 1966:275).

Conclusion

This review of the interactions between the broad social groups and the environment of Palestine has shown that many different permutations are possible. The extent to which environmental constraints, such as the border of aridity, are overcome or the way in which power relations between urban elite, bedouin, bandits and peasantry are worked out are directly dependent upon political and economic investment from outside. The correlation between periods of expanded settlement and flourishing international trade testify to the importance of outside influence in the history of Palestine. Although the urban elite and bedouin form only a small percentage of the total population of Palestine at any particular time, their political influence, especially as the local representatives of inter-regional powers, can be immense. The breakdown or interruption of interregional trade invariably has a profound effect upon the settlement patterns and social relations of Palestine. The power base of the urban elite and their ability to hold control of more marginal areas is directly dependent upon the control and profit from international luxury trade as well as various forms of economic and military investment from outside. As we have seen, all social groups, even the peasantry, are dependent to a greater or lesser extent upon interregional and regional trade centred upon the lowland urban sites along the main trade routes of the Levant. The loss of wealth provided by international trade and the withdrawal of military support when major outside powers decline or are faced with threats in other areas of the world undermines the political and economic control of the urban elite. The result is often a dramatic social transformation within the region as bedouin and bandits begin to exert greater control and agricultural communities take the opportunity to escape the exploitation of the urban elite. The precise ways in which social relations between these various groups are resolved needs to be studied in each particular instance. The next two Chapters will concentrate upon the nature of social transformation in one particular period, i.e. the beginning of Early Iron Age.

Chapter 4

THE EMERGENCE OF ISRAEL:
IRON I TRANSFORMATION IN PALESTINE

Setting the Scene
The previous consideration of settlement patterns throughout the history of Palestine along with an understanding of environmental and social constants allows the emergence of Israel to be set within a broader context. It is hoped that such a study will help to counteract the specialization of much previous scholarship and allow the origins of Israel to be understood as part of extremely complex processes spanning many centuries and covering a vast geographical area (cf. Mendenhall, 1983:95). Israel originated during the third and fourth quarters of the thirteenth century with the shift in land use and settlement patterns of the Palestinian highland and dry land margin. This shift, we have suggested, occurred mainly in response to changes in the economy of the eastern Mediterranean area associated with a drop in trade during the thirteenth century. The discussion of settlement patterns shows that such shifts are endemic to Palestine and are a major feature of its history. They differ in extent but are nearly always the result of economic and political forces from outside the region. The uniqueness of Israel that makes it of such significance in world history lies less in its origin than in the persistence and adaptability of its ideologies as they functioned in various political and economic forms through history, along with the fact that the peoples of Palestine have, for geographical reasons, tended to play significant roles in the wider history of the world. As we have already seen, during the centuries prior to the emergence of Israel, the small highland population concentrated by and large in and near cities, under urban organization and protection. In these areas, chiefly Shechem, Jerusalem, and Hebron, ruling military families headed by kings, governors, prefects and the like, frequently

of non-local ethnic affiliation, held local lands in royal and state tenure, under nominal Egyptian suzerainty. These lands provided part of the local grain requirement together with commodities for trade and commerce, such as wine, oil, fleece, salt, honey, wood, tar, and other locally available products. The urban military families exercised little control over the cultivators of the lands attached to these cities, and over tracts of uncultivated hilly and wooded hinterland none at all. The policing of the urban agricultural lands and their cultivators was subsidized by lowland and Egyptian contributions, as indicated for example by the appeals of Palestinian highland rulers for military reinforcements from Egypt in the Amarna texts. By turn these lands were secure and insecure, while state control in the highlands was tenuous and competitive, as the Amarna texts demonstrate, with effective control in many areas non-existent. This fragmentation into local pockets was fostered by the imperial power of Egypt, which was interested in promoting political fragmentation and dependence rather than mutual interreliance leading to independence.

With pastoralism and other avenues of withdrawal available, the integument enclosing the peasant cultivator in highland city regions was porous and friable at best. To simplify, if the peasant stayed to plant, it was as a benificiary as much as a victim of the commerce of the city. Even when the peasant withdrew, there remained a close tie to the urban economy. This was perhaps less true for nomadic groups, a larger proportion of whose subsistence could perhaps be provided by their pastoralism. There is no questioning the participation and even integration of nomadic groups in agricultural society. To the degree, however, that the nomadic tribe emphasized pastoralism, was a socio-politically distinctive group, and was organized to maintain some domain, it functioned as 'a paramilitary unit in a permanent state of partial mobilization' (Rowton, 1973a:255) and as such figured as an enemy or friend in the commercialized policing of urban agriculture and trade. The bandit or mercenary group with little or no pastoral base was more dependent on commerce (Chaney, 1983:72-83; Horsley 1981:409-32). The bandit either robs the rich or works for them, or both.

The scene is now set to attempt a reconstruction of the emergence of Israel from the perspective of the material gathered together in Chapters 2 and 3. This is an attempt to draw together various categories of evidence within the theoretical framework elaborated in

Chapter 1. In this way it is hoped to approach a growing body of data from a new perspective and to suggest new possibilities and lines of research. The reconstruction offered here will need to be tested against new data, especially from continuing archaeological work, in order to establish or deny its validity. Nevertheless, despite its tentative nature and the reliance upon theory, it is hoped that such a synthesis will be a stimulus to further research and encourage discussion of this important area of study.

The Character of Highland Settlements

The dramatic change in highland settlement pattern, which witnessed a rapid expansion of agricultural settlements in the Palestinian highland and steppes during the thirteenth to the eleventh centuries BCE, generally acknowleged by archaeologists and historians as evidence of the emergence of Israel, needs to be reviewed in the light of long-term settlement patterns. The crucial question is the causal relationship between this settlement shift and the destruction of many of the important urban centres as part of the upheaval experienced throughout the whole of the eastern Mediterranean which Syro-Palestinian archaeology has revealed occurred at around the same time. Israel is seen to be largely or partly responsible for the destruction of urban Palestine either through conquest or revolt.[1] If we are adequately to understand the processes we now label the origins of Israel and their implications for the rise of the monarchy, it is necessary to revise our understanding of the causal connection between the breakup of eastern Mediterranean civilizations and the emergence of the hill country settlements in Palestine.

The direct evidence for the period of the emergence of Israel in Palestine is limited. Nearly everyone agrees that the following pertain: (1) the mention of Israel in the Merneptah stela just before 1200 BCE; (2) the expansion of mostly unwalled villages in the highlands; (3) a widespread destruction that affected nearly all the important urban centres of the region during the period of transition from the Late Bronze Age to the early Iron Age. Yet as any recent textbook will show this evidence is ambiguous and when combined with the problematic traditions of the Hebrew Bible can be used in different ways to support the three main models of the origins of Israel.

The survey work of Y. Aharoni (1957) provided the first direct evidence of settlement expansion in Upper Galilee, where he

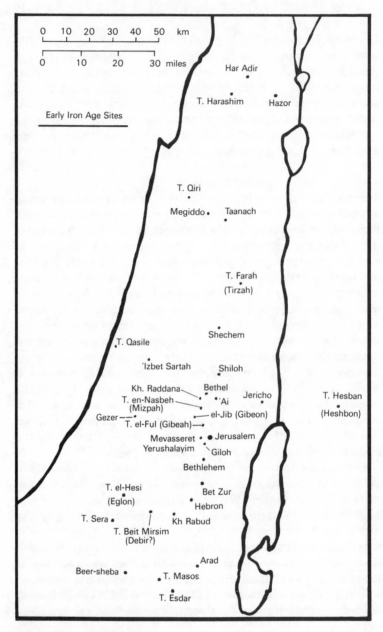

Map 2 Early Iron Age Sites
Reproduced from Hopkins (1985)

discovered a number of small Iron I sites, most of which had not been occupied before this period. This pattern of settlement was further confirmed with his exploration of the northern Negev and enhanced by excavations at the important sites of Beersheba, Arad, Tel Masos, Tel Ira, and Tel Malhata. M. Kochavi (1972) provided important evidence from the central hill country with a survey of the occupied West Bank. As we have already seen, there was a quite dramatic increase in highland settlement from 23 Late Bronze sites to 114 Iron I sites, of which 97 were new foundations (Stager, 1985:3). The total settled area in the survey area considered by Stager increased from 69 ha. in Late Bronze Age to 192 ha. in Iron I.[2] The survey of the Sharon carried out by the Institute of Archaeology at Tel Aviv University provided some of the most surprising data with the discovery of a number of early Iron I sites on the western limits of the heights of the Yarkon Basin (Garsiel and Finkelstein, 1978). The largest of these was 'Izbet Sartah, but other sites were also found in the area. This led the excavators to conclude that 'in the Early Iron Age the process of settlement had reached the very border of the coastal plain' (Garsiel and Finkelstein, 1978:194).

The surveys which are still being conducted will add greatly to our knowledge of this period and aid in understanding the complex processes at work. Yet even from the incomplete picture available at present it is clear that the marginal areas of Palestine experienced significant population and settlement expansion. What were the factors that motivated such a dramatic shift in settlement? The recent excavations of a number of small agricultural sites from the Iron I period shed valuable light on some of the problems involved. The work at Giloh, 'Ai, Khirbet Raddana, 'Izbet Sartah, Tel Masos, and Tel Esdar provides important data for uncovering some of the processes at work in the emergence of Israel.

It is becoming clear from the surveys and excavations at a number of small agricultural sites from various areas of Palestine that we are dealing with an extremely complex process. One of the most puzzling features of the settlement expansion in the highlands and margins is that although many of the Iron I sites were unfortified, recent excavations have shown that a number of other sites were well protected either by their strategic location or man-made defences. A. Mazar (1981:32) describes the small hill country site of Giloh as a 'fortified herdman's village' on the basis of the poor building technique and poor material culture. The primary concern in the foundation of this site appears to have been security, since it was located on a rocky ridge, with no immediate water supply or good agricultural land in the vicinity. Although it was not possible to trace the full extent of the outer wall, it was clear that the site was enclosed by a double outer wall on the south, east, and north-east. Similarly Tel Esdar in the northern Negev has a number of houses built in a wide circle on a flat hilltop with the entrances on the inside for protection (Kochavi, 1978:1169). This need for fortifications or concern for strategic location would appear to point to unsettled conditions and political conflict.

The situation is complicated by the fact that many of the hill country sites, such as 'Ai, Tel el-Ful, and Khirbet Raddana, lack defensive walls. Even more striking is the lack of defensive walls at some of the most exposed sites founded during this period. In particular Tel Masos, the most important Iron I site in the northern Negev, was completely undefended. Similarly, 'Izbet Sartah, although protected by an outer wall, was situated in an exposed area 3km. east of the major Canaanite and Philistine centre of Tel Aphek and could be approached along the ancient road with a 'relatively easy ascent' (Garsiel and Finkelstein, 1978:194).[3] The existence of many small unfortified sites, often in exposed areas, suggests that these sites experienced relatively peaceful conditions.

The archaeological evidence therefore indicates that complex processes were at work. The position of sites such as 'Izbet Sartah and others on the border of the coastal plain is difficult to explain if their origins derive from conquest, infiltration, or ideological conflict. Rather it tends to suggest that such sites as 'Izbet Sartah and those in the Negev were part of the general withdrawal from the more exposed lowlands to other areas once the urban economic decline set in. The primary motivation appears to have been the will to survive rather than any specific ideological conviction. The evidence from Giloh and other sites indicates that conditions in certain regions were unsettled enough that defensive walls were required. It is perhaps more reasonable to assume in such cases that local conditions were the determining factor. The question of whether or not such fortications point to social conflict at an early date is complicated by the fact that dating is imprecise. Social conflict apparently became more acute once the limits of the available land were reached, as will be explained in the following Chapter.

The material culture and economic arrangements of these sites further suggest that the settlement expansion was primarily a result of internal development. It is clear that the economy of these sites was agricultural with a varying pastoral component. Alongside the domestic pottery, such sites also included large numbers of saddle stones, querns, mortars and pestles necessary for carrying out agricultural tasks. The major technological achievement of the hill country sites was the development of terracing to produce agricultural land and protect against erosion. However, the terraces at 'Ai and Raddana were used for growing cereals, rather than the vines, olives or nuts to which they were best suited (Stager, 1976a:13). This suggests that the occupants of these villages were more interested in the short-term expedient of producing food rather than long-term investment in commercial crops. This is again in line with the view that the settlement shift was essentially a short-term risk reduction in response to the dramatic decline in east Mediterranean trade.

The faunal remains at most of these sites also revealed the pastoral element of village economy. The bones of sheep, goats and cattle at such sites as 'Ai, Raddana and Tel Masos show the extent and importance of herding in the marginal areas. Stager (1985:11-15) has recently interpreted various aspects of the four-room house as domestic stables. The large closed courtyard south of building 8 at Giloh has been interpreted by Mazar (1981:12) as a pen for flocks and herds. Similarly, the enclosed area at Tel Esdar formed by the circle of houses probably also provided a pen for the villagers' sheep, goats and cattle (Aharoni, 1982:68). The high percentage of cattle bones, one third of the faunal remains, found in Stratum III at Tel Masos, dated to the end of the thirteenth and mid-twelfth century (Kempinski, 1978:32-33), along with other aspects of the material culture, caused V. Fritz (1981:70) to question the appropriateness of the infiltration model to explain this situation. It would be interesting to compare the faunal remains from hill country sites with those in the steppes since, as Stager (1984:27) suggests, one would expect a greater reliance upon pastoralism in the more arid regions.

The technological achievements of the villagers and the detailed knowledge necessary to survive in the marginal areas again suggests mainly internal developments rather than external invasion or infiltration. Aharoni (1976:60) acknowledged that the houses at Tel Masos witnessed to a 'building tradition, technical ability and obvious affluence of the inhabitants'. The sites were largely dependent upon cisterns for their vital water supplies, and the construction of these indicates considerable technological ability. Callaway (1975:51) notes that 'an appreciable sophistication is evident in the construction of the cisterns. The houses were located only where the Senonian layers are found at Ai and at other Iron Age I sites . . ., indicating that the settlers arrived with experience in cistern building'. Furthermore, many of the cisterns were designed to collect rainwater from the house roofs and were fitted with traps to collect the larger impurities in the surface water. Garsiel and Finkelstein (1978:193, n. 4) point out that the settlements north-east of Shechem and those in the area of the upper affluents of the Kanah brook follow the dispersal of the chalk rocks. By comparison, very few sites are found in the limestone regions which are less suitable for digging cisterns or for agricultural land. It would appear that Giloh, where no such cisterns have been found (Mazar, 1981:33), was abandoned after a short period of settlement precisely because it was devoid of good water supplies and available agricultural land. The almost uniformly poor material culture of these Iron I sites points to the economic decline experienced during this period of transition. An analysis of the pottery at Giloh from building 8, which is representative of the whole site, revealed that 79 per cent of the total pottery repertoire was composed of collared-rim pithoi, cooking pots and storage jars (Mazar, 1981:31). It is noteworthy that Mazar (1981:18-31) discovered clear continuity between Late Bronze Age and Iron I pottery types, particularly with the existence of cooking pots of the Late Bronze Age tradition being slightly more frequent than those characteristic of the Iron Age. Similar pottery repertoires are found at other sites in the marginal areas which also indicate the concern with functional rather than luxury items. A comparable small agricultural site at Tel Menorah in the Beth-Shan valley from the early Iron Age also contained a pottery assemblage in which much of the material displayed clear continuity with Late Bronze ceramic tradition (Gal, 1979:145). The poorer sites founded on the site of Late Bronze Age urban centres, such as Megiddo VI and Hazor XII, also possessed similar pottery assemblages, including the characteristic collared rim jars (Aharoni, 1970:263-64). It would appear that such continuities in the ceramic tradition argue against any explanation of external input resulting in the settlement increase in the highlands and are consistent with indigenous developments as the basis of this settlement shift particularly as there are connections with analogous lowland sites.

The pottery finds at these sites were, however, not entirely uniform. Two decorated vessels were discovered at Tel Harushim and Kibbutz Sasa in Upper Galilee which Aharoni (1982:157) believes must have been brought there by trade. The most surprising finds, however, were at Tel Masos, where in addition to the expected ordinary domestic ware the excavators also found geometric bichrome ware known mainly from the northern coastal plain (Tell Abu Huwam IV and Megiddo VI), fragments of Philistine pottery, decorated 'Midianite ware', as well as a carved ivory lion's head (Aharoni, 1976:66; 1982:166).[4] The excavators interpret these finds as evidence for the importance of Tel Masos on the Negev trade routes connecting the Mediterranean littoral (Aharoni, 1976:66; 1982:166; Kempinski and Fritz, 1977:150). It is clear that all trade and communication had not ceased even if it had seriously declined. More importantly the connections between these sites and lowland areas, witnessed in the pottery finds, suggests that these areas were not necessarily divided by some ideological or military conflict. The continuities and connections show how difficult it is to attach ethnic labels to the archaeological record. De Geus (1976:159), for example, contested the assumptions of the proponents of the conquest model that archaeology had revealed definite aspects of the material culture that were specifically Israelite (see also Bimson, 1978:56-65). All the material discussed so far is consistent with the view that the settlement shift was the result of internal developments following the collapse in trade that took place at the end of the Late Bronze Age. The archaeological record shows that Iron IA culture with its relatively poor material remains, pillared houses and characteristic pottery was widespread throughout Palestine, in the highlands, margins and lowlands, as well as Transjordan (Sauer, 1982:76,81-82). Ahlström (1984:170-172) rejects the assumption of Mazar (1981) that the site of Giloh must have been settled by *invading* Judahites. There are no specific traits which support the view that the inhabitants were Judahite or Israelite and any such conclusion is based upon the use of biblical material to interpret the archaeological evidence. The use of the label 'Israelite' to describe these Iron I settlements usually carries with it the explicit or implicit assumption that the inhabitants originate from outside of Palestine. Yet the archaeological evidence itself is much more in line with the conclusion of Ahlström (1984:171) that 'wherever the people known as Israel lived, they probably were indigenous to Canaan'. Miller (1977:255) pointedly notes that with the exception of the appearance of 'Philistine pottery' '. . . one would not conclude from the material remains themselves that newcomers entered Palestine from the outside at any particular time during LB or Iron I'. The argument for internal developments is further strengthened by recent evidence which demonstrates that the four room house and collared rim ware, until recently thought to be the distinctive traits of Israelite settlement, are much more widespread than previously realised.

The four room house which is typical of the early Iron I sites in the marginal areas of Palestine was believed to have been an 'Israelite' development which was brought with them from outside (see Shiloh, 1970). However the discovery of this house type at Sahab and Khirbet Medaineh in Transjordan (Ibrahim, 1975:74-75) as well as in the lowlands at Tell esh-Sharia (Oren, 1978) seriously undermines such a conclusion. Mazar (1981:11) is forced to conclude that although it is difficult to establish the chronology of the appearance of this house type, 'it seems that no external influence or tradition can be identified as the origin of this characteristic architecture'. Ahlström (1984:171) believes that the four room house develops out of Bronze Age traditions in Canaan where a central courtyard was surrounded by two, three or four rooms. Stager (1985:17) concludes that 'like so much that is considered 'Israelite' in the Iron I period, the pillared house might have had 'Canaanite' antecedents'. The collared rim ware has often been designated as specifically Israelite since the time of Albright. It is characteristic of the many hill country sites and appears to be marked by a distinct geographical boundary with the northern limit being the Jezreel and Akko Valleys and the southern limit marked by Beth Zur and Tell Beit Mirsim (Mazar, 1981:28). However it is not restricted to the hill country sites, but is found as well at a number of lowland settlements. The fact that this type of pottery is absent in the Negev and Upper Galilee shows that it cannot be used to identify 'Israelite' settlements. Furthermore the discovery of large quantities in Transjordan at Sahab and several other sites, including Tell Deir 'Alla (Phase A), Tell el-Mazar, and Khirbet el-Hajjar (Iron I levels and surface) prevents attaching any ethnic label to the form (Ibrahim, 1978:122). Weippert (1971:134-35) also denied that it could be used to identify ethnic groups in such a way. He regarded it instead as a particular fashion of the early Iron Age. Ibrahim (1978:124) concludes that it is the functional role of the vessels that is paramount: 'The presence of the collared-rim jar during the late thirteenth to twelfth centuries cannot be attributed to one single ethnic group. The origins and the long use of the type under discussion, whenever and wherever, ought to be considered in connection with a social economic tradition'.

The evidence discussed above all points to indigenous developments in response to external changes to explain the dramatic shift in settlement pattern at the end of the Late Bronze Age and the beginning of the early Iron Age. Many questions remain to be answered and it is hoped that the detailed surveys and excavation of more rural sites will shed new light on this complex process. The major problem concerns the precise dating of settlements in particular localities in order to illuminate the processes at work in the shift to the marginal areas. The lack of sufficient pottery samples or precise stratification makes this a hazardous process. A. Mazar (1981:35-36) believes that the earliest material comes from 'Izbet Sartah, followed by Giloh, Tel Masos IIb and possibly the earliest occupations at Beth-Zur and Khirbet Raddana. He dates the pottery from these sites to the transitional Late Bronze-Iron I period, c. 1200-1150 BCE. If this is correct then the existence of 'Izbet Sartah at such an early date on the edge of the coastal plain undermines the view that Israel settled first in those areas which were uninhabited and isolated from the urban centres of the lowlands.[5] It is interesting that he dates the sites in Upper Galilee to the twelfth to eleventh centuries and sees a relationship between these sites and 'the destruction of at least some major Canaanite cities'. He claims the pottery evidence shows the Upper Galilee sites must have been founded after the destruction of Hazor. Although he acknowledges that the process is extremely complicated, he also believes the sites in the vicinity of Jerusalem were founded close to the destruction of Bethel, Lachish and Debir. The destruction of urban centres would have completely disrupted the political economy forcing the survivors to seek alternative forms of subsistence independent of the inter-regional and regional economies.

Economic and Political Factors

The destruction of the urban centres of Late Bronze Age Canaan is well documented (see Miller, 1977:254-56), although a comment about this point might be instructive. Albright and his followers seized upon this destruction as ample testimony to the historicity of the biblical account of a planned campaign by Joshua. Yet the evidence is mute and ambiguous since there is no clear indication as to the agents of destruction. As Mendenhall (1983:99) points out, the destruction levels of the Late Bronze cities in Palestine are part of the widespread destruction that took place throughout the eastern Mediterranean, and to a lesser extent in Mesopotamia, over a century or more. We know cities were destroyed, but we do not know who destroyed them. It would appear to be the result of a combination of factors: internecine urban warfare, well attested in the Amarna texts; Egyptian imperial campaigns to the region, again well attested in the documentary evidence; the arrival of the Sea Peoples on the coast and inland lowlands; domestic fires; earthquakes; and conceivably immolation as a magical warding off of the contagion of disease (see most recently Chaney, 1983; also Gottwald, 1979; Ramsey, 1982). Furthermore, the fact that such sites as Jericho, 'Ai and Gibeon, key cities in the biblical account of the 'conquest', provide no archaeological evidence of occupation during this period undermines the conquest model, and forces the search for alternative explanations.

The whole of the eastern Mediterannean had become a vast nexus of international and interdependent trade. The imperial powers and petty kingships of the area were governed by highly centralized royal palace bureaucracies. The high degree of specialization demanded by such systems produced significant economies of scale that supported relatively high concentrations of population. The interrelationships that evolved meant that even localized upheavals could resonate throughout the whole system and produce quite dramatic effects.[6] The direct causes of the traumatic upheaval of the thirteenth century BCE in the eastern Mediterranean are hidden from our view. Whatever the causes, the Mycenaean and Hittite empires fell, Egypt was seriously weakened, and many city-states along the Levantine coast ceased to exist. This precipitated a dramatic decline in interregional trade during this period. The abrupt decline of this trade, which had sustained the power structures of the Palestinian cities and towns, crippled the urban elite and their means to power. It is these dramatic developments which provided the conditions for the emergence of Israel in the Palestinian highland and margins.

As mentioned above, it is clear that it was not just the urban elite who depended upon interregional and regional trade for their livelihood, even though they might be described as the major beneficiaries. Nomad, bandit and even peasant groups were also economically and politically dependent upon such trade. As a result of the instability and material decline, such rural groups, particularly nomads and bandits, would have become increasingly politically independent as is the case in other periods of Palestine's history. The regional expansion of agricultural village settlements in the highlands, we suggest, was a means of risk reduction through a shift to and expansion of agriculture and pastoralism following the general economic collapse. The exploitation of more marginal areas away from the larger urban centres seemingly became politically and economically viable as the close ties to and benefits from urban interregional trade disappeared. We have already seen in Chapter 2 that Richard (1980) and Tubb (1983) describe a very similar process at the end of Early Bronze III following the disruption of Palestinian trade. It is also a common feature of Palestinian history that the lowland peasantry maintain highland seasonal settlements and use these as places of refuge during times of instability (see Marfoe, 1979:23; Frick, 1985:136-38). The seasonal settlements as part of the general pattern of transhumance could become established agricultural settlements when conditions deteriorated sufficiently to encourage such a shift. Approached from this perspective then, Israel emerged in the Palestinian highlands as a result of a dramatic change in settlement and land use mainly in response to the reduction in east Mediterranean trade which had a seismic effect upon the material prosperity of Palestine.

The lack of state control in much of the highland was a major factor in the emergence of Israel. The steppeland east of Jerusalem was of prime importance in this respect as the domain of pastoral nomadism and the refuge for bandit groups. It is here we find the crucial mix of nomads, bandits and village communities in close proximity outside the reach of state power yet dependent on Jerusalemite commerce prior to its collapse in the Late Bronze Age. Pastoral nomads and bandits were in competition with the urban powers in much of the highland, or in their employ in the struggles for control. Such political instability meant the highlands were not exploited to their full agricultural potential. But clearly the unsettled areas are not to be thought of as empty wastelands awaiting a tidal wave of population to sweep over them from outside. The patterns of settlement discussed in Chapter 2 illustrate there had been similar, though not as extensive, expansion of settlement in the highlands and margins. The growing evidence for the view that the Early Bronze IV/Middle Bronze I transition to Middle Bronze II was due to internal factors rather than the result of some external Amorite invasion (Tubb, 1983; Thompson, 1978a; 1978b; de Geus, 1976, Liverani, 1973 and Dever, 1980) provides the closest and most suggestive analogy to the emergence of Israel following the Late Bronze Age collapse. The Early Iron extension of settlement in the highlands might be viewed as a reopening and expansion of this move into the marginal areas rather than the opening up of virgin territory, particularly in the light of seasonal patterns of movement between the highlands and lowlands.

In the piedmont and lowlands, in contrast to the highlands, the population had been denser, the hinterland less extensive, and political and military control tighter. There the peasants had less of an option to stay in place and benefit from commerce at the same time. There too the integument fissured; yet once away, given the pervasive hinterland instability in the Late Bronze period, the peasant, though less contained, became more not less dependent on the commercial sector of the socio-economic system of his erstwhile containment.

In the highland hinterland, sparring bandit and nomad groups, allied to warring urban factions, exercised a typically sporadic and alterable control over the various subregions. To judge from later evidence such interregional conflict, supplemented by inter-village gang warfare, was largely a result of depredation and economic disadvantage. Nevertheless it was carried on largely with the support of urban commerce and exchange and raids on peasants. It was this rural political instability that prevented the establishment of village agriculture on any extensive or permanent basis in the Late Bronze period beyond the lands within the bounds of urban security, even though much of the uncultivated hinterland was fully suited to agriculture and had indeed in many areas at least once before been settled. It was some change in this pattern of rural instability, rather than peasant unrest *per se*, that led to the emergence of Israel.

The change in the highland hinterland from political instability, to political stability, and from hostility among bandit groups and nomad tribal bands to forbearance if not federation, was brought about not by a bandit victory, not to speak of a massive peasant revolt, but by a major economic change in the eastern Mediterranean area as a whole during the thirteenth century. It would appear that Mesopotamia suffered from similar problems, although slightly later and to a lesser extent (Tadmor, 1979). The level of trade declined.

Some would say it plunged. Within a generation, two of the three main trading states—the Mycenaean and Hittite empires—were destroyed. The third empire, Egypt, came under attack by the invading Sea Peoples. Nevertheless Egypt at this time not only maintained its political presence in lowland Palestine but even increased it. Egypt's presence continued to increase for a further two-thirds of a century or more, until the New Kingdom's utter collapse after the reign of Ramses III (1195-1164). Not until then did the Philistines assume full sovereignty in the southern lowlands of Palestine in their place. According to Weinstein (1981), Egypt's presence in Palestine was greater just prior to its collapse than at any time in the entire Late Bronze period, even though its return on expenditure, due to the decline in trade, was ever less. The result is clear: for nearly a century Egypt's imperial budget, so to speak, ran a long-range and eventually catastrophic deficit.[7]

The highland bandit and tribal leaders (not necessarily always different persons) faced a choice: continue to choose sides in imperial or city-state conflicts whose economic basis—in terms of both support and purpose—was melting away, or find some alternative means of subsistence. Sufficient numbers chose the latter, and the means was subsistence agriculture. More precisely, it was a direct exploitation of an expanding subsistence agricultural base in place of an indirect exploitation of a shrinking commercial and commercial agricultural base. Again, the political condition for the exploitation of the highlands for subsistence agriculture was stability. Under the circumstances, stability could only come about by an inter-sub-regional, inter-group, and inter-tribal (again not all mutually exclusive categories) stay of conflict. The political form—whatever it was—that achieved and maintained that stay was referred to eventually by its adherents with the name Israel.

It is important to stress that the main event was not an agreement among generally hostile and aggressive opponents, but the crisis of economic choice faced by the highlanders. Their choice was individual and by groups, then eventually with a collective effect and finally some kind of collective political expression. But the economic choice was primary. When the urban arrangements of which they were a part decayed or collapsed, some alternative had to be found. Agriculture was at first a necessity, then an opportunity. The subregional peace had to do with the lack of gain to motivate continued mutual hostility.

At the socio-political level at which this stay was carried through, it is difficult to choose between the alternative scenarios of mutual forbearance amongst a group of influential leaders or the dominance of a single leader. Band and tribal decision-making tends to be in terms of consensus conceived by and then imposed by the single dominant leader. A more realistic assessment might be that a 'tacit' agreement came about simply because the problem of survival in such marginal areas was for a long time the dominant concern.

A stay in inter-subregional and inter-group conflict did not mean a total stay in conflict altogether, as the existence of fortifications at some of the Iron I sites indicates. The loose coalition of bandit and nomad groups reinforced their truce, drew the political backing of some peasants, and attracted peasant support in the development of villages by exchanging subregional inter-group for regional class conflict. The stay in inter-group conflict and the commitment to subsistence agriculture required among other things that the groups collectively counteract any political advancement among themselves based on an individual's or group's commercial advantage. This tendency could be expressed, and corresponding strategies carried through, in dramatic class terms. One manifestation of this might be preserved in the anti-urban anti-commercial bias of some laws, such as the prohibition against man-stealing and household aggrandizement. Another might be the rooting of Israelite identity in a polemic against Egyptian corvée (particularly significant for the pastoralists of the Negeb and Sinai), of particular relevance in Palestine during the reigns of Ramses II and Ramses III. A third more general and important manifestation was the attack on local urban elites, who had of course been weakened by the drop in trade and Egypt's decline.

Such a reconstruction calls for a further consideration of how the population increase in the highlands came about. The statistical significance of any large-scale external nomadic invasion or infiltration has already been overturned by Mendenhall and Gottwald. This raises the question of how to account for the hill country expansion. It is clear that the settlement of the highland involved movement away (withdrawal) from the urban, especially lowland, areas as well as some external input in the form of migrations. Mendenhall (1983:99) believes the growth in population in Palestine and Transjordan was due largely to the immigration of armed bands and farm families from Anatolia. The question remains how significant these factors were in the formation and growth of Israel as compared with demographic growth in the highlands themselves.

Stager (1985:3-4) maintains that the increase in settlement and total settlement area from 69 ha. in the Late Bronze Age to 192 ha. in Iron I was too great to be accounted for by natural demographic growth.

> This translates into an increase of population at a rate of ca. 2% per year (1250-1150 B.C.) and can hardly be ascribed to natural growth within the zone itself. Even more striking is the number of new foundations in Iron I—97 settlements. Clearly there was a sizable influx of people into the highlands of central Palestine in the 12th century BC.

However such an assumption raises a number of important questions. It is not clear how this figure of 2 per cent has been calculated. If we assume that this figure is correct, then it does seem that the increase is extremely high considering that most estimates of population growth until quite recently range between 0.1 and 0.5 per cent per year. However such figures are based on extended periods of at least 1000 years and do not reflect accurately the potential or actual growth of societies in specific locations. It has already been demonstrated that demographic fluctuations throughout history are often extreme and that population does not experience unilinear or gradual growth. In order to discover actual growth it is necessary to study a defined geographical area over a specific period of time (cf. Ammerman, Cavalli-Sforza and Wagener, 1976:29-33). However, as yet there is little evidence from regional surveys with which to compare the relative shift in agricultural villages in the lowlands and highlands. It is made much more difficult by the inability to date precisely the emergence of small agricultural sites in the margins. There is then a lack of published archaeological evidence to suggest a *large-scale* withdrawal from lowland areas of Palestine corresponding to the increase in highland settlement. From the evidence presented, and particularly in comparison with settlement patterns from other periods, the settlement shift must have received a major initial impetus from the troubled lowlands. However, the resolution of the problem of the statistical significance of the migration from the lowlands to the highlands and margins must wait until more detailed information is made available and more sophisticated demographic studies of Palestine are produced.[8]

The possibility that natural population growth in the highland itself was an important factor in the expansion of settlement must also be seriously considered. A comparative study of pre-industrial agrarian societies shows that natural growth rates are extremely sensitive to even small changes in fertility or mortality rates (Cowgill, 1975:505-25). Harris (1980:66-70) demonstrates how pre-industrial societies regulate population through severe forms of psycho-biological violence and deprivation. The relaxation of such techniques allows a significant increase in reproduction in a short time since the fertility rate rises sharply. This becomes possible when for some reason there is an increase in food production. The extension of agriculture in the Palestine highland with the emergence of Israel allowed a relaxation of population controls. It is commonplace for peasant populations to invest economic surpluses in population increase rather than a higher standard of living since family size is an important consideration in agricultural villages, as we have already seen. The existence of many silos at the Iron I sites may indicate that the village population were now able to retain a far greater share of the agricultural produce than had previously been the case under tighter state control. Alongside the higher fertility of the highland population has to be set the probability of a lower mortality rate since the elevation of the highlands prevented the spread of malaria, which afflicted the stagnant lowlands. There was also a tendency to locate highland villages away from routes, which meant that a population largely dispersed in villages away from highways were less susceptible to epidemic diseases. The increase in population led not to growth in village size but to the proliferation of villages through fission. These villages tended to increase in number faster than in size, as the Iron Age archaeological record shows. In Israel's case the increase was presumably demand-induced through the need for labour intensive activities in the highlands as well as the need for defence (see Harris, 1980:68-70; Meyers, 1983). It is interesting to note that Cowgill (1975:511) argues that the only times in the past when growth rates of 2-4 percent per year were achieved was during the colonization of new environments where all important resources were essentially unlimited. This is suggestive for the emergence of Israel and the expansion of agricultural settlements in the highlands and margins where agricultural land was, relatively speaking, unlimited. Clearly the study of demography for this, and other, periods is a major area of future research. In order to illuminate some of the important factors at work in the emergence of Israel it will be nescessary to clarify and if possible quantify the statistical relationship between the importance of lowland migration and the natural rate of growth in the highlands and steppes.

Israel came into being when the highland hinterland population shifted rather precipitously to agriculture. This hinterland population included not only peasants already involved in agriculture, but also nomad and bandit groups. All three groups combined subsistence food-producing and fighting skills in the same person, although in different degrees. The increasingly extensive tilling of the hinterland was largely motivated by short-term risk aversion and evasion. The formation of independent villages in more marginal areas, in conjunction with bandits and nomads, would have enabled the population to hold off the already weakened urban threat. Israel thus designated a loose federation of highland villages, small towns, pastoral nomad groups, and erstwhile bandits, to preserve and defend local village sovereignty over land and produce, particularly against state encroachment. This was most probably an extension, brought about by the economic crisis, of pre-Israelite decentralized alliances and agreements among hinterland groups.

Such an understanding of the emergence of Israel helps to explain the lack of fortifications around many highland towns and villages, replicating the lowland Late Bronze Age pattern. This lack would appear to contradict models assuming widespread conflict in the emergence and establishment of early Israel. We must reckon with a complex process, since, as we have already seen, there is evidence of fortification at some sites, such as Giloh, and many of the highland sites are inaccessible anyway and so have a kind of natural fortification. The general political instability of these areas might help to explain such factors without appeal to invasion or the primacy of ideologically motivated conflict. Given the piecemeal nature of the process, it is reasonable to assume that local areas would have experienced social conflict to a greater or lesser extent. Most importantly, such a reconstruction helps to explain why agriculture and settlement were extended in the highland *at precisely this time*. Other factors such as appeal to technological innovations have at most considerably less explanatory power. The expansion of agriculture in the highlands and margins only became economically and politically viable following the dramatic decline in interregional trade experienced throughout the Mediterranean basin.

We have characterized Israel as a loose confederation of various groups, at times competitive or hostile with one another, held in equilibrium momentarily by a particular configuration of circumstances. The inherent fragility of this configuration based on short-term objectives meant it was inevitable that the result of a change in circumstances would be either the fragmentation or the fusion of groups in the highland and steppes into a more centralized society. The gradual re-establishment of trade and an upturn in the interregional economy provided the trigger which produced the fusion and the rise of the Israelite monarchy. Indeed one could say this process had begun with the very emergence of Israel.

Conclusion

A restatement of the main point made so far might be helpful. The settlement into villages in the hinterland was given political and incipient ethnic form in the loosely federated people calling themselves Israel. This shift and formation had as much to do with the economic losses suffered directly by trading, transporting, thieving, mercenary, and craft groups more or less dependent on the declining inter-urban economy as with the resultant shrinkage of urban military control over local lands and population. The latter—particularly in the highland—had already long been minimal. The main issue in the emergence of Israel was thus not the regional socio-economic and political forces that led perennially to peasant unrest, though these obviously played a role in the equally perennial spawning of bandit and nomad groups. These forces were not distinctive for the thirteenth century, while the decline in trade was. Instead, the main issue was the supraregional economic forces and their political consequences that forced groups who held military control over separate pockets of the hinterland to turn to agriculture themselves, to supervise and to secure the extensive agricultural development of the hinterland by others for whom hinterland agriculture had at this point come to involve less risk than agriculture under city protection, and to settle for a more or less peaceable stand-off among themselves.

Although heirs to a history of mutual hostility among themselves or their heads, highly decentralized in their regional polity, and—if villages everywhere are any indication—parochial and even reclusive in their separate interests and identities, nevertheless these village groups collectively prevented, for several generations, the restoration of urban dominion over their newly developed lands. Although they did not themselves as a unity permanently dominate the highland region, they were able regularly, mostly within subregions, to fend off threats to local subregional autonomy, particularly during the twelfth century. Early Israel probably owed its collective security as much to its scattered production combined with expanding resources, production, and population as to its decentralized militia descended from the original hinterland armed bands and strengthened by the expression, through cult and otherwise, of its mutual self-interest. The unity of Israel as seen in the Hebrew Bible is the invention of state propaganda from a later period.

The consolidation of the political economical condition for the development of highland agriculture—relative peace, order, and prosperity—was sustained on several interrelated fronts. From the beginning, the following factors were among the most important. Agricultural lands, and especially highland arable, expanded. Iron tools became increasingly available. The mortality slope flattened: a population largely dispersed in villages away from highways is less susceptible to epidemic diseases, and a more consistently maintained mixture of agriculture and pastoralism at the clan level made people less vulnerable to recurrent famine conditions. The birth rate rose in tandem with increased production. Early Israel adhered to an apparently sharpened male reproductive bias in order to favour fighters in defence of its political economy; yet Israel's overall reproductive success overrode the potential of this bias to limit population growth. Greater population meant more labour for the expansion of agriculture. The villages retained the bulk of their product. Regional defence continued to be helped by geography and the low levels of production relative to the lowland. Lowland military elites were preoccupied with the shift from Egyptian to Philistine sovereignty. There was a continual migration of villagers from the lowland to the highland. Decentralized defence was particularly suited to support infrastructural expansion in the hinterland and to counteract the emergence of a more 'expensive' military elite. Early Israel could not however prevent this development in the long run. Finally, as for domestic economy, early Israelite culture fostered an increase in peasant family size and perhaps favoured exogamy in order not to undercut the political basis of its federation.

To repeat, all these factors played a role in the emergence of Israel in that they contributed to its consolidation over a period of several generations. They were interrelated, cumulative, and in concert of gradual not immediate effect. It now remains to investigate how and why this situation changed to such an extent that the highland communities centralized and crossed the threshold to state formation.

Chapter 5

THE FORMATION OF THE DAVIDIC STATE

The Monarchy as an 'Alien' Institution
In light of the reconstruction proposed above concerning the
emergence of Israel, it is important to reassess the processes that
culminated in the formation of an Israelite monarchy. The standard
perception has long been that the monarchy represented a decisive
break with premonarchic Israel. S. Herrmann's treatment (1981:132)
is representative of this position: 'All this confirms the common view
that the monarchy was a late phenomenon in Israel, forced on it by
historical circumstances and essentially alien to its original nature.'
The assumptions of this statement are widely shared and permeate
textbook and specialist monograph alike. The implication seems to
be that 'Israel' should somehow exist beyond or outside the historical
process and that the essence of 'Israel' that exists quite apart from all
but the first two hundred years or so, usually idealistically conceived,
of its history.

Indicative of the strength of this notion that the monarchy is alien
and due almost entirely to Philistine pressure is the striking
agreement between the presentations of M. Noth and J. Bright. Their
reconstructions of the pre-monarchic period represent protagonistic
positions developed from widely differing methodological standpoints.
However, these differences are almost completely resolved in their
discussions of the rise of the monarchy. Noth (1960:165) is of the
opinion that 'the idea of the monarchy became effective so late and
went so much against the grain in Israel . . .' and was due entirely to
Philistine pressure, which threatened the continuity and existence of
Israel as a whole. A very similar line of reasoning is pursued by
Bright, who sees the cause as one and the same, the Philistines. He
concludes that the monarchy was 'an institution totally foreign to
Israel's tradition' (1981:187) yet can go on to add

> But Israel's monarchy was nevertheless unique. It was certainly
> not patterned on the feudal city-state system whether of Canaan or
> Philistia. While it may have borrowed features from the national
> kingdoms of Edom, Moab, and Ammon, it remained a phenomenon
> characteristically Israelite, at its beginning as little a change from
> the old order as possible (1981:189).[1]

Bright's attempts to juggle the two conflicting notions that the
monarchy is both foreign to Israel's traditions yet uniquely and
characteristically Israelite reveals a fundamental methodological
problem common to these standard histories in their treatments of
this period, namely their inability to account for social change.

The disagreements between Noth and Bright over their reconstructions of the pre-monarchic period stemmed from different assessments
of the value of the archaeological record in relation to the biblical
text. With this methodological problem removed, due to the lack of
clear archaeological evidence for the early monarchy, the biblical
traditions assume a position of overwhelming importance as source
material with the result that the events and characters which
preoccupy these narratives have been magnified to such an extent
that virtually all else has been obliterated from view. Noth and
Bright offer accounts which are little more than a reiteration of the
biblical text. As such they serve to perpetuate the theological world-
view of these sources, whether the Deuteronomistic History or some
other earlier or later entity.

Even the most recent work of Soggin (1984), which questions the
reliability of the patriarchal, exodus and conquest traditions for
historical reconstruction, begins with the assumption of the unity of
Israel under David. Once again the Philistines are seen as the
primary cause of Israel's movement to centralization:

> So if we accept the view, presented by the biblical traditions, that
> Israel, unlike the other people in the region (Mesopotamia, Egypt,
> Syria and Palestine), did not originally have a king, it is also
> evident that the monarchy does not seem to have been the
> spontaneous product of the internal development of the nation. It
> came about under the stimulus of external needs, the concentric
> attacks of the Philistines and the Ammonites, against which the
> groups that made up Israel had no effective defence, and which put
> in question the very existence of the people (Soggin, 1984:49).

Soggin (1984:43) admits that because of the absence of material
from the ancient Near East and the few archaeological remains that

can be attributed to the time of David, the reconstruction must be based exclusively on the biblical texts. Some of the methodological problems involved in such a procedure have already been addressed in Chapter 1 and need not be reiterated here. Gottwald (1983:1), while recognizing the problems of the sources, points out that archaeology has scarcely been tapped as a source for the social history of the monarchy. The result of Soggin's analysis is a purely descriptive account of the period of David which assumes the monarchy as a starting point and so fails to ask the all-important questions of how or why the Israelite state came into being.

Despite Mendenhall's innovative work on the emergence of Israel, with his advocacy of comparative study, his view of the rise of the monarchy does not deviate significantly from the standard approach. Mendenhall's portrayal (1975) of the Israelite monarchy as a rapid reversion to Late Bronze Age paganism associated with what he describes as the typical Syro-Hittite monarchies of urban Canaan draws the distinction with pre-monarchic Israel in even sharper relief. The basic assumption remains that the Israelite monarchy represents a decisive, and disastrous, break with what had gone before, being brought about by external Philistine pressure (see Mendenhall, 1983:99).

The same kind of assumption would appear to underlie Gottwald's contrast between egalitarian tribal Israel and its return to the exploitative social set up of the monarchy (1979; 1983). Once again he sees the Philistines as the primary factor in Israel's movement to monarchy (Gottwald, 1979:415; 1983:31). However, he does acknowledge that although the Philistines were the primary factor they were not solely responsible for this social transformation (1986). On the basis of the biblical texts he concludes that the inauguration of the monarchy was introduced by 'free agrarians' following internal corruption as a response to the Philistine threat.

It would appear from this brief review that many of the proponents of the conquest, infiltration and revolt models of Israelite origins are unable to explain significant social change embodied in the movement to statehood except by appeal to external forces.[2]

If one begins with a formalistic definition of 'state', in essence what the state became under David and Solomon, then it is natural that it appears to be diametrically opposed to emergent Israel. Premonarchic Israel defended itself on the basis of a decentralized village and subregional voluntary occasional militia supported by village production in order to preserve village sovereignty. Monarchic Israel, on the other hand, defended itself on the basis of a centralized palace standing army supported by village and state economic production designed to protect the royal family's sovereignty. If Israel is defined permanently and essentially in terms of its premonarchic arrangement thus categorically stated, then the monarchy will be viewed as an alien imposition, an excoriable departure, a morbid accretion, a violation of true Israel. From this point of view the monarchy was, in a word, non-Israelite. It was the unlawful seizure of the nation by a minority who had forsaken their Israelite identity. The most important task is to try to understand the processes involved in this movement from pre-state to state. It is not sufficient to assume the existence of the monarchy as some kind of alien institution, but rather to ask how and why the transition occurred.[3]

The whole question of the rise of the Israelite monarchy is in need of fundamental re-examination (cf. Flanagan, 1981:47). Whatever the reality of the Philistine threat—we might characterize it as a catalyst to Israelite state formation (see also Frick, 1985:25-26)—to portray it as the cause of this transition while concluding that the monarchy is alien to Israel is to ignore the importance of internal developments, in combination with other external forces, necessary for significant social change.[4] It is commonplace for societies, or those in the positions of power who dictate and write history, to externalize crises and social change.[5] On the other hand, as we have already seen in Chapter 2, historians, social scientists and anthropologists are becoming increasingly reluctant to attribute social change to catastrophic or major external events unless all internal stimuli have been discounted (see Kohl, 1981:103-104). More attention is being paid to the dynamic shifts and adaptations of internal patterns which accompany social change (Marfoe, 1979:34-35; Adams, 1974:1).

Clearly the state establishes the great economic advantage of a small class of urban elite officers, warriors, and land owners. In this respect the state represents a marked departure from the lesser degree of stratification that may be posited for early Israel. The state of David and Solomon turns Israel as defined by the state into a virtual imperium in its own right, with the boundaries of its imperial influence extending many times over the traditional heartland of Israel. The rapid amplification of the transition to monarchy, from the modest court of Saul to the proverbial magnificence of Solomon over a period of little more than a generation, magnifies the sense of the state's departing from the 'Israelite' norm. The tendency is to forget that such amplification is itself a historical norm for emergent states. Finally, much of the literature of the Hebrew Bible with its 'prophetic' point of view reinforces the perception which indeed it introduces, that the monarchy is an alien institution, 'like the nations', not like Israel.

As previously stated, if the question of the emergence of Israel has been too much determined by issues of literary interpretation, then the question of the emergence of the monarchy has dealt too little with such issues in a truly critical way. The popular critique of the state that continues the prophetic analysis into our own day and age, including the Marxian critique, is also valid. When absolutized, however, its forms become less valid not more, and less analytically sharp. The prophetic literature of the Bible comes to us in the form of state literature contained in the Scriptures of state churches: by itself and in absolute form, its critique of the state lacks bite and is historically superficial. The idealization of premonarchic Israel, furthermore, supports a wide spectrum of political and religious views today, both for and against the state. There seems to be no single persuasive interpretation of the current political meaning of premonarchic Israel.

All these factors and the perception of the dichotomy between Israel the non-state and Israel the state they support depend on limiting the definition of the real Israel to a premonarchic static ideal. There is no reference to the inherent processive character of the emergence of the monarchy and the points of continuity in the historical process that join the monarchy not only with premonarchic Israel but also the very circumstances of its emergence. Such a limitation leaves many important issues regarding early Israel's infrastructure and political economy unaddressed. We can scarcely make sense out of the development of the monarchy in Israel without recognizing its continuities with early Israel. Indeed, as already indicated, unless these continuities are recognized, the origin of Israel itself is liable to be misunderstood.

Circumscription and the Limits on Early Israel

The study of state formation has become in recent years a major area of research in anthropology (Service and Cohen, 1978; Claessen and Skalnik, 1978a; 1981a; Haas, 1982). The interdisciplinary nature of these studies, drawing upon the expertise of anthropologists, ethnologists, archaeologists and historians, is extremely valuable in suggesting important factors in the emergence of Israel's monarchy. The most suggestive theory for conceptualizing the limits on early Israel's continuation as a loose federation in the highlands of Palestine is Carneiro's theory of state origins (1970), which stresses the importance of environmental and social circumscription. However, it will be beneficial to review some of the recent findings on the origins of states before drawing out the implications of these for the study of Israel.

Cohen (1978b:35) claims that the decisive difference between pre-state polities, particularly chiefdoms, and states is the tendency to fission. He has recently (1981:87) argued that the most important feature of the early state is the ability to develop institutions which counteract the pressures which lead to the fissioning of pre-state polities. These pre-state political systems have an inherent tendency to break up and form similar smaller units. Cohen (1978b:56-57) goes on to show that such pre-state autonomies and chiefdoms can only tolerate a certain level of conflict before they either break up or fuse into new integrative institutions. One major question posed by Cohen's work is why pre-state polities that formed the basis of Israel fused rather than fissioned. It would seem that states emerge where such break-up is impossible or unacceptable, or where one chiefdom opens up new economic resources and thus acquires an advantage over all others.

There is considerable disagreement among political anthropologists as to the specific causes or origins of the formation of the state. Service (1978) classifies the major arguments as variants of conflict or integrative theories. M. Fried (1978) is a leading proponent of the conflict theory, derived from Marxian analysis, which views the state as an attempt to maintain social stratification and the consequent unequal access to resources through a system of specialized institutions. From this perspective, social stratification is seen as one of the key factors in the development towards statehood. Service, by contrast, denies social stratification any such casual role, seeing it rather as a consequence of statehood (see also Claessen, 1978:553-54). He places emphasis upon integration through the functional benefits derived by those who opt for state power. However, the positions are by no means as clearly defined as appears to be the case. Cohen (1978a) demonstrates that both positions have important contributions to make. It would appear that the most fruitful approach to the study of the Israelite state, given the complex interrelationship of different factors involved in the origins of states, is to adopt the systems approach advocated by Cohen (1978a).

The utilization of the anthropological literature for the study of Israelite state origins is complicated by the fact that this material concentrates on so-called 'pristine' or 'primitive' states, such as Egypt, Mesopotamia, China, the Indus Valley and Meso-America. Israel, as Flanagan (1981) has already noted, was a secondary state formation (see Lewis, 1981; Cohen, 1978a; Price, 1978; Fried, 1978). However, although the specific circumstances may differ, with the primary state acting upon the secondary state formation, both still appear to be in gradual process with discernible patterns (Claessen and Skalnik, 1978b:620-21). Fried (1978:37) also makes this point and adds the important observation that secondary states often use parts or all of the organization of some prior state as a model for emulation and improvements. The significance of this for understanding the development of the Davidic monarchy, its bureaucracy, religious personnel and rituals has already been pointed out by Mendenhall (1975:159).[6] Although the distinction between pristine and secondary state formation is useful, it does not mean that the emergence of secondary states is solely the result of external factors. In his study of secondary state formation on the Indian subcontinent, Senevirate (1981:317-38) stresses the importance of the dynamics of internal transformation (1981:318). It is important therefore to pay attention to the combination of internal and external factors in the emergence of secondary states.

The most important overall conclusion to be drawn from the extensive anthropological literature is that no one factor is sufficient or even consistently antecedent to state formation (Cohen, 1978b:32, 70; Claessen and Skalnick, 1978b:629; 1981b:484-85). This casts further doubt upon the standard interpretation of the origin of the Israelite state as due to Philistine pressure. Whatever triggers the process off sets in motion a multiple and complex feedback system involving and acting upon all forms of economic, social, political and religious organizations (Frick, 1985:32; Cohen, 1978a:15; Claessen and Skalnick, 1978b:624-25). It is for this reason that despite wide geographical and temporal differences similar patterns of development can be discerned and strikingly similar end results occur from as far afield as Egypt, Mesopotamia, China, Inca Peru, and pre-colonial West Africa (Cohen, 1978b:70).

A brief word about the typology of social systems is in order before proceeding to discuss the emergence of the Israelite state. The chiefdom has been identified as an important stage in the typological/ evolutionary development from segmentary society to early state. Frick (1985) has made the most detailed study of this stage in Israelite development preceding the formation of the state, which obviates the need to cover the same ground as his important and seminal work. He is well aware of the problems involved in trying to distinguish a chiefdom from the early state (see Service, 1975:304).[7] It is clear that Israel made the transition from segmentary society through chiefdom to early state rather quickly. Thus the present study is more concerned to draw out the processive character of this development rather than to contrast the differences between segmentary society and Israel as a state.

We can already see that a more comprehensive approach would need to take account of other important environmental and social factors, rather than concentrating upon the Philistine threat, which on the basis of the anthropological literature must be viewed as a necessary, though not sufficient, cause of the Israelite state. Although pre-state polities appear to have an inherent tendency to fission or disintegrate, particularly through conflict, states develop where such disintegration is either impossible or unacceptable (Cohen, 1978b:57). The question remains: Why did Israel not disintegrate or succumb to external force?

A modified version of Carneiro's argument (1970) that circum-scription has an important role to play in state origins may help to illuminate this problem. Circumscription theory highlights the environmental and/or social factors which operate as a counterweight against the tendency of a society to disintegrate. Carneiro's original theory held that social and environmental circumscription intensified warfare and this acted as an impetus towards statehood. It is not simply a notion of warfare as the prime mover, as many have argued, since he notes (1970:734) that warfare was a necessary,though not sufficient, condition for the rise of the state. His model is an attempt to explain why states arose where they did as a response to specific cultural, demographic and ecological conditions. Haas (1982:135) cites cases where the conflict was within valleys rather than between valleys and suggests these call into question Carneiro's conclusions. However, this might only be the first stage of the process of centralization within a valley before conflict spreads between valleys.

Carneiro's theory has gained in importance over the last few years (see Cohen 1981:112; Gunarwardana, 1981:134; Lewis, 1981:210-11), although many note, like Cohen (1981:112), that circumscription often leads to statehood but not always. Most recently Hauer (1986) has explored the relevance of this concept for a study of the emergence of the Israelite state with particular reference to Alt's classic study (1966a).

Whether or not circumscription is a sufficient or necessary cause of state formation is irrelevant for our present study. Its importance lies in the explanatory power it holds for illuminating vital aspects of the process that led to an Israelite state in the early Iron Age. The geographical setting of Israel in the central highland of southern Palestine was effectively circumscribed by environmental factors, especially semi-arid steppe and desert regions. This was particularly true of the Judahite highlands, where the first stable state emerged and eventually took over the rest of the Israelite highland. The compact rock plateau that forms the Judahite highland was well provided with natural defences to the west, south and east. The soil distribution gives relatively shallow but fertile terra rossas throughout most of the highland. The deeper alluvial soils and pale rendzinas are also found on moderate slopes in the valleys. The Shephelah has the most easily workable pale rendzinas of moderate depth, with pockets of alluvium and grummsols in the wider valleys. The extreme south and south-west are adversely affected by aridity and form a semi-steppe zone (following Thompson, 1979:49). An understanding of the enviroment is important, as we have seen in the previous chapter, not as mere background to the picture, but in order to outline what kinds of possibilities or restrictions faced a community in adapting to its surroundings during several generations of agricultural and community development (Hopkins, 1985).

The loose federation of groups composing Israel was socially circumscribed by the network of lowland city-states, the incursions of hostile nomadic raiders (the Hebrew Bible names the Midianites and Amalekites), and Philistine pressure from the Mediterranean littoral. It is the combination of environmental and social circumscription with other internal and external factors that provided the impetus to the formation of the Israelite state.

The standard interpretations of the rise of the monarchy, regardless of the position adopted on the origins of Israel, fail to pose or answer the major question of why it is this particular area which centralized and introduced an effective Israelite monarchy. Why is it the population of the highlands which succeeded in subduing and incorporating into its own political structure the surrounding, especially lowland, areas despite the seeming military and economic advantages of urban Canaan or the Philistine pentapolis? The monarchy, far from representing some alien cancer in the Israelite body politic, was fundamentally determined by the nature of the origins of Israel in the hill country and was the result of internal stimuli in response to social and environmental circumscription. It is not the case that there is a straight choice between two polar opposites but rather that pre-state societies and the state involve differing degrees of sharing, stratification and exploitation. For this reason, the origins of Israel in Palestine and the development of the monarchy need to be studied in tandem rather than in opposition. The emergence of an Israelite state also needs to be set in the wider context of the, as yet, little understood process which saw conflicting and almost simultaneous state formations in Edom, Moab and Ammon.[8] The process culminating in an Israelite monarchy is inherent in the emergence of premonarchic Israel, though by no means inevitable, nor is it wholly unique in the patterns of Palestinian history, as the example of Dahir al-Umar in the eighteenth century shows,[9] or the even wider context of state origins.

The importance of understanding the formation of an Israelite state in terms of the preceding economic decline and systems collapse at the end of the Late Bronze Age is borne out by Renfrew's general study of systems collapse:

> The model propounded here suggests that increasing marginality, whether arising from increased population, circumscription or whatever, may be one of the preconditions for the sudden anastrophic formation of a state society. Intriguingly it is likewise a necessary precondition for the catastrophic collapse of a highly centered political system (1979:499).

The significance of this extended view of the historical process has already been investigated in Chapter 2.

Trends Toward Monarchy
How exactly did circumscription work in Israel's case? The society which emerged at the beginning of the Iron Age in the hill country

and margins of Palestine was decentralized, with low production and low military costs. The increase in agricultural production was based at first more on the expansion of agricultural land in these marginal areas than on intensification, increasing population, and increasing stratification. As the availiabity of land declined, expansion would have become less cost-effective and growth more dependent on increasing intensification, while the threat from urban-based militaries in the lowland became greater. This resulted in increasing social conflict through competition for declining resources and meant that the cost of conquest became more attractive. To survive, the hinterland polity of Israel was forced to shift to institutionalized intensification. This was the switch to the monarchy, which when it occurred was a formal political redefinition of dominion over arable, product distribution and labour arrangements carried through in order to regularize the intensification of productive relations and processes, to support increased defence costs. Though formally this shift occurred at a moment in time, as explained above, it was more generally one moment in a lengthy train of events and changing circumstances.

The reversal of some of the primary factors that led to the emergence of Israel set in immediately. If the emergence of the monarchy is in any sense a paradox, the paradox is to be located at Israel's birth rather than at some premature death at the hands of a party of kingmakers. In fact the monarchy was not a paradox, as has been intimated, but the result of the same major shift in highland infrastructure that marked the success of Israel's emergence.

The shift which took place was economic, social and political. Israel had emerged, as we have seen, in the midst of a shrinking economic base following the dramatic decline in interregional trade. Yet from the beginning it grew steadily on an expanding economic base. In other words, the frontier, such that it was, gradually disappeared. Socially, whereas Israel emerged in the midst of a diminished socio-economic stratification with the decline of urban elite control, from the beginning it was characterized by increasing stratification with the growth of wealthy families and increasing competition once the limits of the land were reached. Politically, whereas Israel emerged as a decentralized polity, from the beginning it included within it expanding groups whose interests lay in eventual centralization. Because their interests conflicted, there was no incentive to allow anti-monarchic traditions to counteract centralization.

The tendency in histories of Israel has been to set the monarchy in opposition to the first set of trends, the ones that roughly identify the circumstances of Israel's emergence. Instead, or in addition, the monarchy ought to be seen as a continuation of the second set, which more accurately describe its growth. Of course the opposed tendencies are not exactly equivalent, and thus do not contradict one another. The shrinking economic base refers to trade and the expanding base to agriculture. Diminished stratification refers to the exclusion of top and bottom in the highly fluid and mobile context of hinterland populations, and increasing stratification to the filling out of the vertical dimension of the socio-economic pyramid in the context of the relatively high commitment to settled, stationary village life.

One major factor that acts as a stimulus to this commitment, previously overlooked in favour of the all-encompassing Philistine threat, is the nature of highland farming strategies. Terracing was the most important technique for opening up marginal land in the highland since this preserved shallow soils, removed rocks from the ground to provide terrace walls and prevented erosion on the steep slopes. Terracing demanded long-term investment and continual maintenance or it rapidly disintegrated. Tree crops like the vine, olive, and fig, furthermore, were one mainstay of highland agriculture. It required ten years for the olive to bear fruit and up to fifteen to twenty years for it to reach optimum production. Thus both terracing and tree crops, as Marfoe (1979) has pointed out, called for residential stability. This would have been a crucial factor in the complex forces which resisted disintegration and led to centralization under an Israelite monarchy. Frick (1985:136-38), again following Marfoe, has recognized the importance of highland farming strategies, particularly terracing and intensive orchard cultivation, to act as a buffer against the inherent tendencies of pre-state societies to fission. As Frick (1985:81-82) observes, the growing pressure of population on circumscribed resources led not only to agricultural intensification, but also to political centralization under the sacral leadership of a chief. It is this process of compaction, the combination of environmental and social circumscription, which helps to explain why 'disintegration' was not possible and why Israel crossed the threshold from chiefdom to state.

The rapid expansion of agricultural settlements in the highlands and steppes indicates that from its inception Israelite society and economy were committed to expansion and growth. We have already touched on a number of ways this is so, but perhaps we should look at its economic, social and political development a bit more deliberately in order to specify how precisely Israel changed over time in ways that led, intrinsically and through the process of circumscription, to the monarchy.

1. *The Expansion and Intensification of the Economic Base*

The expansion of agriculture and the growth of population, supporting each other hand in hand, were the foundations of the adaptive success of early Israel. There existed powerful and uninhibited practical and ideological incentives for each. Although the evidence is extremely weak, it would appear that early Israelite highland agriculture allowed only short-term fallowing (see Hopkins, 1983:185-86). Hopkins (1983:185) concludes that 'there is no way to be certain if, for example, a legume rotation was ever practiced in Israel as it was in Roman Italy. Some sort of green-fallow cannot be ruled out on environmental grounds and receives indirect support from the fact that Israel's crop assemblage was rich in legumes (e.g., broad beans, lentils, vetch)'. Soil fertility would also have been replenished, to a certain extent, by the utilization of animal manure (Hopkins, 1983:186).[10] The difficulties of highland farming were overcome, to some extent, by means of terracing and water management through the construction of cisterns. These agricultural technologies, along with deforestation, ensured that enough land was available at the beginning so that careful husbanding of cultivation was not required. Thus it would seem fair to say that with respect to potential agricultural carrying capacity, Israel began with the capacity for major enlargement. The switch to agriculture by itself raised the carrying capacity of the highland, especially areas newly settled by the villagers of early Israel, far above what it had been. The premonarchic period represents essentially the time it took for the growth in population to exceed the point of diminishing returns assuming a relatively higher standard of living. As Galbraith (1980:53) has written concerning poverty, 'the law of secular diminishing returns can be indefinitely postponed in its operation in the rich (industrialized) country. It still works inexorably in the poor rural country'.

Eventually this law of diminishing returns set in and continued to work its disadvantageous effect. Arable was depleted, more marginal lands brought under cultivation, tougher forests attacked, and more labour was required to convert lands to production through terracing, provision of water in some cases, and similar tasks. Once the demographic faucet was turned on, furthermore, it was difficult to turn off. Although it is possible to point to traditions and institutions relating to Israel's need for demographic balance, these measures were limited in practice by the continued opportunities that existed for economic expansion and intensification and by the cultural expectations produced by Israel's earliest experience.

It was only a matter of time before the effects of depletion and overpopulation would lead to the political forms created by landed interests for the furtherance of their power. Along with ecological pressure in favour of the cultivation of the vine and olives, richer people, those with more land, had less incentive to grow food and more to grow cash crops for market. It is impossible to understand early Israel without realizing that the market component of its product was continuously increasing, and that there was a probable correlation between expansion and market avoidance on the one hand and intensification and market acceptance on the other hand. Agglomeration of lands, the switch from expansion to intensification, and from local consumption to urban marketing (with the increasing social integration of the wealthier Israelite farmer with residual urban elites in the highland cities) all worked together. There was no way these trends could be halted given the very decentralized forms which were Israel's initial advantage. The development of the monarchy shows that at most they may have been restrained, perhaps through intense ideological training. The limits placed on intensification by periodic redistribution of arable apparently did not apply. There is little likelihood that village arable was redistributed; redistribution would have limited intensification, and the expand-ability of freehold property gave a great potential for household improvement through intensification available to nearly every family. It is likely that households possessed fragmented land holdings in order to make use of the variety of land types around the village, and also that they reduced risks by grazing livestock; these practices added to the autonomy of individual families and villages (see Hopkins, 1983:189-93).

Because the upswing in interregional trade which occurred throughout the eastern Mediterranean during late Iron IA and Iron IB was one factor in the economic growth of Israel, why did the usual more dominant areas not benefit to a greater extent than Israel and engulf that newer political economy at the earliest opportunity? One answer is of course that they did. Whatever the degree of autonomy exercised by the highland Israelite monarchy—and autonomy in name might not always have meant autonomy in fact—with the collapse of the 'Israelite' and 'Judahite' states, Palestine was again economically fully-integrated into surrounding riverine regions. The answer for early Israel, however, has to do with certain features of circumscription as they worked themselves out in Israel. The lower level of interregional trade meant the higher value of what was traded, and this higher value had a correspondingly greater effect on Israel's lower overall economic level. Israel was well positioned to influence and benefit from trade. In the decades following the breakdown in trade, what traders remained would have been looking for alternative trade routes, and Palestine's inland ways offered one possibility. As long as a deal could be struck with these less-controlled people, goods could be transported rather than siphoned off. The pottery assemblage from Tel Masos, in particular, indicates that it retained an important role in transit trade along the Mediterranean littoral and through the Negev (see Fritz, 1981, and Aharoni, Fritz and Kempinski, 1975:108-09). This points to the possibility of extensive trade relations in the marginal areas.[11]

The process of compaction was reinforced by the fact that the limits of the marginal areas available for agriculture were relatively quickly reached. With such tight environmental and growing social circumscription, the opportunities for the peasant agriculturalists to escape the increasing pressures of intensification and stratification were drastically reduced. Fried (1967:182-226) suggests that the potential for stratification was already present in egalitarian societies, simply waiting for the right conditions to be realized. Once the population expanded to the limits of the land, there developed a chronically precarious balance between population and food resources. Under these conditions, the rise of kingship may have been largely a self-generating process. Furthermore, the inherent fragility of the highland community based upon such short-term objectives increased the possibility that a change in circumstances would lead to greater centralization.

The reintroduction of commercial trade throughout the eastern Mediterranean saw the re-emergence of Egyptian imperial power to the south-west as well as the development of more local regional political and economic centres such as Phoenicia, Edom, Ammon (cf.

1 Samuel 11) and the Aramaean kingdom of Syria (cf. Halpern, 1981b:84). The gradual development of such external pressures from urban Canaan, nomadic raiders, the Philistines and re-emerging or emerging regional and interregional political powers meant that there were numerous social and environmental factors acting and reacting in a multiple feedback process which gave impetus to centralization. The consequent strengthening of the position of various leaders or chiefs, the potential benefits of protection from external threat, and the development of a system of economic redistribution led Israel into chiefdom and ultimately to a centralized state. The greatest effect of the gradual upswing in trade in the eleventh century however was not felt until the time when the monarchy actually did emerge.

2. Increasing Socio-economic Stratification

Although the population of early Israel may be described correctly as more socio-economically homogeneous than the typical population of a Palestinian city-state of the same period, it is essential not to overdraw such homogeneity. This is only the case if a contrast is drawn between Israel's emergent population and the highly class-stratified population of a city-state. It is important to note that the internal constituency of early Israel was not without some form of latent stratification from the time of its emergence. It is to be expected that, on the basis of comparative studies, socio-economic stratification increased in early Israel over time, and in the midst of gradually expanding interregional trade, socio-economic differences present at the outset would be magnified rather than erased or ameliorated. This is particularly true given the comparatively marginal level of the Israelite's town and village economy, in which even a slight advantage in land holdings or commercially based wealth would make a large difference. Furthermore, many items that a few Israelites would have had access to would have increased in value due to the sparseness of interregional trade.

There is some archaeological evidence to support the idea that early Israel possessed some degree of stratification or social differentiation. Stager (1985:18-23) has interpreted the clusters of dwellings, or compounds, at such sites as Ai, Raddana, and Tel Masos, as multiple family compounds comprising two or three individual houses. He notes (1985:23) that, although there is not much evidence of differences in the affluence of individuals, on the basis of Kramer's ethnographical study (1979), the group living in the largest compound at Raddana, site S, 'was probably among the more prominent families in the village'. Interestingly enough, this compound was also equipped with a workshop for copper. Marfoe (1979:21) has also noted that in the highlands of Lebanon the increase in wealth through increased land-holdings was the result of expansion by large families. Thus although the mostly uniform house types in the hill country settlements points to a lack of stratification, the small degree of difference in size of family compounds tends to suggest that social differentiation was present in embryo and increased throughout the Iron I period.

The clearest evidence of such a development is found at Tel Masos. Frick (1985:160-61) believes that the so-called 'Egyptian house', house 314 in Area H, is evidence of a ranked society at this site. House 314, with its different-sized rooms around a central courtyard, is almost twice the size of any of the house types in Area A. It is also significant that the impressive collection of geometric bichrome and Midianite ware, as well as the carved ivory lion's head, were also found in this house. Frick (1985:161) concludes that 'the existence of such a dwelling in an otherwise rather uniform settlement, would seem to constitute evidence for ascribed ranking, especially since the status of this house seems to have remained unchanged throughout the Iron I period'. It is natural that stratification would have made itself felt much earlier at a site such as Tel Masos with its increased wealth through trade than in the hill country sites.

The emergence of stratification within the hill country and marginal settlements as Israel progressed towards centralization and the formation of a state was also affected by a number of interrelated factors. The subregional diversification and isolation in early Israel was greater than is nearly always suggested in the literature. Even within the subregions themselves it is a reasonable guess that villages if not towns were isolated from one another. The ethnographic parallels hardly allow any other construction. This social isolation permitted the continuing economic diversification of the different subregions based on the varying degrees of contact with trading routes and centres and their own productive advantages. Proximity to urban centres and trade routes would give some Israelites more opportunity than others to sell some of their produce, or their labour or military service. The marginality of the Israelite heartland must not be thought of as automatically implying distance from whatever commerce there was. In many cases, such as the southern steppe, trade routes lay in the very midst of the marginal lands. A population along marginal routes stood to gain from the desire of traders to find alternative trade routes to the ones so recently disrupted. This advantage stemmed from the ability of the population to intercept the trade or to participate in its transit. Distance from urban centres might reduce such commercial pressures, but the greater socio-economic equilibrium within areas so removed from commerce would represent a long-term disadvantage as long as other segments of Israelite society were gradually expanding their participation in commerce.

The effect of subregional variability on the increase in stratification was compounded by other factors. Different families, groups, and areas had different relationships with nomadic groups, some of whom would have been particularly well positioned to participate in what commerce there was. Some would benefit more than others from raiding along trade routes or controlling passes. It has been pointed out that this might be one of the reasons for the importance of the territory of Benjamin (cf. Halpern, 1981b:86). Some areas paid tribute to urban or nomad elites while others did not, so that different areas bore the burden of this kind of taxation, which did not cease with the formation of Israel, to different degrees. As villages fissioned, complex relations of dominance and subordination among them developed as a consequence of time and the vicissitudes of growth.

Each village would have had its own internal history of increasing stratification. Even slight initial differences, such as those identified by Stager at Raddana (1985:23), would tend to be magnified over time by the varying economic fortunes of the different families, dependent on varying factors of production and economic relations. Years of hardship are known to have a particularly drastic effect in such situations. As long as there was work for more labour and little limit on fields for the taking, the success of a family was limited by their relative good fortune in reproduction. The bearing and raising of sons bestowed a disproportionate advantage. As richer farmers emerged, they grew increasingly for the market and thus improved their position as a creditor class within the town and village. This kind of opportunity was particularly present in the areas near the old highland cities, which already combined traditionally more secure fields with the proximity of urban markets.

Halpern accurately describes the relationship among the different regional and socio-economic sectors of early Israel as 'loose, sectionally defined, and probably in constant flux' (1981b:75). The agricultural heartland and foundation of early Israel benefited least from this inherent socio-economic variability. The basis of early Israel's general prosperity and therefore its prevailing ideology, namely its agricultural expansion, was quite distinct from the simultaneous basis of economic advantage in early Israel, namely agricultural intensification going hand in hand with some form of participation in commerce, conversely the targets of critical ideology. The inevitable search for economic advantage, of which the emergence of Israel was itself one consequence, in the context of conscription led inevitably to the amplified stratification of the monarchic state.

Biblical indications of socio-economic stratification include the stories of the premonarchic 'judges', or subregional rulers. These figures are worth looking at for a moment, because they are not usually adduced in support of stratification in early Israel (cf. Whitelam, 1979:59-60). It is debatable whether particular elements in these stories go back in origin to premonarchic times, but together these stories are consistent with the picture being suggested here. We are presented with a picture of a number of rich rulers or chiefs, whether established villagers and townsmen or bandits.

The Deuteronomist gave notice but little elaboration to one group of 'minor' rulers who were wealthy enough to have large families and were situated where they could take advantage of whatever trade was developing. They apparently represented a source of relative stability and so were of little interest to the Deuteronomist, who preferred to emphasize traditions that illustrated social disruption in early Israel and thereby justify a strong centralized monarchy like Josiah's. Abdon is said to have had 40 sons, 30 grandsons and 70 asses. With that many asses he could transport a considerable quantity of goods and produce. Ibzan had 30 sons and 30 daughters (probably his sons' wives, for each of whom he was able to provide a suitable bride price). He lived in Bethlehem, an Israelite town that no doubt prospered from its proximity to the trading centre of Jerusalem. Jair of Gilead, a frontier area just off the main routes to Damascus, had 30 sons, 30 asses and 30 towns and villages. There is no reason to doubt that such disproportionate wealth and elite clan networks existed throughout most Palestinian subregions. Furthermore,

Othniel of Hebron is pictured making grants of land from his urban base.

These traditions are difficult to assess accurately due to their position in the Deuteronomistic History and the possibility of editing from the time of the monarchy onwards. Nonetheless recent writers on Israelite history have interpreted these traditions as evidence of stratification in early Israel. Halpern speaks of 'entrenched elites' (1981b:63) and a 'wealthy warrior class' (1981b:88). Bright (1981:171) describes Shamgar, albeit for slightly speculative reasons, as 'presumably . . . a city king of Beth-Anath in Galilee'. Saul and David, at the beginning of his career, are seen as chiefs by both Flanagan (1981) and Frick (1985).

Writers like Bright are equally aware of the bandit nature of the 'major' rulers whose careers for the Deuteronomist illustrate the kind of social disruption and subregional hostility kings were useful for preventing. Bright calls Jephthah a 'bandit' (1981:171) and a 'Gileadite freebooter, an Apiru' (1981:173), and Samson a 'rogue' (1981:171). These are the rulers who dominate the Deuteronomist's account of political turmoil prior to the institution of the state. The norm is for these to threaten to become king, and eventually one of them, David, does. They tend to be opposed, as David was opposed by Saul, by established leaders of the first type: the men of Gideon's town, the sons of Gideon in Shechem, the men of Succoth and Penuel, and the Judahites who turned Samson over to the Philistines in order to remove him as a source of friction between themselves and their Philistine neighbours. From the perspective of the Deuteronomist, the resistance of the good bandit David against Saul was an omen of Josiah's ascendancy over the established sheikhs, elders and other landed notables in his realm.

Among other indications in the biblical literature of stratification in early Israel are the traditions about town and village elders and the continued allowance of debt service. The elders would have been among the wealthier men of a town or village, whose influence was based upon among other things the ownership of greater amounts of land and capital than usual and the partial distribution of these in credit. Laws governing debt service, to the degree they refer to the premonarchic period, demonstrate the unequal distribution of capital (cf. 1 Samuel 8.16 and 25.10). It is important not to mistake the restraint of stratification which can be posited for early Israel for its successful suppression. The indications of an ideology of restraint are at the same time the clearest indications of the prevalence of its object, the existence of stratification. The monarchy that eventually emerged in Israel was based on a social structure whose stratification went back directly to Israel's beginnings.

3. *Increasing Political Centralization*

There is some evidence to suggest that social conflict and political centralization increased throughout the Iron I period. A number of Iron I sites, particularly in the hill country, were destroyed or abandoned towards the end of the eleventh century during the transition from the Iron IB to the Iron II period. It is interesting to note that both 'Ai and Khirbet Raddana, two of the most important archaeological sites in the hill country which have provided such valuable information about the emergence of settlement at the beginning of Iron I, were both destroyed and abandoned c.1050 BCE. Raddana seems to have suffered a violent destruction and was not occupied again until the Byzantine period (Callaway and Cooley, 1971:12). Other sites such as Shiloh and Tel el-Ful suffered destruction around the end of the eleventh century but were reoccupied again after a gap in settlement (Aharoni, 1982:161; Sinclair, 1976:444). A similar fate seems to have befallen sites in the marginal areas of Palestine. Tel Masos, with its wealth and trade connections, along with the smaller Tel Esdar, were destroyed during the same period (Aharoni, 1976:66). It is clear from evidence at other Palestinian sites that the growing social conflict was not restricted to small rural highland or marginal sites. Urban centres such as Megiddo (Yadin, 1979:200) and Tel Abu Hawam (Anati, 1975:11) suffered similar fates during this period.

The growing social conflict which is evidenced at a number of Palestinian sites in all regions seems to have been accompanied, or immediately followed, by increasing political centralization. Frick (1985:161-62) believes that the relationship between Tel Masos and Tel Esdar during the Iron I period points to a two-level settlement hierarchy common in ranked societies. On the basis of the size of Tel Masos, about sixty dunams, in comparison with other sites in the area, the next largest being Tel Esdar at twenty dunams, he suggests that this must have been the central site in this region in the period prior to the emergence of the monarchy. This, along with the connections between the pottery found at both sites, leads Frick to suggest that both sites were linked in a 'two-level hierarchy of settlement types which is characteristic of chiefdoms' (1985:162; cf. Carneiro, 1981:53-54). Frick has identified a most important line of investigation which needs to be followed with regard to the relationship between settlements in other areas, particularly the hill country. This will become possible once the important surveys now being carried out are completed and published. It should also be possible to test such relationships at other sites as more data become available from excavations employing such research strategies. Marfoe (1979:35), among others, suggests that Near Eastern archaeology should 'put greater emphasis on a more rigorous approach to intrasite and intersite variability (a far cry indeed from the basic premise of a 'type' site!) and on regional surveys, both of which would promote a greater sensitivity to small-scale, open-boundary systems'.

This process of centralization continued as Israel moved from chiefdom to state. Aharoni (1976:68), for example, reports that the renewal of settlement which followed shortly after the destruction of such sites as Tel Masos and Tel Esdar was markedly different in character from what had gone before. The unfortified sites were now replaced with impressive fortifications at Arad, Beersheba and Tel Malhata, while Tel Ira was the largest fortified site in the Negev during the monarchy (Aharoni, 1976:70). The change was so marked that Aharoni concluded that 'the tremendous efforts invested in their fortification indicate that this enterprise was carried out under royal initiative'. Clearly the complexity of organization necessary to undertake these projects demanded a high degree of centralization. This movement towards centralization is also in evidence in the hill country where Tel en-Nasbeh emerged as a fortified site during the eleventh century. Its foundation predates the development of a chain of fortified centres which emerged during the monarchic period (see, for example, Ahlström, 1982:27-43; A. Mazar, 1982). The heavy investment in monumental architecture and fortifications, which is well documented for the early monarchy, particularly the Solomonic period, is typical of early states.

The archaeological evidence, admittedly incomplete and fragment-ary, for growing social conflict and increasing political centralization during the eleventh century in Israel is consistent with Carneiro's theory (1970) of state formation in circumscribed areas. He describes (1970:735-36; 1978:207-08; cf. Lewis, 1981:212) how population pressure upon circumscribed resources leads to competition for scarce arable land. Such social conflict results in territorial units transcending the village in size and degree of organization. As such units increased in size they naturally decreased in number with the result that eventually this aggregation of small local groups (cf. Marfoe, 1979) led to chiefdom and ultimately to the state.

As mentioned above, a major task of future research will be to test such theories more fully against new data from excavations and surveys. Flanagan (1981) has already offered a convincing analysis of the biblical narratives and genealogies in light of the anthropological literature on chiefdoms. This work has been advanced by Frick's (1979; 1985) use of archaeological and ethnoarchaeological data to add greater detail to this important period of transition prior to the emergence of the monarchy.

One of the most puzzling features of the formation of states is how or why individuals or villages give up local autonomy for a centralized form of government (Cohen, 1978a:1). Redistribution and military advantage are usually listed as two of the most important features of chiefdoms.[12] The advantages of such features in the context of competition for scarce resources in a tightly circumscribed community such as Israel is of obvious importance. Fried (1967:226) has made the important point that:

> Just as stratification grew within unstratified societies without the conscious awareness of the members of the affected societies, so the state emerged and was hard at work concentrating its power on specific cases long before any reflective individual took the effort to isolate and identify the novelty.

Similarly Claessen and Skalnik (1978b:620-21) view the emergence of the state as an inconspicuous process from a contemporary point of view. Even Godelier (1978:767), from an explicitly Marxist perspective, acknowledges that the domination and exploitation involved in the emergence of states could only have been sustained if they had been presented as an exchange of services.

Legitimation is a crucial aspect of state formation and maintenance (Whitelam, 1984). Thus it is important to bear in mind the perceived benefits of centralization alongside the more commonly studied exploitation of such social systems. Centralization comes about as social actors face certain choices at particular times often unconscious of the wider implications of such actions. As Marfoe (1979:33) points out, social actors respond to environmental pressures and adapt in the most appropriate way. He therefore places much greater emphasis upon the way culture change is brought about by the shifts in balance between dynamic social systems (1979:35). Thus the emergence of Israel and the formation of the state need to be understood as adaptations to particular environmental and social pressures. Much previous scholarship has adopted the theological bias of the biblical traditions and prefered to emphasize the discontinuities between pre-monarchic Israel and the monarchy. The social transformation which occurred when Israel crossed the threshold to statehood needs to be analysed and understood much more in terms of the social and environmental pressures acting upon the highland and marginal communities from their inception at the end of the Late Bronze Age.

In retrospect, however, centralization can be seen as the means by which an emergent landed class attempted to preserve the power and privilege created for them by their increasing wealth. Centralization was eventually perceived to serve the interests of these few rather than the many. The biblical traditions reflect growing social conflict and increasing centralization in the stories of the struggle between Saul and David. These traditions may well reflect a struggle between an increasingly dominant group of larger landowners whose primary social bonds had gradually shifted from the village to the regional level and a much larger subordinate group of poorer villagers whose political and economic integrity was being threatened. The interests of the villages of Israel were presumably represented at the regional level by the rural priesthood, which may help to explain why the struggle appears in the sources as between wealthier landowners and the priesthood.[13] The sources which concentrate on the conflict between the houses of Saul and David, which betray a Davidic bias (Whitelam, 1984), no doubt schematized what in actuality was a complex matrix of special interests and their realization in political groupings. The evidence is not available, however, for anything other than a theoretical statement of such complexities.

It has already been argued that the increase in social conflict which emerged during the eleventh century was accompanied by intensification in response to the competition for diminishing resources. It would appear that increasing Israelite production became increasingly attractive to the lowland elites, such as the Philistines. The gradual expansion in trade, moreover, presumably also benefited the Philistines who became politically more centralized and enlarged their lowland dominion. This must have been an important feature in the social conflict evident in the archaeological record. Furthermore such pressures from the lowlands can only have compounded Israel's social circumscription and added significantly to the regional costs of defence. In sum, those in Israel who were increasingly called upon to bear the greater defence burden and who in one sense were better positioned to do so through their wealth were, at the same time, increasingly able through their power to shift this burden back down to the village smallholders. Seen in this light, monarchy was a means of 'redistributing' the cost of defence that increased along with but at a greater rate than the total product of Israel. The internal dynamics of this redistribution was veiled at the time, as it has been in the historiography of Israel, by the overwhelming consciousness of the Philistine threat.

The second trend saw the emergent landed class attempting to retain amongst themselves control of their participation in trade rather than allowing control to transfer, through the machinations of the wealthiest of them, to the lowland. There is little if any hint in the written sources that the highland landed were involved in such trade in the first place. This bias of the sources, however, should occasion no surprise given the tendency of elites to externalize threat. The almost exclusive attention given to the Philistines in the sources, which come from a Davidic state that had good reason to obscure its linkage with the Philistine elite, results from the same tendency. There is no reason not to take the comparative view and assume that the pattern of highland elite participation in interregional trade applies to the emergent elite of eleventh century BCE Israel, whether they themselves conceived of such activity in this way or not. This might be indicated by Saul's offer of intensified arable and vineyards to his retainers (1 Samuel 22). Though not noted in the text, the product of these would have served the retainers as commodities. The same must be supposed regarding the increased pastoral product of the vast and progressively integrated drylands controlled by David early in his career (cf. 1 Samuel 30).

The monarchy represented, therefore, the means by which a subgroup of emergent landed elite in Israel imposed greater costs of national defence upon village smallholders and retained political control over their participation in trade among themselves. The creation of the monarchy by a privileged subgroup of Israelites represented little threat to themselves. The right of the state to redistribute lands functioned to the advantage of those who already bore a larger share of defence. The expansion of the monarchy was mostly a result of internal forces let loose by the initial political transmutation.

Conclusion

The emergence of Israel and the inauguration of the monarchy must be seen as part of long-term trends and processes if progress is to be made towards a more realistic appraisal of this phase of Palestinian history. Both premonarchic and monarchic Israel represent different adaptations to social and environmental pressures. Israel had emerged in the highlands and margins of Palestine following the shift in settlement pattern in response to the collapse of Mediterranean trade. The monarchy was the result of shifts within Israel brought about by increasing pressures on tightly circumscribed resources. The potential of this approach of concentrating upon long-term processes at work in the history of Palestine is suggestive for understanding much that is obscure about the development of the Israelite monarchy.

Our purpose has been to stress the continuous and processive character of events as opposed to the usual demarcation between the emergence of Israel and the development of the Israelite state. Consistent with this stress on continuity and process, Chapters 4 and 5 have concerned not two subjects but one, and the chapter division should not be allowed to suggest otherwise. While Chapter 4, furthermore, clearly continues the emphasis of the earlier chapters on the importance of outside influences on the history of social change in Palestine, it might appear at first that Chapter 5, with its focus on internal developments, departs from that emphasis. This is an inconsistency in appearance only. The purpose of focusing on internal developments in Chapter 5 is not to deny outside influence on the formation of the state, but to emphasize the continuity of this formation with the process of the emergence of the Iron Age highland population. It is to stress, in other words, the systemic character of the process of the emergence of Israel as a whole, from early villages to Davidic state, and the primary dependence of that single process on interregional influences that go far beyond the conceptually contained influence of the Philistines.

Harris (1980:101) has pointed out that advanced chiefdoms were thoroughly committed to the relief of reproductive pressures not through regulation of fertility but through territorial expansion, military plunder, and the continual intensification of production. A particularly important aspect of the growth of chiefdoms, as we have seen, is that military advantages of size set in motion a process which proceeds rapidly with ever-quickening pace (Carneiro, 1981:64). The chiefdom as it crosses the threshold to state becomes a self-perpetuating and self-justifying process (Harris, 1980:102-103). This would help to explain the rapid rise and expansion of the Davidic monarchy as it subdued and replaced the Saulides of Gibeah, before expanding into the lowlands, the coastal plain and Transjordan. The utilization of studies on state formation theory suggests, therefore, that it was the population of the central hill country that centralized and expanded at the expense of surrounding areas precisely because of the pressures of social and environmental circumscription. The lowlands failed to compete because were not nearly so tightly circumscribed. Lowland farming strategies did not depend to the same extent on residential stability so that in the face of social or political pressure the rural population were able to move more easily to pastoralism and towards the more marginal areas to escape effective state control. This in turn created greater pressure on the resources of these marginal regions, leading to further competition and eventually to centralization.

Furthermore, circumscription theory not only helps to explain the fusion of local autonomous groups into an Israelite monarchy, but also aids in understanding the later fissioning of the state into separate southern and northern monarchies. The limits to the extent of Israel's expansion were set by the environmental constraints of sea and desert to the west and east, with the more powerful riverine civilizations of Egypt and Mesopotamia to the south and north. The resurgence of international trade throughout the eastern Mediteranean accompanied by the revival of the imperial powers to the south and north meant that Solomon was unable to relieve internal demographic pressures through military expansion or the opening up of new economic resources. Such opportunities, which had been responsible for the rapid expansion of the early monarchy, were now denied to Israel. The result was that greater financial and labour burdens had to be placed upon Israel's own infrastructure in order to support the burgeoning superstructure. The build up of these pressures resulted in the disintegration of the state into northern and southern monarchies which now found themselves once more, as so often in the history of Palestine, subject to the whims of interregional powers.

Chapter 6

THE IDEA OF EARLY ISRAEL IN HISTORY

The emergence of Israel and the formation of an Israelite state during the early Iron Age in Palestine, we have argued, represent distinctive adaptations of various groups to environmental and social pressures. The social transformation which took place following the decline of interregional trade and the subsequent formation of the monarchic state has been set within the context of long-term settlement patterns in Palestine. The tentative and temporary nature of this investigation, as of all historical investigations, poses many problems that cannot be treated at the same time in depth. This study has relied heavily upon the growing body of archaeological evidence interpreted in terms of comparative historical and anthropological studies. The biblical traditions, which have been the focal point of most previous reconstructions of this period, have played a secondary role in our investigation. It is the nature of these traditions, addressed only briefly in Chapter 1, and their understanding of Israel that form the focus of much of the present Chapter.

Earlier attempts by Albright and others to identify the emergence of Israel from particular traits in the material culture have failed with the increasing discoveries of distinctive pottery types or architectural features in many regions of Palestine that defy ethnic labels. Our assumption, shared by many historians and archaeologists, that the emergence of numerous rural sites in the highlands and margins of Palestine during the transition from the Late Bronze to the early Iron Age is to be identified with a single people, 'Israel', itself begs the question. Most importantly, assumptions about the unity of premonarchic Israel are brought into question. The prevailing understandings of the identities of the many Israels of history and of the ideas of Israel that correspond to those identities are tied closely to the problem of the nature and functions of the religious traditions preserved in the Hebrew Bible and the ways in which they have been interpreted by various communities from their inception to the present day. The most obvious question raised by the preceding discussion is why the biblical traditions obscure the nature of the emergence of 'Israel' in the highlands and steppes of Palestine. It is also important to ask why the monumental investment of scholarly effort from the early nineteenth century onwards perpetuated the biblical picture of the origins and unity of early Israel. In discussing briefly some episodes in the history of the idea of Israel, we will be interested in the continuing interplay between two levels: what Israel was conceived or experienced to be, and what the social, political and economic position was of those who thought of themselves as Israel.

The concentration of scholarly attention in recent years upon the nature and function of the canon has stressed the adaptability and fluidity of the traditions (Sanders, 1972; 1976; 1984; Blenkinsopp, 1981). In the words of Sanders (1976), the traditions survived precisely because they were 'adaptable for life'. Israel was not a monolithic entity but like any dynamic historical community was composed of shifting factions and social groups that experienced many changes throughout its eventful history. Traditions developed and were adapted and preserved if they addressed in some meaningful way the overriding questions of the identity and lifestyle of the community as it faced changing historical circumstances. Thus at any given time there might be many ideas, some of which have been preserved in the Hebrew Bible, about the identity, make-up and origins of Israel. It is important therefore to attempt to identify the vested interests and factions involved in the formation of particular traditions. However, the richness and diversity of the material preserved in the Hebrew Bible is such that it is not easy to produce a straightforward account of its development. The adaptability, fluidity and pluralism of traditions that have become particularly evident in the wake of the discovery of the Dead Sea Scrolls are the major obstacles to understanding the emergence of Israel from the perspective of the biblical traditions. Soggin (1984:31-32) has recently warned against the dangers of accepting 'uncritically the picture which Israel had of its own origins' simply by paraphrasing the biblical texts or supplementing them by alleged parallels from the ancient Near East.[1]

The formation of the Davidic state, described in Chapter 5, was crucial in shaping and defining the nature and identity of Israel as it is mainly presented in the Bible. It was the state which provided the standard of Israelite identity even though there were always factions within 'Israel' with identities that differed from this standard. From the destruction of the monarchy to the present, the Torah or Pentateuch and its interpretations have served the same function. Thus prior to the Babylonian exile—the deportation of the monarchic elite of the state of Judah who inherited the identity of Davidic Israel—the nature and identity of Israel as it is now usually conceived was largely determined by the state, its beneficiaries and interpreters. After the exile, it is the history of the Torah and its interpretations which governed the idea and identity of Israel. Such interpretations were dictated by those in positions of power and the specialized scribes attached to them beholden to a succession of suzerain authorities. The identities of Israel at given times, from the monarchy onwards, were determined by small, though extremely influential, minorities who projected these identities and sought legitimacy, with more or less success, from the rest of the community.

Because in origin the temple represented the state and yet was rebuilt soon after the final destruction of the state, the history of the Torah and its interpretations divides into two periods, before the final destruction of the temple in 70 CE and after. The Second Temple period is also the most important for the final development of the biblical traditions themselves and decisively shaped the presentation of the history of the community through Scripture. The parties and polemics over hundreds of years which led to the final forms of the Scriptures are the major historiographical problem faced by the historian wanting to extract information from these traditions about the emergence of Israel or the development of the early monarchy. It was the destruction of the temple in 70 CE which marked an important watershed that occasioned the emergence of Rabbinic Judaism and the post-apostolic episcopal Christian movement as the two surviving distinctive Jewish groups. Thus the prevailing interpretations of Torah by these two groups have had a profound influence on the identity and nature of Israel to the present day (cf. Grose, 1983). The events of 70 CE therefore have had perhaps more influence than any other on the history of the idea and identity of Israel from then until now.

The various responses to the loss of the temple made possible the continuation of the meaningfulness of Israel from 70 CE on despite the loss of both state and temple. It is essential to underscore the importance of the presence and absence of the temple in the history of the meanings of Israel. As has already been indicated, the great historical importance of the ideology of early Israel lies not so much in itself but in the set of later developments through which it was adapted and preserved. *This* history is what gives the origin of Israel its meaning and poses the problem of investigating the origins of Israel in such a way that the historian is forced to look for sources other than the biblical traditions themselves in order to understand the origins of the community.

The Davidic Idea of Israel
We have already seen that the major difference between early states and such pre-state polities as chiefdoms is the development of institutions that counteract inherent tendencies to fission. It is widely recognized that one of the most important factors in the survival and development of early states is the manner in which they are able to legitimize their existence and functions. Marcus (1974:83) identifies the exercise of power as a major difference between states and simpler chiefdoms: states have a monopoly of power that represents a quantum leap over chiefdoms. Physical coercion, or its threat, are important for the maintenance of state authority but by no means decisive. Early states invest a great deal in the development of an ideology of legitimacy and the means by which to propagate such an ideology to all levels of society simply because it is cost effective over against the use of force (Harris, 1980:102). The ideology of legitimacy is conveyed to different levels of society by a variety of means ranging from the literary output of a royal bureaucracy, to monumental architecture, iconography and ceremonial.

The dynamics of this process within the early Davidic state is an important topic for future research (Whitelam, 1984). However, for the present study it is more important to note the dramatic effect that the Davidic court must have had upon shaping the idea of Israel and its origins. A comparison with other early states ought to prove most instructive in this regard. However, for the present it is sufficient to suggest some lines of thought on how the emergence of Israel has been obscured by the shaping of the identity of Israel in traditions preserved in the Hebrew Bible. Two of the most influential collections of traditions within the canon of the Hebrew Bible are to be found in the Pentateuchal material traditionally assigned to J and the Josianic redaction of the Deuteronomistic History. This brief review is meant to be suggestive and illustrative of the problems involved rather than an exhaustive study of this material.

Much more work remains to be done on the way in which the traditions preserved within the Hebrew Bible might reveal the Davidic perception of the emergence of Israel. As is typical of histories written for other agrarian states, the Davidic understanding of how Israel came into being must have been heavily influenced by how the house of David gained power. In the past scholars have recognized the close association between David and the portrayal of Abraham in the Pentateuchal traditions (Clements, 1967). The lack of any reference to a temple suggests that the material usually assigned to J is Davidic rather than Solomonic.[2]

Strikingly these traditions represent Israel in terms of bedouin chiefs and groups, of the types described in Chapter 3, located in the south-western Palestinian borderlands and southern Judahite highlands. The most surprising fact is that the people of Israel are not represented in terms of rural peasants located in the central highlands and steppes of Palestine. The narratives concentrate upon leading bedouin figures like Abram and Jacob. Significantly Abram is portrayed in the service of a Palestinian monarch Malki-sedeq, while the priority of Judah (Genesis 49) and its claim to the throne are emphasized.

Furthermore, the narratives deal not simply with great men but express a notion of the unity of Israel through the blessing and oath to Abram in Genesis 12. The oath to Abram to make his name great (Genesis 12.2) parallels the dynastic promise to the house of David (2 Samuel 7.9) (cf. Weisman, 1985). The idea of Israel as a national unity is conveyed in the expression *goy gadol* found in Gen. 12.2. Whether or not J concluded with a story about the conquest has long been debated by scholars. Nevertheless the narrative of Balaam and Balak envisages a promising future for Israel in nationalist terms. It is this understanding of Israel represented in terms of bedouin leaders who monopolize the national identity that obscures the emergence of Israel. Neutralizing the Philistines, with whom David, like Abram, must have formed a treaty and whom David employed in his private army, the Davidic scribe makes the Egyptian state the foil of Israel's national identity, and through the 'exodus' portrays the emergence of *landed* Israel in terms of a crisis in the perennial tension between Egypt and loyal bedouin of south-western Palestine, the adopted eponyms of the nation (see Breuilly, 1982).

The Pentateuchal traditions, particularly those traditionally assigned to J, need to be investigated much more carefully in order to discover how they might reflect the political economy of the early monarchy, an economy without a temple that established itself in the south and south-west, and thereby legitimize the state of David. The Davidic/Solomonic presentation of how a single 'Israel' came into being has heavily influenced later perceptions about the nature and identity of Israel. It is this perception of Israel, rather than the spread of rural villages in the Palestinian highlands, which has been adapted by later communities. The history of Israel has been presented in these traditions in terms of the circumstances of the rise of David's house to power. The real circumstances of Israel's emergence as the adaptation of various groups to the economic decline suffered by Palestine at the end of the Late Bronze Age have been forgotten, since they never served the purpose of any ruling elite, and certainly not David's need to emphasize the unity of Israel under his rule. The royal bureaucracy, like all such groups, was concerned to play down social conflict and emphasize the unity achieved under David.

The Idea of Israel in the Deuteronomistic History
The presentation of Joshua as a royal figure in the Deuteronomistic History (see Porter, 1970; Nelson, 1981b) parallels in many ways the similar portrayal of Abraham in the Pentateuch. Nelson (1981a; 1981b) recently has given substance to the theory of Cross (1973) of a double redaction of the Deuteronomistic History, in contrast to Noth's classic statement of a unified exilic work. In so doing he has demonstrated that the figure of Joshua and his exploits are little more than a retrojection of Josiah. The traditions about Joshua act in effect as a justification for the Josianic reforms and attempts to unify Israel. In particular the military success of the obedient Joshua in leading Israel provides a model of and for Josiah's nationalist policy. Nelson (1981b:540) concludes that

> the Joshua of Dtr is in many ways a thinly disguised Josianic figure who acts out the events of Dtr's own day on the stage of the classical past. Against the backdrop of Gilgal, Ai, and Hazor, he struts out a deuteronomistic script recalling contemporary events

involving Jerusalem, Bethel, and a Judaean expansion to the north. While all this was obvious to Dtr's seventh-century readers, the passage of years and later exilic redaction have made Joshua's make-up and costume less transparent than originally intended.

The consequence of Nelson's study is that once again in traditions that form the basis of the Hebrew Bible the emergence of Israel has been obscured by royal scribes concerned to legitimize the policies of the occupant of the Davidic throne. Chaney (1983:67) has already pointed out that the 'conquest' account in the book of Joshua has been shaped by the intense nationalism of the Josianic reform and so obscured the nature of Israel's emergence. The concept of a total conquest of the land (Josh. 11.23) is seen by Nelson (1981a:124) as reflecting the nationalist designs of Josiah.

The presentation of the history of Israel in the Pentateuchal traditions and the Deuteronomistic History is seen in terms of royal figures at the head of unified national entities. The concern with the land and the boundaries of the land are important elements in these traditions. The thin disguises of Abraham and Joshua legitimize the present reality of David and Josiah. They tell us little, if anything, about the actual emergence of Israel in Palestine. It is no coincidence that the reigns of David and Josiah represent the two major periods when the rulers of this area could claim political autonomy from the interregional powers who normally held sway in Palestine. The royal elites and their scribes have shaped Israel's past to reflect their own present. They have shaped the perceptions and presuppositions of nineteenth and twentieth century biblical historians to such an extent that it is only in recent years, with the increasing use of comparative studies and new archaeological data, that the circumstances surrounding the emergence of Israel have become evident. For this reason it is worth-while to consider briefly the assumptions that have governed so much of biblical historiography in the modern era.

Israel in Recent Historiography
The biblical presentation of the origins of Israel in terms of a unified, even national, entity led by heroic figures has found its ready reflection in modern historiography. German and American biblical scholarship, which has dominated the study of the 'history of Israel' for most of the present century, is founded upon a concept of history based on the study of the origins and development of nation states

and the great statesmen who determined the course of history. Modern historiography has worked in the shadow of ideas of nationalism which emerged in the eighteenth century and have become the dominating force of politics in the nineteenth and twentieth centuries (Taylor, 1985:125). Leopold von Ranke's search for a 'scientific' history, developed in the context of nationalist aspirations, has shaped modern historiography (see Barraclough, 1979). History has been broadly understood to be the study of unique events and individuals presented in narrative form. The basis of this type of history has been the study of written evidence, stemming from the elite themselves, which revealed the motivations of great statesmen who supposedly determined the course of political and military events.

Biblical historians for the most part have shared the presuppositions and concerns of the intellectual environment in which they have worked. The concern for written texts, great personalities, and political events dovetailed nicely with the presentation of the history of Israel found in the biblical texts. The further reinforcement of such bias can be seen from a brief review of other aspects of German and American historiography.

Iggers (1980:217) has recently described the profound influence that the work of von Ranke has exercised over German historiography:

> Well into the mid-twentieth century, German historians followed the model set by Leopold von Ranke of a narrative, event-oriented history which concentrated on politics narrowly conceived as the actions of government in pursuit of national interest (*raison d'état*) relatively unaffected by social and economic considerations. Moreover, since the mid-nineteenth century, German university-based historians have been committed to an interpretation of the national past that saw the culmination of German history in Bismarck's establishment of a German Empire under Prussian dominance, a state that maintained the privileged political position of the propertied classes and left considerable authority in a monarchy surrounded by an aristocratic aura.

It is interesting to note that the purpose of von Ranke's *Histories of the Latin and Germanic Nations from 1494 to 1514* had been to describe the history of these nations 'in their unity' (cited by White, 1973:164). The considerations and concerns of much German biblical historical scholarship become understandable when viewed within such an intellectual climate.

Clements (1983:173) has pointed out that the legacy of Bismarck and the development of German unity which had a profound effect upon German universities left its mark on the biblical historiography of Ewald, Duhm and Wellhausen. There is a pronounced concern with the nation-state, its origins, and the leading personalities who were responsible for the unity of Israel. It is noticeable that even Wellhausen, who questioned the historicity of the 'Patriarchs' and stressed the importance of the exilic period in shaping the literature, believed that Israel was a unity under Moses, who founded the nation. This concern with the origins of national unity is clear in his study of the history of Israel, originally published in the Encyclopaedia Britannica, which opens with a section on 'The Beginning of the Nation' (Wellhausen, 1885:429-40). Similarly Alt's seminal essays (1966) on the settlement of Israel and formation of the state reflected this interest in the origins and unity of national identity. The debate over charismatic kingship which Alt initiated also illustrates the central importance attached to trying to understand the unique. The introduction to Noth's *History* (1960:1-7) illustrates the concern with the identity of Israel as a 'nation'. His amphictyonic hypothesis, which was one of the domain assumptions of biblical scholarship until recently, was essentially an attempt to describe the origins and unity of Israel.

The context in which American biblical historiography developed is considerably more complex than that for German scholarship. Sasson (1981) has recently argued that while German scholarship drew its models for the reconstruction of Israelite history from the achievements of Bismarck, so American scholars were concerned with their own past as immigrants. The dominant model in American biblical historiography has undoubtedly been that of the chosen people in search of territory. The work of Albright, Wright and Bright has had a profound influence upon American and British biblical scholarship. Once again the emphasis has been upon the representation of Israel as a unity and the historical authenticity of the traditions about early Israel.

Recent years have witnessed the development of Israeli biblical historiography.[3] The formation of the modern state of Israel has reinforced and continued these basic assumptions and concerns of American and German biblical historiography with the origins and development of an Israelite nation. B. Mazar's preface (1970) to the volume on the Patriarchs in the *The World History of the Jewish People* stresses the importance of the study of 'the origins of the

Hebrews, the formation and crystallization of the nation . . .' The primary focus of Israeli scholarship has remained with the actions and motivations of leading personalities and a descriptive account of political and military events.

The study of the history of Israel has reached a significant point in its development. The pioneering work of Mendenhall and Gottwald has made biblical specialists aware of the importance of comparative historical and social scientific studies and opened the way to an exciting phase in the study of the history of early Israel. The phenomenal changes which have taken place in biblical studies in recent years mean that serious questions need to be raised about the relationship between biblical studies and the study of the history of early Israel. In particular the primary role of the biblical text as the major source for the history of early Israel needs to be re-examined. It is important that those who study the history of Israel begin to reflect the profound changes that have taken place in historiography in the USA, France, Britain, and to a lesser extent West Germany, during the post-Second World War period with the alignment between history and the social sciences, especially economics and demography (see Barraclough, 1979; Iggers and Parker, 1980).

Conclusion
This broad and schematic overview of the transformation and reshaping of the traditions of Israel emphasises the problems the historian faces in trying to recreate its origins at the end of the Late Bronze Age. Our understanding of that emergence has been obscured by the way in which the monarchic and exilic communities have appropriated and shaped the traditions and the way that this has been reinforced by recent historiography. Thus it has become almost impossible to appreciate the nature of the emergence of rural villages in the highlands and margins from a complex of material that has been decisively shaped by questions and concerns of later communities and their polemical debates. Sanders (1972:118) has remarked that 'the Torah as we have it was shaped by the experience of Israel's destitution and transformation'. Clearly Israel's past has been determined by its later present.

The way in which we have approached the investigation of long-term settlement patterns and the history of the traditions has been governed by the importance of what Braudel has termed *la longue durée*. The reconstruction which we have offered of the transformation of Palestinian society in the early Iron Age and the emergence of an Israelite monarchy, despite some speculation and numerous assertions, is of course tentative. The nature of historical research is such that no interpretation can claim to be definitive. Our proposals offer a broad sweep of important problems that require further detailed, long-term research in order to verify or negate their assumptions and conclusions. The investigation into the history of Israel, particularly its emergence, has reached an exciting stage. Our understanding of this period promises to be profoundly affected by the results of new archaeological work, especially the regional surveys still in their early stages, and new approaches to the nature and understanding of the traditions that form the Hebrew Bible. We can only hope that our researches and suggestions will prove sufficiently attractive to stimulate further debate on many of the issues raised here. The study of the history of Israel is becoming such a complex task that, like recent archaeological digs, it requires the co-operation of a team of experts drawn from many disciplines. The dialogue is only just beginning and it promises to be a most exciting phase in the history of scholarship.[4]

NOTES

Notes to Preface

1. There is no entirely satisfactory term for the region under considera-tion, and every usable term involves a degree of indeterminacy. Palestine has the advantage of being perhaps the most standard term in the history of scholarship.

2. In a work that adamantly questions one kind of conventional periodization, a word ought to be said about our adoption of another. The terms Bronze Age and Iron Age are fraught with difficulty. Their precise definition continues to elude historians, and the congruence of 'Israel' with the Iron Age is simplistic in the extreme. We have already noted our awareness of this difficulty. Some such terms are required, however, for any discussion to proceed, and it was felt that such archaeological terms were, for the purposes of this book, the least problematic. In consulting experts in the field, we found that agreement was adequate to proceed on this basis, since most of our points do not hang on dated chronology.

3. We do not assume that by referring to the Early Iron Age highland settlement as 'Israel' that anything qualitative has been said about 'early Israel'. We focus our history of 'Israel' on this highland settlement because it is the clearest archaeological datum that precedes the eventual emergence of the kingdoms of Israel and Judah. The reference to 'Israel' in the Merneptah stela may not refer to the settlement of the highland or to any social group directly ancestral to monarchic Israel. The authors are continuing their study of the relationship between the Egyptian New Kingdom and Palestine highland settlement and hope to report on that study in due course.

Notes to Chapter 1

1. Critiques and appraisals of the standard works can be found in G.W. Ramsey (1982), J.M. Miller (1977), M. Weippert (1971) and M. Chaney (1983). There have been relatively few studies on method: the most extensive are those of J. Bright (1956), G. Mendenhall (1961), and M. Weippert (1971).

2. The classic work on the Deuteronomistic History is that of M. Noth (1981). H.W. Wolff (1975) has an important essay on the theology of this corpus. For the theory of the double redaction of the Deuteronomistic History see F.M. Cross (1973) and R.D. Nelson (1981a).

3. Barton (1984a; 1984b) gives a lucid appraisal of the influence of literary approaches to the biblical text.

4. The latest attempt by Halpern (1983) offers a number of interesting suggestions and makes good use of the Amarna material. Yet the thesis is heavily dependent upon a rather speculative use of the biblical text. Miller (1982:215) is a strong advocate of the view that 'any convincing treatment of Israelite history must begin with a systematic literary critical analysis of the biblical materials'. Mendenhall (1961:34-35, 50 n.9) made the point long ago that most of the important new results in historical studies have had little to do with literary analysis and have been much more dependent upon new evidence produced by archaeologists. He also cites Albright as a pioneer in the recognition of the importance of social sciences for the study of Israelite history. Mendenhall (1978:32) has argued more recently that archaeological evidence alone cannot produce a history.

5. This approach to history is not only advocated by the *Annales* school but also by such historians as J.H. Plumb (1969:105):

> The aim of history, I believe, is to understand men both as individuals and in their social relationships in time. Social embraces all of man's activities—economic, religious, political, artistic, legal, military, scientific—everything, indeed, that effects the life of mankind. And this, of course, *is not a static study but a study of movement and change. It is not only necessary to discover, as accurately as the most sophisticated use of evidence will allow, things as they actually were, but also why they were so, and why they changed*; for no human societies, not one, have ever stood still. (Emphasis added.)

Braudel (1980:64-84; 25-54) denied the commonplace distinction between history and sociology. He saw them as essential elements in the same enterprise. Similarly, according to Barraclough (1979:42), Bloch professed more than once to see no real distinction between history and sociology. It is no longer possible to draw such clear boundaries between the concerns of history, anthropology, sociology, archaeology, geography, etc. (see Wolf, 1981).

6. Ramsey (1982:107-124) raises some of these problems while advocating reading the biblical narratives as story. Although he claims that 'the reconstruction of the history of biblical times will always be a legitimate and important historical undertaking', he does not indicate how this enterprise is to proceed in light of the difficulties raised.

7. Thompson (1978b) has called for an archaeologically based history and offered some tentative suggestions.

8. For a discussion of the uses and limitations of analogies see Hodder, 1982:11-27. Elton (1983:95) takes a more negative line with his view that analogy by itself cannot prove anything in history. He recognises the fact that it can act as a stimulus to thought and enquiry but is still in need of evidence for proof. By contrast, Price (1980:156) argues that

Derived from a paradigm, a research strategy directs the search for information and determines the relevance of answers to the questions . . . A research strategy generates theory, the test of which is not primarily or exclusively against data, but against a hierarchical network of increasingly more general and inclusive theory to the level of the paradigm, the broadest and most general statement of the problem and of the investigative strategies and priorities.

9. Braudel's insistence on the importance of studying history from the perspective of *la longue durée* has been endorsed by W. McNeill (1961:30,45; 1982:84). As he argued (1982:84) in the Prothero lecture to the Royal Historical Society,

With appropriate concepts and sensitivity, a questioning historian can stumble on significant patterns in the past of which men of the age were often quite unaware, which are yet real and testable and important because they may endure for centuries and millennia and affect civilizations and continents, so as to constitute, like the ecosystem itself, an ever changing framework within which human history as a whole runs its course.

Keddie (1984) has recently produced an important programmatic essay on the study of material culture to illuminate the various phases of development and decline throughout the history of the Middle East.

10. There have been some good historical geographies of Palestine, like those of George Adam Smith and F.M. Abel, but these have not played a significant role in biblical historical studies. The works of A. Alt and to a slightly lesser extent M. Noth, or more recently the works of D. Baly (1974) and Y. Aharoni (1962), also represent attempts to do historical geography and have been quite influential. Wagstaff (1985) has recently produced a good historical geography of the Middle East.

11. Many aspects of Israel's culture which until recently were believed to be unique have been shown to have parallels throughout the ancient Near East. These include not only its view of history or the development of prophecy but also many aspects of the material culture.

Notes to Chapter 2

1. Different ports played a significant role at different periods, including Gaza, Jaffa, Caesarea, Haifa, Akko and Tyre. As will become clear later in this chapter, it was outside economic and political factors which governed the rise and fall of particular ports.

2. This way of analysis goes back at least to Ibn Khaldun in the fourteenth century. See Issawi, 1966:258-59.

3. It should be noted that the archaeological terminology and precise dating of particular periods is a matter for some debate among specialists. The alternative terminology adopted by different scholars, particularly for

the Early Bronze-Middle Bronze periods, is often confusing. For part of the debate and proposals for a more acceptable schema, see Dever (1980) and Richard (1980).

4. Richard (1980:10-11) rejects the views of Mazar and Callaway that the decline was due to Egyptian campaigns along the Palestinian coast since no Egyptian objects have been discovered in late or post-Early Bronze III contexts. Lapp's theory of a Kurgan nomadic invasion from beyond the Caucasus has never achieved great support and is a more extreme example of invasion theories to explain cultural change.

5. Richard (1980) and Dever (1980) both explain Syrian influences on Early Bronze IV/Middle Bronze I sites as due to cultural interaction rather than invasion, whereas Prag (1984) accounts for Syrian influence particularly through 'small migrations along the plateau fringes and into the river valleys'.

6. Hatcher (1977) discusses why the pattern does not seem to apply to England during the period 1348-1530 CE, reputedly a period of long-term population decline in the face of high living standards.

7. McNeill (1976) offers many examples of the devastation of disease throughout history of which the most striking is the lethal European diseases carried by Cortez and his Spanish troops which completely devastated the Aztec population. McNeill (1976:1-4, 176-207) believes that this is a prime factor in Spain's conquest of the civilizations of Peru and Mexico by less than six hundred men. It is difficult to see how this could have been achieved on the basis of technological superiority alone. See also Braudel (1974:43-51).

8. For a growing concern with Palestinian demography see Gottwald, 1979:790, 792 (with good bibliography). Frick (1985:141-57) has an good discussion of some of the problems relating to attempts to estimate population from archaeological data. Archaeologists are showing increasing concern with demography following more detailed archaeological surveys of Palestine. See most recently Shiloh (1980:25-35) and Broshi and Gophna (1984). The volume by Zubrow (1976) contains more technical information on the study of demography in general; see especially Ammerman, Cavalli-Sforza and Wagener, 1976:27-61.

9. Kempinski (1983:25) claims that the end of the fourth millennium experienced a more arid climate, although he does not cite specific evidence.

10. For the details of Roman technology that partly made this possible, see now K.D. White's very good up-to-date survey (1984).

11. Callaway (1970:18) discovered unlimed cisterns at 'Ai and Raddana. See most recently Frick (1985) for the evidence, with up-to-date bibliography, that these technological innovations played little role in the initial surge in hillcountry settlement at the beginning of Iron I. See also Hopkins (1985).

12. The Lenskis' categorization of 'advanced agrarian' societies, on the basis of the work of V. Gordon Childe (1951; 1964), makes sense for putting

mature iron-using societies of historically more stable regions than Palestine in comparative perspective. But for analyzing comparative shifts in settlement along Palestine's margins over the entire agrarian epoch, it is of less obvious value.

13. There are examples of the converse of the pattern of peasant revolt following on economic development. During the eighteenth century, for instance, Dahir al-Umar of Galilee and Acre was reported to have instituted measures early in his rule genuinely favourable to village peasants under his sovereignty. It is, after all, well attested that depopulation helps rather than harms a peasantry, other factors being equal.

14. J. Kautsky (1982) argues in detail and quite convincingly, in response to writers like Lenski, that peasant unrest and revolt have no significant or lasting effect on agrarian politics.

15. Braudel (1984:21-88) discusses the nature and typology of world economies, including the distinction and differences between core and peripheral areas. The latter is drawn from Wallerstein (1974) and seems applicable to the changing fortunes of Palestine in relation to the changes in trade and trade routes. This distinction is also used by Taylor (1985).

There are a number of good new studies dealing with the trade axis between Europe and Asia, see especially the excellent study of Charlemagne and Muhammad by Hodges and Whitehouse (1983), as well as Braudel (1984).

16. The study of population by McEvedy and Jones (1978) can be used to show that during most periods the population of Palestine was typically about one-tenth of its neighbouring riverine empires.

17. See Kriedtke (1983), Wallerstein (1974; 1980) and Braudel (1984) for a description of the rise of the European powers. Braudel (1984:469-71) sets the decline of the Ottoman empire much later than most historians, during the eighteenth and early ninetenth centuries. However the decline began in Palestine much earlier, particularly since the dominant centre of the economy moved from Aleppo and Alexandria in the sixteenth century, to Smyrna in the seventeenth, and Istanbul in the eighteenth.

18. For a description of the influence of world economy on settlement in a small region in Palestine, see Karmon (1953).

Notes to Chapter 3

1. This categorization goes back at least to Ibn Khaldun, a theorist of the fourteenth century. Until this century there was much lore based on this distinction. It is an obvious oversimplification, but with appropriate qualification it retains schematic and heuristic value. See also Eickelman, 1981: 63-72, especially p. 65 n. 4; Braudel, 1982:459.

2. The geographical descriptions are based, in the main, on Orni and

Efrat (1966), Karmon (1971) and Baly (1974).

3. Amiran (1953:193-4) vividly illustrates the fluctuations of lowland settlement.

4. Obviously it is difficult to generalize about the nature of Palestinian cities over such a long period of time. For a study of Israelite cities which draws upon archaeological and sociological material see Frick, 1977:77-170. Frick makes use of the important study of pre-industrial cities by G. Sjöberg (1960). Most recently H. Kennedy (1985:3-27) has produced a study of urban development from the Roman to the Islamic period with a good bibliography. For Mamluk cities see Lapidus, 1984.

5. Foreign urban elites have been a constant throughout Palestinian history. Lapidus (1984) provides a good description of this phenomenon during the Mamluk period.

6. There is a voluminous literature on the *apiru*, including Mendenhall (1973), Weippert (1971), Gottwald (1979), and Chaney (1983). The general conclusion is that this is a socio-political rather than ethnic designation (*contra* de Vaux, 1978). Loretz (1984) has recently produced a detailed treatment of the whole problem.

7. Rowton (1973a; 1973b; 1974) has been responsible for introducing the concept of enclosed nomadism in the discussion following his extended treatment of the problem in a whole series of articles.

8. E. Marx (1984b:1-15) has recently demonstrated how strong this attachment can be even under the rapidly changing economic conditions of recent times. Even though wage labour outside the tribal area is often now the major source of cash income, traditional affiliations and economic pursuits are still retained for reasons of security. In particular, the bedouin working on construction sites in the towns and cities prefer to keep their homes and families in the tribal territory for security, especially given the volatile political situation.

9. The terms emic and etic were introduced into anthropology by the linguist K. Pike. Emic is used to denote the view of the social actor, whereas etic designates the explanation and analysis of the observer. For a detailed discussion of these terms, see Harris, 1980:32. Gottwald (1979:638, 785 n.558) has recently introduced these terms into biblical studies.

10. The term is usually written as Shasu in English—capitalized and unitalicized—as though it were the name of a specific group, which is probably not the case.

11. It is interesting to note that Mendenhall (1983:101) is the only person to mention *shasu* in this recent collection of essays on the emergence of Israel.

12. For a detailed study of the texts and reliefs see Giveon (1971) and Ward (1972).

13. Ward adopts Helck's distinction (1968:477f.) that *apiru* was used of groups north of the Dead Sea and *shasu* of groups south of it. This would

appear to be too artificial a distinction given the paucity of evidence. On the relationship between the two terms see below and Gottwald (1979:458-59).

14. Giveon prefers the Semitic etymology, 'to plunder', followed by Gottwald (1979:458), while Ward (1972:58-59) opts for the more usual Egyptian etymology, 'to travel, wander about'. It might also be noted that the Coptic *shos*, 'shepherd', indicates the pastoral emphasis of *š3sw*. All three etymologies are consistent with different aspects of bedouin life.

15. The precise references to these activities can be found in Giveon and Ward. There are references to the *shasu* in connection with the term *mhwt*, which Gottwald (1979:457) points out is an imprecise term that denotes a unit of social organization based on kinship (see Giveon, 1971:255-57).

16. It is not certain that the Amarna texts refer to *shasu*, although Albright (1975:111) takes Amarna *Sutu* in this sense.

17. Rowton (1974:5) points out that at times of weak state control great bedouin tribes opt for enclosed nomadism in Syria and Palestine, just like the nomads of central Asia in Iran.

18. Owen (1981:35) estimates that taxation was between 10-50 percent during different periods.

Notes to Chapter 4

1. The major exception to this is, of course, the work of G.E. Mendenhall, who has campaigned for a long time for such a reappraisal. See most recently Mendenhall (1983:95).

2. Stager's figures are based on Kochavi (1972), supplemented by data from Campbell (1968), Sapin (1968-1969), and Stager. Stager notes that his Table I does not subdivide the Late Bronze sites into Late Bronze I or Late Bronze II, and therefore covers a period of 350 years. Thus he notes that it is possible that some sites occupied in both the Late Bronze and Iron I periods were unoccupied at some point before 1200 BCE and therefore ought to be included in the new foundations.

3. Mazar (1981:17) reports that recent excavations at 'Izbet Sartah have revealed a defensive wall not unlike that at Giloh. However, it is not clear whether this wall stems from the beginning of settlement or later when pressures of centralization brought about the need for defence.

4. Frick (1985:161) argues that these finds indicate a ranked society at Tel Masos. He points out that the material was all found in the large structure House 314 in Area H rather than in any of the four-roomed houses at the site.

5. Miller (1977:257) notes the possibility that there may have been a cultural expansion from the coastal plain eastwards into the central hills, rather than a westward expansion from Transjordan. He cites unpublished

work of Callaway and Stager in support of this view.

6. See Renfrew, 1979:487-88. Chapter 2 has already dealt with the concept of world economies and the interconnections of Mediterranean trade.

7. Weinstein (1981:21-22) notes that there was more Egyptian pottery during Late Bronze IIB and Iron I than during any other phase of the Bronze or Iron Ages. Significantly there was hardly any Egyptian pottery from Hazor or the hill country sites. Thirteenth and twelfth century Egyptian pottery is found at sites in southern Palestine, along the coast, the coastal plain, the Shephelah, the plain of Esdraelon and the Jordan valley.

8. The study of demography in Palestine has developed in recent years. See especially Wilkinson (1974), Shiloh (1980), Gottwald (1979:790, 792-93), and Stager (1985). The most recent and best study of this complex problem is Frick (1985:141-57). He offers a concise and clear appraisal of previous attempts to estimate the population size of Iron Age Palestine and the problems involved.

Notes to Chapter 5

1. Mayes (1977:331) regards the monarchy not so much as an alien institution but rather a new, though inevitable, step in the progression towards unity. We would challenge the view that the monarchy was inevitable, although agree that it is inherent in the nature of early Israel. Buccellati (1967), in his important study of Syria, had already emphasized the crucial point that such a notion denied the internal dynamics of Israelite society.

2. A recent major exception to this is Frick's study (1985) of the formation of the state which has anticipated many of our own conclusions.

3. Gottwald (1985) has attempted to deal with this problem from the perspective of 'free agrarians'. Frick (1985) is so far the only major study published which poses these important questions and attempts to answer them from the perspective of the anthropological study of state formation. Hauer (1986) generously allowed us to use his own unpublished study and also offered valuable comments on an earlier draft of our work discussed at the SBL/ASOR Seminar on the Sociology of the Monarchy, Dec. 1984 (Coote and Whitelam, 1986).

4. Talmon (1979:5, 9) recognizes that the monarchy was a result of internal social factors and external political pressures.

5. This is an important avenue of study for the development of traditions of conquest within the monarchy and for the later community. Renfrew (1979) has shown the importance of such traditions in relation to the Mayan and Mycenaean collapse. Frick (1985:43) has drawn attention to the importance of Renfrew's study for understanding responses to the collapse

experienced throughout the eastern Mediterranean and Palestine in particular.

6. Similarly Kohl (1981:112) argues that societies with historically interacting areas adopt basic organizational principles not solely as a common solution to natural problems, but because they have been tried, tested and proven to work by earlier societies with which they are familiar. Recourse to an idealist interpretation—the 'genius' of a people or the 'form' of a civilization—is not necessary to explain this common and important phenomenon.

7. Mendenhall (1975) was the first biblical scholar to recognise the period of Saul as a chiefdom. Gottwald (1979:297-298, 322-323) and Flanagan (1981) have also stressed the importance of this aspect of Israelite development. Frick (1979; 1985), however, offers the most comprehensive treatment, drawing upon the anthropological literature in addition to archaeological, demographic and agricultural information. A word of caution is also in order since Lewis (1981:207) believes that Service has elevated a special form of Hawaiian and Polynesian chiefly organization into a universal stage of political evolution without concern for its rarity or particularity. He believes that non-state polities are much more complex and exhibit greater variety than just chiefdoms. See also Tringham (1974) for a critique of Renfrew's study (1974) of the archaeological aspects of chiefdoms. Carneiro (1981) has an extensive treatment of chiefdoms which questions some basic assumptions of earlier studies.

8. Haas (1982:5) suggests that one of the effects of state emergence in a particular area is the stimulation of state development in surrounding areas. Price (1978) discusses this general phenomenon in the context of a 'cluster-interaction' model. An important area of future study is the complex process of state formation in Transjordan in comparison with the rise of an Israelite state (cf. Talmon, 1979:10-12).

9. Dahir al-Umar, who originated from a Bedouin family, gained control of most of Palestine from his base in Galilee during the eighteenth century when Ottoman control was weak. The career of Dahir and the way in which he was able to extend his control provides a striking analogy with the rise of David. For an extensive study of Dahir al-Umar see A. Cohen, 1973.

10. Hopkins (1983:185-86) believes that the law of the sabbatical year (Exod. 23.10-11) is not fully descriptive of Israel's land-use strategies or its maintenance of fertility. He points out that such a system of fallowing one year out of seven would indicate an extremely high intensity cropping system and could not have been supported in the pre-industrial Mediterranean world without irrigation.

11. The dispersal of 'Midianite' pottery suggests that trade relations extended considerable distances. See Ingraham (1981:59-84) and Parr (1982:127-33) for a discussion of some of the problems involved in trying to interpret this material.

12. Carneiro (1981:61) has recently questioned the importance of redistri-

bution as a basic feature of chiefdoms. He argues that the chief appropriates and concentrates rather than distributes.

13.   See Halpern (1981b:76-79) for a treatment of the monarchy from this perspective.

Notes to Chapter 6

1.   This methodology needs to be carried out consistently for all periods of Israel's history rather than assuming as Soggin does that the material on the reign of David is historically reliable. He does note (1984:27-28) that even the traditions about David have been subjected to later shaping but nonetheless accepts them as historically trustworthy. Ahlström (1982:81, n.21) has recently recognized the applicability of Carr's view (1961:13) of the problems of history writing to the study of Israel's history: 'Our picture has been preselected and predetermined for us, not so much by accident as by people who were consciously imbued with a particular view, and thought the facts, which support that view, worth preserving'. In regard to the problem of the way in which the emergence of Israel has been obscured by the later community it is worth noting Soggin's use (1984:19) of the remarkable view of Albright (1918:113f.): 'The long memory possessed by semi-civilized peoples for historical fact is a pious fiction of over-zealous apologists. . .' The use of the past to legitimize the present is well illustrated by the use and amendment of genealogies in traditional societies (see Wilson, 1977; Flanagan, 1981).

2.   It is interesting to note that this feature of J did not preclude reinterpretation under Solomon and his successors or the priestly elite of the Persian and Hellenistic periods. However, it was a decisive feature that allowed the recomposition and canonical reinterpretation of these traditions during the Babylonian exile and the period during which the 'official' Jewish and Christian communities and Scriptures became differentiated. For the view that J is exilic see Van Seters (1983).

3.   It is interesting to note that a British model of the history of Israel has not been developed in the same way as American and German scholarship. Sasson (1981) suggests that this is due to the British tradition of the study of the Greek and Latin classics.

4.   Indicative of the kind of comparative historical work required to assess the political issues raised in this final chapter is the recent outstanding work of Taylor (1985).

WORKS CITED

Abel, F.M.
1933-1938 *Géographie de la Palestine*, 2 Vols. Paris: J. Gabalda.

Adams, R. McC.
1974 'The Mesopotamian Social Landscape: A View from the Frontier', in *Reconstructing Complex Societies*, ed. by C.B. Moore. Cambridge: ASOR:1-11.

Aharoni, Y.
1957 'The Settlement of the Israelite Tribes in Upper Galilee', (Hebrew) Ph.D., Jerusalem.
1966 *The Land of the Bible. A Historical Geography*, London: Burns and Oates.
1970 'New Aspects of the Israelite Occupation in the North', in *Near Eastern Archaeology in the Twentieth Century. Essays in Honor of Nelson Glueck*, ed. J.A. Sanders. Garden City: Doubleday:254-67.
1976 'Nothing Early and Nothing Late: Rewriting Israel's Conquest', *BA* 39:55-76.
1982 *The Archaeology of the Holy Land. From the Prehistoric Beginnings to the End of the First Temple Period*, London: SCM.

Aharoni, Y., V. Fritz and A. Kempinski
1975 'Excavations at Tel Masos (Kh. el-Meshash); Preliminary Report on the Second Season, 1974', *Tel Aviv* 2:97-124.

Ahlström, G.W.
1982 *Royal Administration and National Religion in Ancient Palestine*, Leiden: Brill.
1984 'Giloh: A Judahite or Canaanite Settlement', *IEJ* 34:170-72.

Albright, W.F.
1918 'Historical and Mythical Elements in the Joseph History', *JBL* 37:111-143
1935 'Archaeology and the Date of the Hebrew Conquest of Palestine', *BASOR* 58:10-18.
1939 'The Israelite Conquest of Canaan in the Light of Archaeology', *BASOR* 74:11-23.
1975 'The Amarna Letters from Palestine', in *The Cambridge Ancient History*, 3rd edn Vol. II Part 2, ed. I. Edwards, *et al.* Cambridge: Cambridge University Press:98-116.

Alt, A.
1966a 'The Formation of the Israelite State in Palestine' in *Essays on Old Testament History and Religion*, Oxford: Blackwell:171-237.
1966b 'The Settlement of the Israelites in Palestine', in *Essays on Old Testament History and Religion*, Oxford: Blackwell:135-69.

Amiran, D.
1953 'The Pattern of Settlement in Palestine' *IEJ* 3:65-78, 192-209, 250-60.

Amiran, R., I. Beit-Arieh and J. Glass
1973 'The Interrelationship between Arad and Sites in Southern Sinai in the early Bronze Age II (Preliminary Report)', *IEJ* 23:193-97.

Ammerman, A.J., L.L. Cavalli-Sforza and D.K. Wagener
    1976   'Toward the Estimation of Population in Old World Prehistory', in *Demographic Anthropology. Quantative Approaches*, ed. E.B.W. Zubrow. Albuquerque: University of New Mexico: 27-61.

Anati, E.
    1975   'Abu Hawam, Tell' in *Encyclopedia of Archaeological Excavations in the Holy Land* I ed. M. Avi-Yonah and E. Stern. London: Oxford University Press: 9-12.

Avi-Yonah, M.
    1974   'Historical Geography of Palestine', in *Compendium Rerum Iudaicarum ad Novum Testamentum, Vol. I* ed. S. Safrai and M. Stern. Assen: Van Gorcum:78-116.
    1976   *Gazetteer of Roman Palestine*, Jerusalem: Hebrew University of Jerusalem.
    1977   *The Holy Land from the Persian to the Islamic Periods*, London: Thames and Hudson.

Baer, G.
    1982   *Fellah and Townsman in the Middle East. Studies in Social History*, London: F. Cass.

Baly, D.
    1974   *The Geography of the Bible* (New and Revised Edition). Guildford and London: Lutterworth.
    1984   'The Geography of Palestine and the Levant in Relation to its History', in *The Cambridge History of Judaism. Vol. I Introduction; The Persian Period*, ed. W.D. Davies and L. Finkelstein. Cambridge: Cambridge University Press: 1-24.

Barr, J.
    1980   'Story and History in Biblical Theology' in *Explorations in Theology* 7, London: SCM:1-17.

Barraclough, G.
    1979   *Main Trends in History*, New York: Holmes and Meier.

Barton, J.
    1984a   'Classifying Biblical Criticism', *JSOT* 29:19-35.
    1984b   *Reading the Old Testament*, London: Darton, Longman and Todd.

Bates, D.G.
    1971   'The Role of the State in Peasant-Nomad Mutualism', *Anthropological Quarterly* 44:109-31.

Beit-Arieh, I.
    1983   'Central-Southern Sinai in the Early Bronze Age II and its Relationship with Palestine', *Levant* 15:39-48.

Bimson, J.
    1978   *Redating the Exodus and Conquest*, Sheffield: JSOT.

Blenkinsopp, J.
    1977   *Prophecy and Canon. A Contribution to the Study of Jewish Origins*, Notre Dame: University of Notre Dame.
    1981   'Interpretation and the Tendency to Sectarianism: An Aspect of Second Temple History', in *Jewish and Christian Self-Definition. Vol. II Aspects of Judaism in the Graeco-Roman Period*, ed. E.P. Sanders. London: SCM:1-26.

Bloch, M.
    1954   *The Historian's Craft*, Manchester: Manchester University Press.

Blok, A.
    1972   'The Peasant and the Brigand: Social Banditry Reconsidered', *Comparative Studies in Society and History* 14:494-503.

Boserup, E.
    1965   *The Conditions of Agricultural Growth*, London: Allen and Unwin.
    1981   *Population and Technology*, Oxford: Blackwell.

Braudel, F.
    1972   *The Mediterranean and the Mediterranean World in the Age of Philip II. Vols. I-II*, London: Collins.
    1974   *Capitalism and Material Life 1400-1800*, London: Fontana.
    1980   *On History*, London: Weidenfeld and Nicholson.
    1982   *Civilization and Capitalism 15th-18th Century Vol. II. The Wheels of Commerce*, London: Collins.
    1984   *Civilization and Capitalism 15th-18th Century Vol. III. The Perspective of the World* London: Collins.

Braun, E. and S. Gibson
    1984   ''En-Shadud: An Early Bronze I Farming Community in the Jezreel Valley', *BASOR* 253:29-40.

Breuilly, J.
    1982   *Nationalism and the State*, Chicago: University of Chicago Press.

Bright, J.
    1956   *Early Israel in Recent History Writing. A Study in Method*, London: SCM.
    1981   *A History of Israel*, 3rd edn, London: SCM.

Brinkman, J.A.
    1984   'Settlement Surveys and Documentary Evidence: Regional Variation and Secular Trends in Mesopotamian Demography', *JNES* 43:169-80.

Broshi, M.
    1980   'The Population of Palestine in the Roman-Byzantine Period', *BASOR* 235:1-10.

Broshi, M. and R. Gophna
    1984   'The Settlements and Population of Palestine during the Early Bronze Age II-III', *BASOR* 253:41-53.
    1986   'Middle Bronze Age II Palestine: Its Settlements and Population', *BASOR* 261:73-90.

Bryson, R., H. Lamb and R. Donley
    1974   'Drought and the Decline of Mycenae', *Antiquity* 48:46-50.

Buccellati, G.
    1967   *Cities and Nations of Ancient Syria. An Essay on Political Institutions with Special Reference to the Israelite Kingdoms*, Rome: University of Rome.

Callaway, J. A.
    1969   'The 1966 'Ai (Et-Tell) Excavations', *BASOR* 196:2-16.
    1970   'The 1968-1969 'Ai (Et-Tell) Excavations', *BASOR* 198:7-31
    1975   ''Ai', in *Encyclopedia of Archaeological Excavations in the Holy Land I*, ed. M. Avi-Yonah and E. Stern. Oxford: Oxford University Press:36-52.

Callaway, J.A. and R.E. Cooley
    1971   'A Salvage Excavation at Raddana, in Bireh', *BASOR* 201:9-19.

Campbell, E.F.
    1968   'The Shechem Area Survey', *BASOR* 190:19-41.

Carneiro, R.L.
    1970   'A Theory of the Origins of the State', *Science* 169:733-38.
    1978   'Political Expansion as an Expression of the Principle of Competitive Exclusion', in *Origins of the State*, ed. R. Cohen and E.R. Service. Philadelphia: Institute for the Study of Human Issues: 205-23.
    1981   'The Chiefdom: Precursor of the State', in *The Transition to Statehood in the New World*, ed. G.D. Jones and R.R. Kautz. Cambridge: Cambridge University Press.
Carpenter, R.
    1966   *Discontinuity in Greek Civilization*, Cambridge: Cambridge University Press.
Carr, E.H.
    1961   *What is History?*, Harmondsworth: Penguin.
Carroll, R.P.
    1979   *When Prophecy Failed: Reactions and Responses to Failure in the Old Testament Prophetic Traditions*, London: SCM.
    1981   *From Chaos to Covenant: Uses of Prophecy in the Book of Jeremiah*, London: SCM.
Chaney, M.
    1983   'Ancient Palestinian Peasant Movements and the Formation of Pre-monarchic Israel', in *Palestine in Transition: The Emergence of Ancient Israel*, ed. D.N. Freedman and D.F. Graf. Sheffield: Almond: 39-90.
Childe, V.G.
    1951   *Man Makes Himself*, New York: New American Library.
    1964   *What Happened in History*, Harmondsworth: Penguin.
Childs, B.
    1979   *Introduction to the Old Testament as Scripture*, London: SCM.
Claessen, H.J.M.
    1978   'The Early State: A Structural Approach', in *The Early State*, ed. H. Claessen and P. Skalnik. The Hague: Mouton: 533-596.
Claessen, H.J.M. and P. Skalnik
    1978a   *The Early State*, The Hague: Mouton.
    1978b   'Limits: Beginning and End of the Early State' in *The Early State*, The Hague: Mouton: 619-35.
    1981a   *The Study of the State*, The Hague: Mouton.
    1981b   'Ubi Sumus? The Study of the State Conference in Retrospect', in *The Study of the State*, The Hague: Mouton: 469-501.
Clarke, D.
    1973   'Archaeology: The Loss of Innocence', *Antiquity* 48:6-18.
Clements, R.
    1967   *Abraham and David*, London: SCM.
    1983   *A Century of Old Testament Study*, Guildford: Lutterworth.
Cohen, A.
    1973   *Palestine in the 18th Century*, Jerusalem: Magnes Press.
Cohen, A.
    1965   *Arab Border Villages in Israel*, Manchester: Manchester University Press.
Cohen, R.
    1978a   'Introduction', in *Origins of the State*, ed. R. Cohen and E.R. Service. Philadelphia: Institute for the Study of Human Issues: 1-20.
    1978b   'State Origins: A Reappraisal', in *The Early State*, ed. H.J.M. Claessen

and P. Skalnik. The Hague: Mouton: 31-75.

1981   'Evolution, Fission, and the Early State', in *The Study of the State*, ed. H.J.M. Claessen and P. Skalnik. The Hague: Mouton: 87-115.

Cohen, R.

1979   'The Iron Age Fortresses on the Central Negev', *BASOR* 236:61-79.

Conder, C. and H. Kitchener,

1880   *Map of Western Palestine in 26 Sheets from Surveys Conducted for the Committee of the Palestine Exploration Fund*, London: Palestine Exploration Fund.

Coon, C.S.

1951   *Caravan: The Story of the Middle East*, New York: H. Holt.

Coote, R.B. and K.W. Whitelam

1986   'The Emergence of Israel: Social Transformation and State Formation following the Decline in LBA Trade', *Semeia* 37: 107-47.

Cowgill, G.L.

1975   'On Causes and Consequences of Ancient and Modern Population Changes', *American Anthropology* 77:505-25.

Croix, G. Ste.

1981   *The Class Struggle in the Ancient Greek World*, London: Duckworth.

Cross, F.M.

1973   'The Themes of the Book of Kings and the Structure of the Deuteronomistic History', in *Canaanite Myth and Hebrew Epic*, Cambridge, Mass: Harvard University Press: 274-89.

Curtin, P.D.

1984   *Cross-Cultural Trade in World History*, Cambridge: Cambridge University Press.

Danin, A.

1985   'Palaeoclimates in Israel: Evidence from Weathering Patterns of Stones in and near Archaeological Sites', *BASOR* 259:33-43.

Dauphin, C.M. and J.J. Schonfield

1983   'Settlement of the Roman and Byzantine Periods on the Golan Heights. Preliminary Report on Three Seasons of Survey (1979-1981)', *IEJ* 33:189-206.

Desborough, V.R.

1972   *The Greek Dark Ages*, London: E. Benn.

Dever, W.G.

1976   'Beginnings of the MBA in Syria-Palestine', in *Magnalia Dei: The Mighty Acts of God. Essays on the Bible and Archaeology in Memory of George E. Wright*, ed. F.M. Cross. New York: Doubleday: 3-38.

1977   'The Patriarchal Traditions: 1. Palestine in the Second Millenium B.C.E.: The Archaeological Picture', in *Israelite and Judaean History*, ed. J. Hayes and J. Miller. London: SCM:70-120

1980   'New Vistas on the EBIV ('MBI') Horizon in Syria-Palestine', *BASOR* 237:35-64.

1982a   'Monumental Architecture in Ancient Israel in the Period of the United Monarchy', in *Studies in the Period of David and Solomon*, ed. T. Ishida. Winona Lake: Eisenbrauns: 269-306.

1982b   'Retrospects and Prospects in Biblical and Syro-Palestinian Archaeology', *BA* 45:103-107.

Edbury, P.

1985   *Crusade and Settlement*, Cardiff: University College Cardiff.

Eickelman, D.F.
1981   *The Middle East: An Anthropological Approach*, Englewood Cliffs: Prentice Hall.
Elton, G.R.
1983   'Two Kinds of History', in *Which Road to the Past*, ed. R.W. Fogel and G.R. Elton. New Haven: Yale University Press: 71-121.
Falconer, S.E. and B. Magnes-Gardiner
1984   'Preliminary Report of the First Season of the Tell el-Hayyat Project', *BASOR* 255:49-74.
Febvre, L.
1973   *A New Kind of History and Other Essays*, New York: Harper Torch.
Finley, M.
1973   *The Ancient Economy*, Berkeley: University of California Press.
Finn, E.A.
1879   'The Fellahheen of Palestine. Notes on the Chief Traits in their Character, their Faults, and their Virtues', *PEFQ*: 72-87.
Fisher, W.B.
1961   *The Middle East. A Physical, Social and Regional Geography*, 4th edn London: Methuen.
Flanagan, J.
1981   'Chiefs in Israel', *JSOT* 20:47-73.
1982   'Models for the Origin of Iron Age Monarchy: A Modern Case Study', *SBL Seminar Papers*, Chico: Scholars: 135-56.
Frick, F.
1977   *The City in Ancient Israel*, Missoula: Scholars.
1979   'Religion and Sociopolitical Structure in Early Israel: An Ethno-Archaeological Approach, *SBL Seminar Papers*, Missoula: Scholars: 233-53.
1985   *The Formation of the State in Ancient Israel*, Decatur: Almond Press.
Frick, F. and N.K. Gottwald
1975   'The Social World of Ancient Israel', *SBL Seminar Papers I*. Missoula: Montana: 165-77.
Fried, M.
1967   *The Evolution of Political Society*, New York: Random House.
1978   'The State, the Chicken, and the Egg; or, What Came First?', in *Origins of the State*, ed. R. Cohen and E.R. Service. Philadelphia: Institute for the Study of Human Issues: 35-47.
Fritz, V.
1981   'The Israelite "Conquest" in the Light of Recent Excavations at Khirbet el-Meshash', *BASOR* 241:61-73.
Gal, Z.
1979   'An Early Iron Age Site near Tel Menorah in the Beth-shan Valley', *Tel Aviv* 6:138-45.
Galbraith, J.K.
1980   *The Nature of Mass Poverty*, Harmondsworth: Penguin.
Gamst, F.C.
1974   *Peasants in Complex Society*, New York: Holt, Rinehart and Winston.
Garsiel, M. and I. Finkelstein
1978   'The Westward Expansion of the House of Joseph in the Light of the 'Izbet Sartah Excavations', *Tel Aviv* 5:192-98.

Gauthier-Pilters, H. and A.I. Dagg
    1981   *The Camel: Its Evolution, Ecology, Behaviour, and Relationship to Man*,
                Chicago: University of Chicago Press.

Geertz, C.
    1977   'Centers, Kings and Charisma: Reflections on the Symbolics of Power',
                in *Culture and its Creators: Essays in Honor of E. Shils*, ed. J. Ben-David
                and T. Clark. Chicago: University of Chicago Press.

Gerstenblith, P.
    1980   'A Reassessment of the Beginning of the Middle Bronze Age in Syria-
                Palestine', *BASOR* 237:65-84.
    1983   *The Levant at the Beginning of the Middle Bronze Age*, Winona Lake:
                Eisenbrauns.

de Geus, C.H.J.
    1971   'The Amorites in the Archaeology of Palestine', *UF* 3:41-60.
    1976   *The Tribes of Israel. An Investigation into some of the Presuppositions of*
                Martin Noth's Amphictyonic Hypothesis, Assen: Van Gorcum.

Gilbert, A.S.
    1975   'Modern Nomads and Prehistorical Pastoralists: The Limits of Analogy',
                JANESCU 7:53-71.

Giveon, R.
    1971   *Les bédouins Shosou des documents égyptiens*, Leiden: Brill.

Godelier, M.
    1978   'Infrastructures, Societies and History', *Current Anthropology* 19:763-
                71.

Gonen, R.
    1984   'Urban Canaan in the Late Bronze Period', *BASOR* 253:61-73.

Gophna, R.
    1984   'The Settlement Landscape of Palestine in the Early Bronze Age II-III
                and Middle Bronze Age II', *IEJ* 34:24-31.

Gottwald, N.K.
    1974   'Were the Early Israelites Pastoral Nomads?', in *Rhetorical Criticism:*
                Essays in Honor of James Muilenburg, ed. J. Jackson and M. Kessler.
                Pittsburgh: Pickwick: 223-55.
    1978   'The Hypothesis of the Revolutionary Origins of Ancient Israel. A
                Response to Hauser and Thompson', *JSOT* 7:37-52.
    1979   *The Tribes of Yahweh. A Sociology of Liberated Israel, 1250-1050 BCE*,
                London: SCM.
    1983   'Early Israel and the Canaanite Socio-Economic System', in *Palestine in*
                Transition, ed. D.N. Freedman and D.F. Graf. Almond: Sheffield: 25-
                37.
    1986   'Social History of the United Monarchy: An Application of H.A.
                Landsberger's Framework for the Analysis of Peasant Movements to
                the Participation of Free Agrarians in the Introduction of the Monarchy
                to Ancient Israel', Paper presented to the ASOR/SBL Seminar on the
                Sociology of the Monarchy, Dec. 1983. *Semeia* 37: 77-106.

Grose, P.
    1983   *Israel in the Mind of America*, New York: A. Knopf.

Gunarwardana, R.
    1981   'Social Function and Political Power: A Case Study of State Formation
                in Irrigation Society', in *The Study of the State*, ed. H.J.M. Claessen and
                P. Skalnik. The Hague: Mouton: 133-54.

Haas, J.
  1982   *The Evolution of the Prehistoric State*, New York: Columbia University
            Press.
Haddad, E.N.
  1920   'Political Parties in Syria and Palestine', *JPOS* 1:209-14.
Halpern, B.
  1981a   *The Constitution of the Monarchy*, Chico: Scholars.
  1981b   'The Uneasy Compromise: Israel between League and Monarchy', in
            Traditions in Transformation: Turning Points in Biblical Faith, ed. B.
            Halpern and J. Levenson. Winona Lake: Eisenbrauns: 59-96.
  1983   *The Emergence of Israel in Canaan*, Chico: Scholars.
Halpern, M.
  1963   *The Politics of Social Change in the Middle East and North Africa*
            Princeton: Princeton University Press.
Hanson, P.
  1975   *The Dawn of Apocalyptic*, Philadelphia: Fortress.
Harris, M.
  1980   *Cultural Materialism. The Struggle for a Science of Culture*, New York:
            Vintage Books.
Hatcher, J.
  1977   *Plague, Population and the English Economy 1348-1530*, London:
            MacMillan.
Hauer, C.
  1986   'From Alt to Anthropology: The Rise of the Israelite State', *JSOT* 36:3-
            15.
Hauser, A. J.
  1978   'Israel's Conquest of Palestine: A Peasants' Rebellion?', *JSOT* 7:2-19.
Hayes, J. and J.M. Miller
  1977   *Israelite and Judaean History*, London: SCM.
Helck, J.
  1968   'Die Bedrohung Palästinas durch einwandernde Gruppen am Ende der
            18. und am Anfang der 19. Dynastie', *VT* 18:472-80.
Hennesey, J.B.
  1967   *Foreign Relations of Palestine during the Early Bronze Age* London: B.
            Quaritch.
Herion, G.
  1981   'The Role of Historical Narrative in Biblical Thought: The Tendencies
            Underlying OT Historiography', *JSOT* 21:25-57.
Herrmann, S.
  1981   *A History of Israel in Old Testament Times* (revised and enlarged edn),
            London: SCM.
Hobsbawm, E.J.
  1972   *Bandits*, Harmondsworth: Penguin.
Hodder, I.
  1982   *The Present Past. An Introduction to Anthropology for Archaeologists*,
            London: Batsford.
Hodges, R. and D. Whitehouse
  1983   *Mohammed, Charlemagne and the Origins of Europe. Archaeology and
            the Pirenne Thesis*, London: Duckworth.
Hopkins, D.
  1983   'The Dynamics of Agriculture in Monarchical Israel', *SBL Seminar*

Papers: 177-202.

1985   *The Highlands of Canaan: Agricultural Life in the Early Iron Age*, Decatur: Almond.

Horowitz, A.

1974   'Preliminary Palynological Indications as to the Climate of Israel during the Past 6000 Years', *Paleorient* 2:407-14.

Horsley, R.A.

1981   'Jewish Banditry and the Revolt against Rome, A.D. 66-70', *CBQ* 43:409-32.

Horsley, R.A. and J.S. Hanson

1985   *Bandits, Prophets, and Messiahs: Popular Movements in the Time of Jesus*, New York: Winston.

Hourani, A.

1981   *The Emergence of the Modern Middle East*, London: Macmillan.

Hütteroth, W.-D. and K. Abdulfattah

1977   *Historical Geography of Palestine, Transjordan and Southern Syria in the Late 16th Century*, Erlangen: Fränkische Geographische Gesellschaft.

Ibrahim, M.M.

1975   'The Third Season of Excavations at Sahab, 1975 (Preliminary Report)', *ADAJ* 20:69-82.

1978   'The Collared-rim Jar of the Early Iron Age', in *Archaeology in the Levant. Essays for Kathleen Kenyon*, ed. R. Moorey and P. Parr. Warminster: Aris and Phillips: 116-26.

Iggers, G.G.

1980   'Federal Republic of Germany', in *International Handbook of Historical Studies. Contemporary Research and Theory*, ed. G.G. Iggers and H.T. Parker. London: Methuen: 217-32.

Iggers, G.G. and H.T. Parker

1980   *International Handbook of Historical Studies. Contemporary Research and Theory*, London: Methuen.

Ingraham, M.L., *et al.*

1981   'Saudi Arabia Comprehensive Survey Program: Preliminary report of the Northwestern Province (with a note on a brief survey of the Northern Province)', *ATLAL: The Journal of Saudi Arabian Archaeology* 5:59-84.

Isaac, B. and I. Roll

1982   *Roman Roads in Judaea I: The Legio-Scythopolis Road*, Oxford: British Archaeological Reports.

Issawi, C.

1966   *The Economic History of the Middle East 1800-1914. A Book of Readings*, Chicago: University of Chicago Press.

1982   *An Economic History of the Middle East and North Africa*, New York: Columbia University Press.

Karmon, Y.

1953   'The Settlement of the Northern Huleh Valley since 1838', *IEJ* 3:4-25.

1971   *Israel a Regional Geography*, London: Wiley and Son.

Kautsky, J.

1982   *The Politics of Aristocratic Empires*, Chapel Hill: University of North Carolina.

Keddie, N.R.
1984   'Material Culture and Geography: Toward a Holistic Comparative
          History of the Middle East', *Comparative Studies in Society and History*
          26: 709-735.
Kempinski, A.
1978   'Masos, Tel (Khirbet El-Meshash)', *The Encylopedia of Archaeological
          Excavations in the Holy Land, III*, ed. M. Avi-Yonah and E. Stern.
          Oxford: Oxford University Press: 816-19.
1983   'Early Bronze Age Urbanization in Palestine: Some Topics in a Debate',
          IEJ 33:.235-41.
Kempinski, A. and V. Fritz
1977   'Excavations at Tel Masos (Khirbet el-Meshash), Preliminary Report on
          the Third Season, 1975', *TA* 4:136-58.
Kennedy, H.
1985   'From *Polis* to *Madina*: Urban Change in Late Antiquity and Early
          Islamic Syria', *Past and Present* 106:3-27.
Kenyon, K.
1973   'Palestine in the Time of the Eighteenth Dynasty', *Cambridge Ancient
          History*, 3rd edn Vol. II, Part 1. Cambridge: Cambridge University Press:
          526-56.
Kochavi, M.
1972   *Judaea, Samaria, and the Golan: Archaeological Survey, 1967-1968*,
          (Hebrew) Jerusalem: Carta.
1978   'Tell Esdar', in *The Encyclopedia of Archaeological Excavations in the
          Holy Land, IV*, ed. M. Avi-Yonah and E. Stern. Oxford: Oxford
          University Press: 1169-1171.
Kohl, P.L.
1981   'Materialist Approaches in Prehistory', *American Review of Anthropology*
          10:89-118.
Kramer, C.
1979   *Ethnoarchaeology: Implications for Archaeology*, New York: Columbia
          University Press.
Kriedtke, P.
1983   *Peasants, Landlords and Merchant Capitalists. Europe and the World
          Economy 1500-1800*, Leamington Spa: Berg.
Kupper, J-R.
1957   *Les nomades en Mésopotamie au temps des rois de Mari*, Paris: Les Belles
          Lettres.
LaBianca, O.S.
1982   'Ancient Mediterranean Food Systems', Paper presented to the ASOR/
          SBL Meeting in New York December 1982.
Ladurie, E. Le Roy
1970   *The Territory of the Historian*, Hassocks, Sussex: Harvester Press.
1972   *Times of Feast, Times of Famine: A History of Climate since the Year
          1000*, London: Allen and Unwin.
Lapidus, I.
1984   *Muslim Cities in the Late Middle Ages*, Cambridge: Cambridge
          University Press.
Lapp, P.
1967   'The Conquest of Palestine in the Light of Archaeology', *Concordia
          Theological Monthly* 38:283-300.

Lenski, G.E.
    1966   *Power and Privilege. A Theory of Social Stratification*, New York: McGraw-Hill.
    1981   'Review of N.K. Gottwald *The Tribes of Yahweh*', *RelStRev* 6:275-78.
Lenski, G. and J. Lenski
    1978   *Human Societies: An Introduction to Macrosociology*, 3rd edn. New York: McGraw Hill.

Levenson, J.
    1984   'The Temple and the World', *JR* 64:275-98.
Lewis, H.S.
    1981   'Warfare and the Origin of the State: Another Formulation', in *The Study of the State*, ed. H.J.M. Claessen and P. Skalnik. The Hague: Mouton: 201-21.

Lewis, I.
    1968   *History and Social Anthropology*, London: Tavistock.
Lewis, N.M.
    1966   'The Frontier of Settlement, 1800-1950' in *The Economic History of the Middle East 1800-1914*, ed. C. Issawi. Chicago: Chicago University Press: 258-68.

Liverani, M.
    1973   'The Amorites', in *Peoples of Old Testament Times*, ed. D.J. Wiseman. Oxford: Clarendon: 100-33.
    1979   'The Ideology of the Assyrian Empire', in *Power and Propaganda*, ed. M.T. Larsen. Copenhagen: Akademisk Forlag: 297-317.

Loretz, O.
    1984   *Habiru-Hebräer. Eine sozio-linguistische Studie über die Herkunft des Gentiliziums 'ibri vom Appelativum habiru*, Berlin: De Gruyter.

Loyn, H.
    1980   'Marc Bloch', in *The Historian at Work*, London: Allen and Unwin: 121-35.

Luke, T.
    1965   'Pastoralism and Politics in the Mari Period', Unpublished Diss. University of Michigan.
McEvedy, C. and R. Jones
    1978   *Atlas of World Population History*, London: Allen Lane.
McNeill, W.
    1961   'Some Basic Assumptions of Toynbee's *A Study of History*', in *The Intention of Toynbee's History: A Cooperative Appraisal*, ed. E.T. Gargan. Chicago: Loyola University Press: 27-46.
    1976   *Plagues and Peoples*, New York: Doubleday.
    1982   'A Defence of World History (The Prothero Lecture)' *Transactions of the Royal Historical Society* 32:75-89.

Mabry, J.
    1984   'The Organization of MBII Settlement in Palestine: The Urban-Rural Hierarchy', paper presented to the ASOR meeting Chicago, Dec. 1984.

Marcus, J.
    1974   'The Iconography of Power among the Classic Maya', *World Archaeology* 6:83-94.
Marfoe, L.
    1979   'The Integrative Transformation: Patterns of Socio-Economic Organization

in Southern Syria', *BASOR* 234:1-42.

Marx, E.

1984a 'Changing Employment Patterns of Bedouin in South Sinai', in *The Changing Bedouin*, ed. E. Marx and A. Shmueli. New Brunswick: Transaction Books: 173-86.

1984b 'Economic Change among Pastoral Nomads in the Middle East', in *The Changing Bedouin*, ed. E. Marx and A. Shmueli. New Brunswick: Transaction Books: 1-15.

Matthews, V.H.

1978 *Pastoral Nomadism in the Mari Kingdom (ca. 1830-1760 B.C.)*, Cambridge, MA: ASOR.

Mayes, A.D.H.

1977 'The Period of the Judges and the Rise of the Monarchy', in *Israelite and Judaean History*, ed. J. Hayes and J.M. Miller. London: SCM: 285-331.

1983 *The Story of Israel between Settlement and Exile*, London: SCM.

Mazar, A.

1981 'Giloh: An Early Israelite Settlement Site near Jerusalem', *IEJ* 31:1-36.

1982 'Three Israelite Sites in the Hills of Judah and Ephraim', *BA* 45:167-78.

Mazar, B.

1970 *The World History of the Jewish People. First Series: Ancient Times Vol I Patriarchs*, London: W.H. Allen.

1981 'The Early Israelite Settlement in the Hill Country', *BASOR* 241:75-85.

Mendenhall, G.E.

1961 'Biblical History in Transition', in *The Bible and the Ancient Near East: Essays in Honor of W.F. Albright*, ed. G.E. Wright. London: RKP: 32-53.

1962 'The Hebrew Conquest of Palestine', *BA* 25:66-87.

1973 *The Tenth Generation*, Baltimore: Johns Hopkins University Press.

1975 'The Monarchy', *Interpretation* 29:155-70

76 '"Change and Decay All Around I See": Conquest, Covenant and *The Tenth Generation*', *BA* 39:152-57.

1978 'Between Theology and Archaeology', *JSOT* 7:28-34.

1983 'Ancient Israel's Hyphenated History', in *Palestine in Transition*, ed. D.N. Freedman and D.F. Graf. Sheffield: Almond: 91-103.

Merrillees, R.S.

1986 'Political Conditions in the Eastern Mediterranean during the Late Bronze Age', *BA* 49:42-50.

Meyers, C.

1981 'Review of N.K. Gottwald, *The Tribes of Yahweh*', *CBQ* 43:104-109.

1983 'Procreation, Production, and Protection: Male-Female Balance in Early Israel', *JAAR* 51:569-93.

Miller, J.M.

1977 'The Israelite Occupation of Canaan', in *Israelite and Judaean History*, ed. J. Hayes and J.M. Miller. London: SCM: 213-84.

1982 'Approaches to the Bible through History and Archaeology: Biblical History as a Discipline', *BA* 54:211-16.

Nelson, C.
1973   *The Desert and the Sown: Nomads in the Wider Society*, Berkeley: University of California, Institute of International Studies.

Nelson, R.D.
1981a   *The Double Redaction of the Deuteronomistic History*, Sheffield: JSOT.
1981b   'Josiah in the Book of Joshua', *JBL* 100:531-40.

Noth, M.
1960   *The History of Israel*, London: Black.
1981   *The Deuteronomistic History*, ET: Sheffield: JSOT.

Oppenheim, L.
1967   'Essay on Overland Trade in the First-Millennium B.C.', *JCS* 21:236-54.

Oren, E.D.
1973   'The Overland Route between Egypt and Canaan in the Early Bronze Age', *IEJ* 23:198-205.
1978   'Esh-Shari'a, Tell (Tel Sera')', in *Encyclopedia of Archaeological Excavations in the Holy Land*, IV, ed. M. Avi-Yonah and E. Stern. Oxford: Oxford University Press: 1059-69.

Orni, E. and E. Efrat
1966   *The Geography of Israel* (2nd revised edn), Jerusalem: Israel Program for Scientific Translations.

Orwell, G.
1954   *Nineteen Eighty-Four. A Novel*, Harmondsworth: Penguin.

Owen, R.
1981   *The Middle East in the World Economy 1800-1914*, London: Methuen.
1982   *Studies in the Economic and Social History of Palestine in the Nineteenth and Twentieth Centuries*, London: Macmillan.

Pacey, A.
1983   *The Culture of Technology*, Oxford: Blackwell.

Parr, P.
1982   'Contacts between North West Arabia and Jordan in the Late Bronze and Iron Ages', in *Studies in the History and Archaeology of Jordan I*, ed. A. Hadidi. Amman: Dept. of Antiquities: 127-33.

Plöger, O.
1968   *Theocracy and Eschatology*, Richmond: John Knox Press.

Plumb, J.H.
1969   *The Death of the Past*, London: Macmillan.

Porter, J.R.
1963   *Moses and Monarchy: A Study in the Biblical Tradition of Moses*, Oxford: Blackwell.
1970   'The Successsion of Joshua', in *Proclamation and Presence* ed. J.I. Durham and J.R. Porter. London: SCM: 102-32.

Prag, K.
1974   'The Intermediate Early Bronze-Middle Bronze Age: An Interpretation of the Evidence from Transjordan, Syria and Lebanon', *Levant* 6:69-116.
1984   'Review Article: Continuity and Migration in the Southern Levant in the Late Third Millenium: A Review of T.L. Thompson's and some other arguments', *PEQ* 116:58-68.

Price, B.J.
1978   'Secondary State Formation: An Explanatory Model', *Origins of the State*, ed. R. Cohen and E.R. Service. Philadelphia: Institute for the Study of Human Issues: 161-84.
1980   'The Truth is Not in Accounts but in Account Books: On the Epistemological Status of History', *Beyond the Myths of Culture: Essays in Cultural Materialism*, ed. E.B. Ross. New York: Academic Press: 155-80.

Rainey, A.
1982   'Historical Geography—The Link between Historical and Archaeological Interpretation'. *BA* 45:217-23.

Ramsey, G.W.
1982   *The Quest for the Historical Israel. Reconstructing Israel's Early History*, London: SCM.

Reifenberg, A.
1952/1955 *The Struggle between the Desert and the Sown: Rise and Fall of Agriculture in the Levant*, Jerusalem: Government Press.

Renfrew, C.
1973   *Social Archaeology. An Inaugural Lecture*, Southampton: University of Southampton.
1974   'Beyond a Subsistence Economy: The Evolution of Social Organisation in Prehistoric Europe' in *Reconstructing Complex Societies*, ed. C.B. Moore. Cambridge, Mass: ASOR: 64-85.
1979   'Systems Collapse as Social Transformation: Catastrophe and Anastrophe in Early State Societies', in *Transformations. Mathematical Changes to Culture Change*, ed. C. Renfrew and K.L. Cooke. New York: Academic Press.

Richard, S.
1980   'Toward a Consensus of Opinion on the End of the Early Bronze Age in Palestine-Transjordan', *BASOR* 237:5-34.

Ripinsky, M.
1983   'Camel Ancestry and Domestication in Egypt and the Sahara', *Archaeology* 36:21-27.

Rowton, M.B.
1968   'The Topological Factor in the Habiru Problem', *Assyriological Studies* 16:375-85.
1973a   'Autonomy and Nomadism in Western Asia', *Oriens Antiquus* 42:247-58.
1973b   'Urban Autonomy in a Nomadic Environment', *JNES* 32:201-15.
1974   'Enclosed Nomadism', *JESHO* 17:1-30.
1976   'Dimorphic Structure and Topology', *Oriens Antiquus* 15:17-31.

Sanders, J.A.
1972   *Torah and Canon*, Philadelphia: Fortress.
1976   'Adaptable for Life: The Nature of the Function of Canon', in *Magnalia Dei. The Mighty Acts of God. Essays on the Bible and Archaeology in Memory of G. Ernest Wright*, ed. F.M. Cross. New York: Doubleday: 531-60.
1984   *Canon and Community. A Guide to Canonical Criticism*, Philadelphia: Fortress.

Sapin, J.
  1968-1969 'Le Plateau Central de Benjamin: Essai de géographie humaine et historique (Secteur Râmallah Nebi Samwi)' MA Thesis, Ecole Biblique, Jerusalem.
  1981-82 'La géographie humaine de la Syrie-Palestine au deuxième millénaire avant J.C. comme voie de recherche historique', *JESHO* 24:1-62; 25:1-49; 25:113-86.

Sasson, J.
  1981 'On Choosing Models for Recreating Israelite Pre-Monarchic History', *JSOT* 21:3-24.

Sauer, J.A.
  1982 'Prospects for Archaeology in Jordan and Syria', *BA* 45:73-84.

Schäfer, P.
  1977 'The Hellenistic and Maccabaean Periods', in *Israelite and Judaean History*, ed. J.H. Hayes and J.M. Miller. London: SCM: 539-604.

Senevirante, S.
  1981 'Kalingra and Andhra: The Process of Secondary State Formation in Early India', in *The Study of the State*, ed. H.J.M. Claessen and P. Skalnik. The Hague: Mouton: 317-38.

Service, E.R.
  1975 *Origins of the State and Civilization: The Process of Cultural Evolution*, New York: Norton and Co.
  1978 'Classical and Modern Theories of Government', in *Origins of the State*, ed. R. Cohen and E.R. Service. Philadelphia: Institute for the Study of Human Issues: 21-34.

Service, E.R. and R. Cohen
  1978 *Origins of the State. The Anthropology of Political Evolution*, Philadelphia: Institute for the Study of Human Issues.

van Seters, J.
  1981 'Histories and Historians of the Ancient Near East: the Israelites', *Orientalia* 50:137-95.
  1983 *In Search of History. Historiography in the Ancient World and the Origins of Biblical History*, New Haven: Yale University Press.

Shiloh, Y.
  1970 'The Four Room House. Its Situation and Function in the Israelite City', *IEJ* 20:180-90.
  1980 'The Population of Iron Age Palestine in the Light of a Sample Analysis of Urban Plans, Areas, and Population Density', *BASOR* 239:25-35.

Shmueli, A.
  1984 'The Desert Frontier in Judea', in *The Changing Bedouin*, ed. E. Marx and A. Shmueli. New Brunswick: Transaction Books: 17-38.

Shils, E.
  1975 *Center and Periphery. Essays in Macrosociology*, Chicago: University of Chicago Press.

Sinclair, L.A.
  1976 'Gibeah', *Encyclopedia of Archaeological Excavations in the Holy Land*, *II*, ed. M. Avi-Yonah. London: Oxford University Press: 444-46.

Sjöberg, G.
  1960 *The Preindustrial City: Past and Present*, Glencoe: Free Press.

Smith, G.A.
1894   The Historical Geography of the Holy Land, London: Hodder and Stoughton.
Smith, M.
1971   Palestinian Parties and Politics that Shaped the Old Testament, New York: Columbia University Press.
Snodgrass, A.M.
1971   The Dark Age of Greece. An Archaeological Survey of the Eleventh to the Eighth Centuries B.C., Edinburgh: Edinburgh University Press.
Soggin J.A.
1984   A History of Israel. From the Beginnings to the Bar Kochba Revolt, A.D. 135, London: SCM.
Stager, L.
1976a   'Agriculture', IDBSV: 11-13.
1976b   'Farming in the Judaean Desert during the Iron Age', BASOR 221:145-58.
1985   'The Archaeology of the Family in Ancient Israel' BASOR 260:1-35.
Steensgaard, N.
1974   The Asian Trade Revolution of the Seventeenth Century. The East India Companies and the Decline of the Caravan Trade, Chicago: University of Chicago Press.
Stern, E.
1982   Material Culture of the Land of the Bible in the Persian Period 538-332 B.C., Warminster: Aris and Phillips.
1984a   'The Archaeology of Persian Palestine', in The Cambridge History of Judaism, Vol. I, ed. W.D. Davies and L. Finkelstein. Cambridge: Cambridge University Press: 88-114.
1984b   'The Persian Empire and the Political and Social History of Palestine in the Persian Period', in The Cambridge History of Judaism, Vol. I, ed. W.D. Davies and L. Finkelstein. Cambridge: Cambridge University Press: 70-87.
Stiebing, W.H.
1980   'The End of the Mycenean Age', BA 43:7-21.
Tadmor, H.
1979   'The Decline of Empires in Western Asia ca 1200 B.C.E.' in Symposia, ed. F.M. Cross. Cambridge, Mass.: ASOR: 1-14.
Talmon, S.
1979   'Kingship and the Ideology of the State', in World History of the Jewish People: The Age of the Monarchies: Culture and Society, Vol. IV/2. ed. B. Mazar. Jerusalem: Massada Press: 3-26.
Tamari, S.
1982   'Factionalism and Class Formation in Recent Palestinian History', in Studies in the Economic and Social History of Palestine in the Nineteenth and Twentieth Centuries, London: Macmillan: 177-202.
Taylor, P.J.
1985   Political Geography. World Economy, Nation State and Locality, London: Longman.
Tcherikover, V.
1979   Hellenistic Civilization and the Jews, New York: Atheneum.

Thompson, T.L.
1975   *The Settlement of Sinai and the Negev in the Bronze Age*, Wiesbaden: L. Reichert.
1978a   'Historical Notes on Israel's Conquest of Palestine: A Peasant's Rebellion?', *JSOT* 7:20-27.
1978b   'The Background to the Patriarchs: A Reply to William Dever and Malcolm Clark', *JSOT* 9:2-43.
1979   *The Settlement of Palestine in the Bronze Age*, Wiesbaden: L. Reichert.
1980   'History and Tradition: A Response to J.B. Geyer', *JSOT* 15:57-61.

Thornier, D.
1971   'Peasant Economy as a Category in Economic History', in *Peasants and Peasant Economies*, ed. T. Shanin. Harmondsworth: Penguin: 202-18.

Tringham, R.
1974   'Comments on Professor Renfrew's Paper' in *Reconstructing Complex Societies*, ed. C.B. Moore. Cambridge, Mass.: ASOR: 88-90.

Tubb, J.
1983   'The MBIIA Period in Palestine: Its Relationship with Syria and its Origin', *Levant* 15:49-62.

de Vaux, R.
1978   *The Early History of Israel*, 2 vols. London: Darton, Longman and Todd.

Wagstaff, J.
1985   *The Evolution of Middle Eastern Landscapes. An Outline to A.D. 1840*, London: Croom Helm.

Waldbaum, J.
1978   *From Bronze to Iron. The Transition from the Bronze Age to the Iron Age in the Eastern Mediterranean*, Göteborg: Paul Astroms.

1980   'The First Archaeological Appearance of Iron and the Transition to the Iron Age', in *The Coming of the Age of Iron*, ed. T.A. Wertime and J.D. Muhly. New Haven: Yale University Press: 69-88.

Wallerstein, I.
1974   *The Modern World System. Capitalist Agriculture and the Origins of the European World-Economy in the Sixteenth Century*, New York: Academic Press.
1980   *The Modern World System II. Mercantilism and the Consolidation of the European World-Economy 1600-1750*, New York: Academic Press.

Wapnish, P.
1981   'Camel Caravans and Camel Pastoralists at Tell Jemmeh', *JANESCU* 13:101-21.

Ward, W.A.
1972   'The Shashu 'Bedouin'. Notes on a Recent Publication' *JESHO* 15:35-60.

Weinstein, J.M.
1981   'The Egyptian Empire in Palestine: A Reassessment', *BASOR* 241:1-28.

Weippert, M.
1971   *The Settlement of the Israelite Tribes in Palestine. A Critical Survey of Recent Scholarly Debate*, London: SCM.
1979   'The Israelite "Conquest" and the Evidence from Transjordan' in *Symposia*, ed. F.M. Cross. Cambridge, Ma.: ASOR: 15-34.

1982   'Remarks on the History and Settlement in Southern Jordan during the Early Iron Age', in *Studies in the History and Archaeology of Jordan I*, ed. A. Hadidi. Amman: Dept. of Antiquities: 153-62.
Weisman, Z.
1985   'National Consciousness in the Patriarchal Promises', *JSOT* 31:55-73.
Wellhausen, J.
1885   *Prolegomena to the History of Israel*, Edinburgh: Black.
White, H.
1973   *Metahistory: The Historical Imagination in Nineteenth Century Europe*, Baltimore/London.
White, K.D.
1984   *Greek and Roman Technology*, London: Thames and Hudson.
Whitelam, K.W.
1979   *The Just King: Monarchical Judicial Authority in Ancient Israel*, Sheffield: JSOT.
1984   'The Defence of David', *JSOT* 29:61-87.
Wilkinson, J.
1974   'Ancient Jerusalem: Its Water Supply and Population', *PEQ* 106:33-51.
Wilson, R.
1979   'Israel: Self-help or Client State?', in *The Economies of the Middle East*, London: Macmillan: 54-70.
Wilson, R.R.
1977   *Genealogy and History in the Biblical World*, New Haven: Yale University Press.
Wolf, E.R.
1969   *Peasant Wars in the Twentieth Century*, New York: Harper & Row.
1981   *Europe and the People Without History*, Berkeley: University of California Press.
Wolff, H.W.
1975   'The Kerygma of the Deuteronomistic Historical Work', in *The Vitality of Old Testament Traditions*, ed. W. Brueggemann and H.W. Wolff. Atlanta: John Knox: 83-100.
Wright, G.E.
1961   'The Archaeology of Palestine', in *The Bible and the Ancient Near East: Essays in Honor of William Foxwell Albright*, New York: Doubleday: 73-112.
1962   *Biblical Archaeology*, 2nd edn. Philadelphia: Westminster.
1971   'The Archaeology of Palestine from the Neolithic through the Middle Bronze', *JAOS* 91:276-93.
Wright, H.E.
1968   'Climatic Change in Mycenaean Greece', *Antiquity* 42:123-27.
Wrigley, E.A.
1969   *Population and History*, London: Weidenfeld and Nicholson.
Yadin, Y.
1963   *The Art of Warfare in Biblical Lands*, London: Weidenfeld and Nicholson.
1979   'The Transition from a Semi-Nomadic to a Sedentary Society in the Twelfth Century BCE' in *Symposia*, ed. F.M. Cross. Cambridge, Mass.: ASOR: 57-68.

Yoffee, N.
1982   'Social History and Historical Method in the Late Old Babylonian
        Period', *JAOS* 102:347-53.
Zenner, W.P.
1972   'Aqiili Agha: The Strongman in the Ethnic Relations of the Ottoman
        Galilee', *Comparative Studies in Society and History* 14:168-88.
Zubrow, E.B.W.
1976   *Demographic Anthropology: Quantitative Approaches*, Albuquerque:
        University of New Mexico.

INDEX OF AUTHORS